THE SECULARIZATION OF CHRISTIANITY

THE SECULARIZATION OF CHRISTIANITY

An Analysis and a Critique

E. L. MASCALL

Professor of Historical Theology in the University of London, Emeritus Student of Christ Church Oxford, Priest of the Oratory of the Good Shepherd

I am debtor both to the Greeks and to the Barbarians, both to the wise and to the unwise. *Romans 1:14*

Conscience summons *Dasein's* Self from its lostness in the 'they'. *Heidegger.*

HOLT, RINEHART AND WINSTON

NEW YORK CHICAGO SAN FRANCISCO

Library of Congress Catalog Card Number: 66-15656

First published in the United States, April, 1966

Second printing, September, 1966

85504-0116

Printed in the United States of America

TO THE RIGHT REVEREND FATHER IN GOD
JAMES HERBERT LLOYD
BY DIVINE PERMISSION
LORD BISHOP OF LEWES
WITH AFFECTION AND RESPECT

ACKNOWLEDGMENTS

GRATEFUL ACKNOWLEDGMENT is made to the following for their permission to include excerpts from the books listed:

Alec R. Allenson, Inc., Naperville, Illinois, for an excerpt from *Type and History in Acts,* by M. D. Goulder (1964); Cambridge University Press, London, for an excerpt from *The Background of the New Testament and its Eschatology,* edited by W. D. Davies and D. Daube (1954); The Clarendon Press, Oxford, for excerpts from *Roman Society and Roman Law in the New Testament,* by A. N. Sherwin-White (1963); Faber & Faber Ltd., London, for an excerpt from F. N. Davey's Introductory Essay to the original two-volume (1940) edition of E. C. Hoskyns' *Fourth Gospel;* Faith Press Ltd., London, for an excerpt from *Theology and History,* by E. L. Mascall (1962); Harper & Row, Publishers, Inc., New York, for excerpts from *The Church and the Reality of Christ,* by John Knox, copyright © 1962 by John Knox; for excerpts from *Historical Introduction to the New Testament,* by Robert M. Grant, copyright © 1963 by Robert M. Grant; and for excerpts from *The Man Born to Be King,* by Dorothy L. Sayers, copyright © 1949 by Dorothy L. Sayers; Hillary House Publishers Ltd., New York, for excerpts from *The Formation of the Christian Dogma,* by Martin Werner (1957); Humanities Press, Inc., New York, for excerpts from *Religion and the Scientific Outlook,* by T. R. Miles (1959); The Macmillan Company, New York, for excerpts from *The Secular Meaning of the Gospel,* by Paul M. van Buren, copyright © 1963 by Paul M. van Buren, and for excerpts from *Miracles,* by C. S. *Lewis* (1947); Charles Scribner's Sons, New York, for excerpts from *Paul Tillich and the Christian Message,* by G. H. Tavard (1961), and for an excerpt from *The New Testament in Current Study,* by R. H. Fuller (1962); Sheed & Ward, Ltd., London, for excerpts from *Sense, Nonsense and Christianity,* by Hugo Meynell (1964); The Shoe String Press, Hamden, Connecticut, for excerpts from *Christian Theology and Natural Science,* by E. L. Mascall; The Society for Promoting Christian Knowledge, London, for excerpts from *The Miracles and the Resurrection,* by G. H. Boobyer; The Westminster Press, Philadelphia, Pennsylvania, for excerpts from *Honest to God,* by John A. T. Robinson (1963); for excerpts from *History, Sacred and Profane,* by Alan Richardson (1964); and for an excerpt from *Tradition in the Early Church,* by R. P. C. Hanson (1963).

CONTENTS

PREFACE

THE UNUSUAL AND, I fear, somewhat untidy structure of this book may well seem to the reader to call for some explanation. This will best be provided by an account of the circumstances of its composition.

When the Bishop of Woolwich, Dr J. A. T. Robinson, burst upon a startled world with his famous little paper-back *Honest to God*, it seemed clear to me that he was saying something which, if it was true, was very important, and that therefore it was very important to find out what he was saying and whether it was true or not. It thus seemed worth while, in spite of the comparative shortness of his book, to make a very careful analysis of the successive stages of his argument. Before I had really got down to this task there came into my hands a longer and much more professionally theological work by Dr Paul van Buren, *The Secular Meaning of the Gospel*, which seemed to have much in common with the Bishop's book and for which, indeed, the Bishop himself, in replying to his critics, had expressed warm commendation. In consequence, the two main chapters of the present work consist of detailed analyses and critiques of the two works in question. Such analyses are bound to make severe demands on the reader and even more severe demands on the analyst, but without them it seems impossible to pass any valid or useful judgment on the positions maintained in the two works. The matter is the more important since these two books do not stand alone; they are outstanding expressions of a radical and destructive attitude to traditional Christianity which has obtained a foothold in many academic circles in the United States and the United Kingdom, though until the publication of *Honest to God* it was little known to the general public and to the majority of the parochial clergy.

In such a situation as this the radicals and the revolutionaries are in a position of psychological advantage. They can always point to the cases of the Inquisition *versus* Galileo and of Wilberforce *versus* Huxley in order to show without further argument that the radicals are always clear-headed and right and the conservatives always stupid and wrong. Nevertheless, every case needs to be examined on its own merits and it does not follow that if the radicals were right on two particular issues they are necessarily right on a third; and to meet any criticism with triumphant shouts of 'Galileo!' 'Huxley!' or even 'Colenso!' can become little less than a form of intellectual intimidation and blackmail. In any case, even when the radicals have performed a useful task in challenging established positions, the verdict of posterity is not always in their favour. Nobody now accepts the views about the date and composition of the New Testament books and the history of the primitive Church which characterised the Tübingen school in the days of Baur; nobody now holds that Catholic sacerdotalism and sacramentalism were introduced into the Christian Church from the pagan mystery-religions. I would therefore plead that the reader will do his best to approach my discussions of Dr Robinson and Dr van Buren in the same spirit of sympathetic but alert detachment in which, whether successfully or unsuccessfully, I have tried to write them. And I would ask for special attention to those parts of my examination in which, before making any judgment whether they are true or false, I have tried to find out exactly what are the positions which these two scholars are concerned to defend. This seems to me to be the more necessary since this vital stage has been by-passed in many of the comments, both favourable and unfavourable, which they have provoked.

Apart from the two chapters just mentioned, the rest of this book is devoted to the intellectual setting in which the thought of Dr Robinson and Dr van Buren is located. This, it seems clear, consists of three main elements, derived respectively from philosophy, science and biblical study, all of which, it is alleged, demand a complete recasting of Christian belief. The philosophical and scientific impacts are the subject of Chapters One and Four; there seemed to be advantages in dealing with philosophy before and science after the detailed examinations of the writings in question. I have written on both of these matters elsewhere (on the philosophical impact in *Words and Images*, on the scientific impact in *Christian Theology and Natural Science*), but there seemed still to be something to add. The third element—that of biblical study—is one with which I must frankly admit that I am very much less at home. For neither my best friends nor my worst enemies could describe me as a biblical scholar, though I think I can claim to have made as much effort to keep up with recent work on the Bible as most biblical scholars have made to keep up with recent work in the philosophical and scientific fields or in that of systematic theology. However, while such a situation has its obvious drawbacks, it has also some compensating advantages. It is easier to act as an umpire if one is not a player in the game, provided, of course, that one knows what the game is and what are the rules by which it is played. This analogy, of course, breaks down at one important point, but this strengthens rather than weakens my case. In a mere game the rules are entirely arbitrary, though one set of rules may make for a jollier game than another; the umpire has only to apply them. In an intellectual pursuit, on the other hand, the rules are imposed by the nature of rational argument, and if the umpire objects that the contestants are not arguing validly they cannot reasonably reply, 'But we are following the rules that we have agreed to adopt.' Admittedly, every branch of learning has its own techniques which correspond to the nature of its subject-matter, and only when one has thoroughly immersed oneself in the subject and entered into the fraternity of its practitioners can one become competent in handling them. Nevertheless, the outsider, if he has made the effort to understand what the experts are doing, can perform a useful and indeed necessary task of discrimination and arbitration; he can help them to see the wood as well as the trees, to correct inadvertent errors of reasoning and to keep their own specialism in its correct proportion and relation to others. And—I say this with reluctance and with great respect—when the theologian who is not a biblical expert interests himself in the work which the biblical experts are doing, he cannot, I think, help being struck by the fact that they are abnormally susceptible to one of the chief occupational diseases of the scholar, that of taking the conclusions at which they have arrived at any moment as being final and irrefutable. Time after time the guileless outsider finds himself confronted with categorical assertions which, if he ranges a little more widely, he will find contradicted by equally categorical assertions made by authorities no less eminent than the former. It hardly needs remarking that the phrase 'the assured results of modern criticism' has become something of a joke in theological circles, even among those who show most assurance about their own results. Now, as St Thomas Aquinas remarked, of all arguments that based upon sheer human authority is the weakest. Whatever truth there is in the maxims *Experto crede* and *Ne sutor supra crepidam*, we ought, when we are presented with an argument, to examine it carefully for possible defects and not allow ourselves to be dazzled by the rhetoric or the prestige of its proponent. The trustful outsider can therefore legitimately be shocked by the assurance with which many biblical scholars tend to state their more controversial conclusions, and this is of none more true than of those on whom the theological radicals rely. It is thus not out of mischief but in genuine perplexity and with at least a faint sense of protest that, in my last chapter, I have drawn the reader's attention to cases where the more confident assertions of biblical radicals are questioned by other scholars of not less competence than their own. 'Who shall decide, when doctors disagree?' But at least the doctors ought not to conceal the fact of disagreement. And it is, I think, not irrelevant to call in the judgment of the historian or the literary critic to correct the aberrations of the biblical scholar.

As I write this Preface I have before me on my desk two books, both of which are concerned with the Acts of the Apostles primarily, and consequentially with the Gospels; the first is by an accomplished biblical theologian, the second by a distinguished Roman historian. I shall give an extract from each.

Mr M. D. Goulder writes as follows:

> For a good many years now, Acts has been the Church's first history book; and it is required in history books that they supply us with fact. The Church has unhesitatingly turned to Acts for information, and has expected to read in its pages an account of what actually happened after the resurrection, the plain, ungarnished 'truth'. . . . But what if this confidence in the factual integrity of Acts should be undermined? For our studies have established at least one thing: that factual integrity was not the only standard that St Luke set himself. It is not, or not only, as the liberal and form critics supposed, that St Luke intended to write a 'true' account, but was hindered by his

> limitations of knowledge. It is that St Luke never intended to write a 'true' account of the Church's early years at all, in the sense that his book should exclude any story for which he had no evidence in Christian tradition. Symbol was a factor of weight at least comparable to fact with him. . . . St Matthew believed that things for which he had no evidence and which were in fact untrue, came to pass that it might be fulfilled which was spoken by the prophets. St Luke believed this too, but he was not content to write about them in two or three lines as did his predecessor. And as he wrote, his method made plain to him subconsciously that he was selecting, taking a sentence from this type and a phrase from that, writing an account of an ideal incident, the birth, or the ascension of the Saviour, or the coming of his Spirit. And it was in this gift that he excelled. It is the myths of St Luke which dominate the Christian calendar.[1]

And here is the passage from Mr A. N. Sherwin-White:

> However one accepts form-criticism, its principles do not inevitably contradict the notion of the basic historicity of the particular stories of which the Gospel narratives are composed, even if these were not shored up and confirmed by the external guarantee of their fabric and setting. . . . For Acts the confirmation of historicity is overwhelming. . . . Any attempt to reject its basic historicity even in matters of detail must now appear absurd. Roman historians have long taken it for granted.[2]

In the present somewhat overcharged theological atmosphere it is difficult to escape the suspicion that one is either defending vested interests on the one hand or arousing the passions of the mob on the other. And a book like the present one, which is largely devoted to a critical analysis of the work of other scholars, can easily be written off as destructive, negative and unhelpful. I can only say that its intention is to be constructive, positive and, as far as may be, even useful. What I have sought to destroy is itself destructive, and what I have denied are negations. I must refer the reader to other books which I have written for more positive and systematic expositions and commendations of the Church's faith. And, without aspiring to any higher position than that of an ant crawling about the plinths of

[1] *Type and History in Acts*, pp. 179f, 205.
[2] *Roman Society and Roman Law in the New Testament*, pp. 188f.

their pedestals, I may perhaps remind him that Origen wrote *Contra Celsum*, Irenaeus *Adversus haereses*, Athanasius *Contra Arianos*, Augustine *Contra Donatistas*, and Thomas Aquinas *Contra Gentes* and *Contra murmurantes*. In so far as I have attacked the outlook of certain contemporary writers it is because I believe in something that I hold to be more embracing, more balanced, more lasting, more inspiring, and more firmly based in both reason and revelation. I hope, *Deo volente*, to write more about this at some future time. And I would, in concluding this Preface, commend to the reader the following words of that great Christian scholar C. H. Turner:

> It is perhaps most often when defective theologies work themselves out to full and explicit completeness in forms which are felt to be irreconcilable with the Christian religion, that a definite step is taken forward; in this sense error is normally a condition precedent of the exacter comprehension of truth.[1]

[1] *Catholic and Apostolic*, p. 126.

CHAPTER ONE

THE CHANGELESS AND THE CHANGING

The substance of the ancient doctrine, contained in the 'deposit of faith' is one thing; its formulation is quite another.

—Pope John XXIII.

I

ONE OF THE most imperative duties with which the Christian theologian is confronted is that of relating the revealed datum of Christian truth, final, absolute and fundamentally permanent as he must by his Christian commitment believe it to be, to the essentially incomplete, relative and constantly changing intellectual framework of the world in which he lives. This is a task of great importance and of no less difficulty, and it is, I venture to suggest, highly unfortunate that many of those writers who have recently addressed themselves to it because they were convinced of its importance have assumed it to be very much easier than in fact it is.

It is important for three reasons. In the first place, Christians themselves, however well instructed and thoughtful they may be, inevitably share in the intellectual climate and perspective of their time, even if they are conscious that it is, in one way or another, uncongenial to their Christian beliefs. The twentieth-century Christian is bound to be a twentieth-century man by the very circumstance of his birth and upbringing, just as the first-century Christian was a first-century man and the thirteenth-century Christian a thirteenth-century man. Complete independence of the temporal process is just not possible for a being whose existence is rooted in time, even if those roots penetrate below time into eternity. And if the Christian manages to discover some enclave in which to retreat which seems on the surface to have escaped from the flux of the ages, he will in all probability be deluding himself. Even the twentieth-century Carthusian or Athonite monk is a twentieth-century Carthusian or Athonite monk; he is not a Carthusian of the age of St Bruno or an Athonite of the age of St Athanasius of Trebizond, and if he succeeded in becoming one he would not be escaping from time into eternity but only from the twentieth century into the eleventh or the tenth. And it is, in fact, an impressive feature of any really vigorous religious community that, without disloyalty to the basic immutability of the Christian religion and to the particular features of its own temporal history, it is able to adapt itself to the special needs and outlook of each successive epoch. It is thus performing in the concrete business of life itself (never, of course, perfectly, but with a greater or lesser degree of success) the task with which the theologian is concerned in the sphere of the intellect. Nor is the ordinary Christian, whose life is not in the cloister but in 'the world', in an essentially different situation. He, too, has to live out the permanent and absolute truth of the Christian Gospel in one particular epoch of an ever-changing world, and since for him this task is not as *simple* as it is for the professed religious it may well be more rather than less *difficult*; though the opposite of 'simple' is not 'difficult' but 'complex', and the opposite of 'difficult' is not 'simple' but 'easy'.

The theologian, then, has a direct duty to Christians as such, in helping them to live by an essentially unchanging Gospel in an essentially changing world, but, as we have seen, this does not mean that the unchanging Gospel can be expressed in unchanging terms; it would be much easier for us if it could. On the contrary, the terms themselves—and their meanings—are constantly changing, and it is this that makes the theologian's task one of extreme difficulty. That there is an unchanging nucleus of belief and practice to which the Christian is committed he is bound to hold; that any particular expression of it is absolutely permanent and immutable and complete he may well doubt. For words change their meanings and formulas their emphases, and what needs saying at one time may not be just what needs saying at another. In spite of the labours of such scholars as Prestige, can we be quite sure that we know precisely what the Council of Nicaea meant by *homoousios*? Is there no case for the argument of some modern Armenian theologians that what the Roman and later Byzantine churches understood the Definition of Chalcedon to mean, while admirably orthodox in itself, is not what the Council of Chalcedon in fact intended? Have not many present-day Roman Catholic scholars been anxious to maintain that, while it was inevitable in the actual circumstances of the Middle Ages that the Papacy should take the form which it did and that the theology of Trent and Vatican One should place such extreme emphasis upon the Papacy as almost to make it seem to be the sole and ultimate constitutive principle of the Church, a more balanced ecclesiology will see the Papacy as one element in an organic whole of the Church's structure, and the particular form which it has taken under the pressure of the historical circumstances as very largely relative and, even so, not in all respects commendable? Has not one of the best known of them told us that '*every* dogma of the Church expresses at the same time both the irreformable divine revelation and what is human and reformable',[1] that 'even "irreformable" utterances of the teaching office can, without ever being falsified, come to be seen in a better and more balanced way' and 'in this sense be, not negatively but very positively, corrected and improved, as for example the Council of Chalcedon improved on the irreformable definition of the Council of Ephesus'?[2] Has not the editor of Denzinger's *Enchiridion* himself warned us that 'all human statements, even those in which faith expresses God's saving truths, are finite', in the sense that 'they never declare the *whole* of a reality', and that 'anyone who proposes to regard these propositions of faith, because they are wholly true, as in themselves *adequate* to the matter in question, i.e. as exhaustive statements, would be falsely elevating human truth to God's simple and exhausting knowledge of himself and of all that takes its origin from him'?[3] Thus, because both the thought-forms and the needs of the concrete situation of Christians in one age differ from those in another, the theologian has a continual duty to relate the unchanging Gospel to the contemporary situation in order that Christians themselves shall

[1] H. Küng, *The Council and Reunion*, p. 167.

[2] ibid., p. 165; cf. *The Living Church*, pp. 308f.

[3] K. Rahner, *Theological Investigations*, I, pp. 43, 44. Cf., for the practical as distinct from the theological side of this question, Albert Mirgeler, *Mutations of Western Christianity*, *passim*.

understand their faith as adequately as is possible and feel at home in it as contemporary men and women. And here I will anticipate a point which I shall be making at greater length later on, namely that this does not mean that the Christian is, in St Paul's phrase, to be 'conformed to this world'.[1]

The second reason why this task of the theologian is important is concerned with the apologetic and evangelistic work of the Church. Clearly, if the Church is to commend its message to those who are outside it, it must speak to them in words that they can understand, even if it is doing this in order to bring about a radical transformation in their outlook and their beliefs. And thirdly, it is important so that Christians shall be able to see the relevance of their faith to the problems of contemporary society and to bring their influence to bear upon the solution of those problems in accordance with the beliefs which Christianity holds about man's nature, his end, his predicament and his resources.

For all these three reasons, then—for Christian instruction, apologetics and social action—the task of relating the unchanging Gospel to the contemporary situation is of the utmost moment to the theologian, and it cannot be side-tracked on the ground that the contemporary situation is constantly changing and that what will be relevant to it at one moment will not be relevant at another. For, however much it may change from one epoch to another, the contemporary situation is what the Church is, in fact, faced with at any given moment in its existential location; it is to twentieth-century man that the Church must speak in the twentieth century, not to first-century or thirteenth-century or seventeenth-century or thirtieth-century man. But I would draw attention to the fact that I have said 'the Church . . . in the twentieth-century', not 'the twentieth-century Church'. There are twentieth-century Christians, but there is not, in the strict sense, a twentieth-century Church, any more than there is a twentieth-century Gospel. The Church, like the Gospel, is one throughout the ages, however much its forms of speech, worship and life may vary from time to time.

I have said that this task is one of great difficulty, and, because it involves the correlation of two factors, it can be thrown off its balance by the exaggeration of either to the depreciation of the

[1] Rom. xii. 2.

other. We have seen both these tendencies in Protestant theology in recent years. It was the peculiar characteristic of the movement of biblical theology which Dr Karl Barth inaugurated with his famous Commentary on the Epistle to the Romans in 1919, and of which he has been for so many years the leading exponent, that it looked upon contemporary thought, if not contemporary political history, as altogether irrelevant to the primary concern of the Christian theologian. To quote from the article on Karl Barth in the *Oxford Dictionary of the Christian Church*:

> Barth's primary object was to lead theology away from what he believed to be the fundamentally erroneous outlook of modern religious philosophy, with its positive attitude to science, culture, and art, its sympathy with mysticism and its stress on feeling, and to bring it back to the principles of the Reformation. It was to be a return to the Prophetic teaching of the Bible, of which he believed that the Reformers were the most authentic exponents. . . . The Christian message, he held, affirmed the Supremacy and Transcendence of God, whose infinite superiority to all human aspirations meant the worthlessness of human reason. Since the Fall, which brought man wholly under the domination of sin, his natural capacities, including his reason, had been radically perverted, so that all 'natural theology', as expounded e.g. by the Scholastics and the modern Roman Catholic Church, as well as all religion grounded in experience, as found in, e.g., F. D. E. Schleiermacher and the Hegelians, has now become impossible. God's sole revelation is in Jesus Christ and the Word of God is his one and only means of communication with man.[1]

It is true that not all theologians of the biblical school have been as extreme in their position as Barth himself, as was shown by his attacks on Brunner for being a concealed believer in natural theology; the controversy between Barth and Brunner on this issue in 1934 reached an unusual pitch of theological notoriety.[2] But while Barthians such as Dr Karl Heim and Dr W. A. Whitehouse have discussed at some length the relations between Christian theology and such a profane human activity as natural science, they have tended to do this by

[1] op. cit., p. 135.
[2] Eng. Trans.: *Natural Theology*. By E. Brunner and K. Barth. (London, 1946.)

discussing Christian theology and natural science separately and concluding that there is no relevant relation between them.[1] It is only fair to add that quite recently—roughly since 1956—Barth has shown a certain modification of his previous position.[2] It is nevertheless true that the biblical school as a whole has conceived the primary task of the Christian theologian as the proclamation and exposition of the Bible in biblical terms, and has considered both the examination of the Christian documents by modern critical techniques and the expression of Christian truth in contemporary non-biblical idiom as outside the proper concern of the Christian theologian as such.

In reaction to this there has more recently appeared another school in Protestant theology, of which the best known if not the most coherent exponent is Dr J. A. T. Robinson, which takes as its starting-point the outlook of contemporary secularised man and demands that the traditional faith of Christendom should be completely transformed in order to conform to it. The most extreme exponent of this point of view is perhaps Dr Schubert M. Ogden, but Dr Paul van Buren runs him pretty close, with Dr Robinson as a fairly good third. I have thought it worth while to devote two chapters of this present book to a very detailed examination of the two writers last mentioned, and I shall not anticipate that examination here. I would, however, make one or two remarks on the general issue. In the first place, there is a very perplexing tendency among writers such as these to retain the word 'Christianity' while applying it to something that nobody would normally describe as Christianity and then to say that this new thing is '*real* Christianity' or '*authentic* Christianity' or 'the *essence* of Christianity' or 'what Christianity *really is*'. This has the great advantage for the expositor that it enables him to cash in on the respect which still lingers in many minds for Christianity, while rendering it unnecessary to prove by argument that the beliefs which he is recommending are substantially identical with the religion that, as a matter of historical fact, has passed under that name. It has the disadvantage for everyone else of introducing mental confusion by

[1] K. Heim, *Christian Faith and Natural Science; The Transformation of the Scientific World View; The World, its Creation and Consummation.* W. A. Whitehouse, *Christian Faith and the Scientific Attitude; Order, Goodness, Glory.*

[2] Cf. the last two essays in *The Humanity of God.*

the *kerygmatic* character of the Christian message, that is to say its character as a proclamation of the unique salvific and eschatological act of God in Jesus. Myth must go, but kerygma remains. This remarkable result is achieved by reinterpreting the Christian message in terms of the existentialist philosophy of Heidegger, and it is worth remarking, in view of the common repudiation by traditional Protestant theologians of *all* systems of philosophy as seductive artefacts of fallen man, that Bultmann is committed to the particular philosophical system of Heidegger every bit as much as the most doctrinaire textbook Thomist could be to the Aristotelianism of Aquinas. What this means is that the mythology is not to be eliminated but to be reinterpreted in such a way as to make evident that transformation from 'inauthentic' existence, dominated by anxiety and despair, to 'authentic' existence in freedom and faith which takes place when, in response to the preaching of the Word of God, a man accepts God's forgiving grace. Christian beliefs are thus to be evaluated entirely in terms of their effect upon one's present existence.

It is no part of my present concern to make a detailed examination of Bultmann's system. That has been done exhaustively in the books to which I have referred, and extremely adequately in those of Malevez and Owen. I shall only remark on one or two points which will be relevant to my later discussion. First, as many critics have pointed out, Bultmann lumps together, under the all-inclusive term 'myth', a variety of quite different items. Thus, Hebraic cosmogony (and presumably Hellenic cosmogony, too), belief in demons, the resurrection of Christ, traditional trinitarian and Christological concepts, are all classed together, apparently for no better reason than that they are all uncongenial to the outlook of twentieth-century man. However, only a moment's thought is needed in order to see that there is no logical or metaphysical incompatibility in accepting some of these notions and rejecting others. Nevertheless, while Bultmann is extremely tender to the modern man's intellectual prejudices about matters like the three-storey universe and miracles, he is quite unsparing in the demands which he makes upon him for existential commitment of the Heideggerian type and quite determined that this commitment shall take place only as a result of the preaching of the Word of

God as contained in the New Testament. But, as Meynell has observed, in view of the treatment by Bultmann of both the miraculous and the eschatological element in the Gospels as mythological, 'for Bultmann, the crucial nature of the present moment seems to consist in nothing but the individual's subjective disposition to treat it as though it was really crucial'.[1] His insistence on the place played in this by preaching, when combined with the demythologising of the Gospel narrative, seems to give a serious point to the gibe quoted by Dr R. H. Fuller,[2] that the Christ-event took place not in the years A.D. 1–30 but every time that Bultmann enters the pulpit at 11 a.m. on Sunday. And, to quote Meynell again, 'if religious beliefs are to be evaluated entirely in terms of their effect on one's present existence, it is difficult to see why the notion of God should be any more acceptable than that of angels, saints and demons'.[3] (We might comment that for van Buren it is not!) Lastly, we may once again observe with Meynell that the claim that man can achieve authentic existence only in the hearing of the word as proclaimed in the New Testament is either trivial or probably false.

> It is [he remarks] at least arguable that a man may experience a feeling of release from his past and freedom for his future, and become morally better, by listening to the preaching of the Koran or the Buddhist scriptures as well as the New Testament. Once this is granted, if the Word of God is *defined* as that which projects man out of inauthentic and into authentic existence, it follows that either other forms of preaching than that which characterises the New Testament are the Word of God, or it is true merely by definition that freedom from one's past and for one's future is 'authentic existence' only when it occurs in response to this particular word of preaching. If the first horn of this dilemma is taken, the uniqueness of the New Testament and the Christ which it proclaims goes by the board, and it must be admitted on Bultmann's premisses, as it actually is by Jaspers and Buri, to be the vehicle of authentic existence, or the Word of God, to Western man in no more proper a sense than the Buddhist Scriptures are so to the Burmese and Siamese, or the Koran to the Arabs. If the second horn of the dilemma is

[1] op. cit., p. 264.
[2] *The New Testament in Current Study*, p. 21.
[3] op. cit., p. 267.

> taken, the sense in which the New Testament is the unique vehicle of the Word of God, and the Cross and Resurrection which it preaches the unique Word of God, is a trivial one, a mere matter of definition. In this case, to say that it is this form of preaching alone which can project man into authentic existence is merely to refuse to call by this name identical states which happen to have been brought about by different means.[1]

I suppose Bultmann's reply to this would be that, either as an empirical fact or as a conviction of blind faith, there is no other preaching than that of the Christian Gospel that brings about a state of existence which can be properly described as 'authentic'. I do not think, however, that the empirical evidence has been produced, nor am I clear what is the standard of authenticity by which it could be judged. I imagine that the sincere Buddhist or Mohammedan would claim that his 'existence' was just as 'authentic', in any normal sense of the word, as that of the Christian; otherwise he would presumably abandon Buddhism or Islam for Christianity. If, on the other hand, Bultmann's assertion is made as a matter of blind faith, he would seem to be making demands on the intellect every bit as exacting as those which in his demythologising programme he has repudiated. It is, I think, difficult not to sympathise with Buri and Jaspers in their contention that, if you are going to demythologise the Gospel with Bultmann, you had better take the further step of dekerygmatising it as well. It might indeed be suggested that to combine Bultmann's attitude to the Gospels with his attitude to preaching is to substitute magic for myth.[2]

[1] ibid., pp. 269–70.

[2] The way in which the notion of 'myth' can legitimately and fruitfully be used in Christian theology, without in any way impugning the fundamental factuality of the Gospels, is well shown in Père L. Bouyer's *Rite and Man*, with its detailed use of psychological and anthropological data, Père J. Daniélou's *Primitive Christian Symbols* and Dr Hugo Rahner's *Greek Myths and Christian Mystery*. Bouyer writes:

> A vision of the world that is both religious and contemporary cannot be conceived as simply by-passing the myth, but it must be conceived as a necessary dialectical integration of a scientific concept, which has itself become far more subtle than the one proposed by Bultmann in the name of an outmoded rationalism, and of a mythic concept whose permanent value can no longer be doubted. . . .
>
> How did the faith of the Jews and later that of the Christians break up and remake what was till then most constant and universal in the mythic order of the universe? It did this by substituting for the cyclic

Before leaving Bultmann for the time being, it may be worth while to notice that, in spite of the vigorous polemic which Barth has directed against his handling of the Scriptures, they are at one in their emphasis upon the centrality in religion of the preaching of the Word of God as a sheer kerygmatic activity. For both of them, it is not reasoned argument based upon the Scriptures, but proclamation of the Word from the pulpit, that is the Church's primary task and *raison d'être*; where they differ is in the fact that for Barth the critical study of the Scriptures is no business for the theologian as such, whereas for Bultmann it is a highly important prolegomenon to the task of preaching the Word, though one whose proper place is the lecture-room and the study. In their agreement upon the Word of God as an object of proclamation rather than a medium of rational persuasion, their common inheritance of the Protestant spirit can be seen to dominate their obvious conflict in the matter of theological method.

I must at this point make some reference, however brief, to the outstanding figure of Paul Tillich, whose mature thought is now available to us in the three volumes of his *Systematic Theology*, published at intervals over the period since 1951. For Dr Tillich, the fundamental principle of Protestantism is not its unquestioning acceptance of the Bible as the Word of God, but its determination to protest against *every* human activity, idea, formula and judgment as a challenge to, and an infringement of, the transcendence of God. It is therefore not surprising that, in

---

vision of the universe, in which the same powers ceaselessly reproduce the same invariable order of phenomena, a really transcendent intervention which by means of a unique saving event, effected a definitive modification in reality. In other words, in the Christian message as formulated in the Scriptures, Bultmann attributes to the myth the very thing through which both Jews and Christians transcended the earlier mythic formulas.

Conversely, the timeless truth which Bultmann aims at substituting for the saving event is the exact analogue of the rationalisation of the mythic view of things which is the substance of the Greek philosophical interpretations of the natural mysteries. In other words, it is the Gospel in its pristine tenor that really surpasses the myth, while integrating whatever it contained of lasting value. An endeavour such as Bultmann's, on the other hand, unwittingly ends up in the same impasse that confronted Greek rationalism in its comprehension of reality: it devitalised the myth without being able to transcend it. (op. cit., pp. 218f.)

spite of his insistence that the 'theological norm', by which all formulations must be assessed is man's '*New Being* in Jesus as the Christ', he has been accused of taking Christianity, in even its most uncompromisingly Protestant forms, as merely one, even if the highest and in a sense the final, member of a class of essentially homogeneous and comparable activities collectively called 'religions'. Thus he has been unsparingly attacked by Dr Kenneth Hamilton, whose standpoint is that of a more-than-Kierkegaardian anti-rational biblicism, for, as it is alleged, first constructing a system of religion on a non-biblical basis and then finding within this a place for Christianity as he understands it; hence the title of Hamilton's book *The System and the Gospel*. The contrast between these two very different understandings of Protestantism is further brought out in two other books by these two writers bearing very similar titles, namely Tillich's *The Protestant Era* and Hamilton's *The Protestant Way*. A much more temperate, and therefore a much more useful, discussion of Tillich is contained in Dr J. Heywood Thomas's *Paul Tillich: An Appraisal*, but, in my view, the most penetrating and sympathetic attempt to assess both the strong and the weak points of Tillich's work is Fr George H. Tavard's *Paul Tillich and the Christian Message*, a book of which Thomas speaks in terms of high praise. (It is perhaps significant of the influence that Tillich's thought has had in America that all of the writers just mentioned are domiciled in the United States.) I am content to direct the reader to these two last-mentioned works for a discussion of Tillich, whom I find one of the most stimulating and at the same time provocative of contemporary theologians. His significance in the present theological situation seems to me to lie in his determined attempt to develop on Protestant principles a theology which will do justice both to the authenticity of human religion as such and also to the uniqueness, finality and all-inclusiveness of Christianity. The basic criticisms which Hamilton makes of him are, I think, justified only if one accepts Hamilton's anti-rationalist presuppositions. On the other hand, it does seem to me that Tavard has accurately fastened on certain ambiguities in Tillich's discussion which introduce real weaknesses into his system. For example, his determination to avoid abstractness, and to concentrate on man in his actual existential situation, leads him to identify man's fallenness with the transition from essence to existence and so, if not exactly to identify man's createdness with his fallenness, at least to make it very difficult to discern where one ends and the other begins.[1] His assertion that the grace of God justifies man not only without reference to his merits but even without reference to his faith seems to drive the doctrine of justification beyond the point of paradox to that of absurdity;[2] though we ought to remember that existentialist writers frequently exaggerate, in order to make their points, and introduce the necessary corrections elsewhere. And, as Tavard very clearly shows, Tillich's denunciation of the Chalcedonian Christology rests upon a misunderstanding of its language, and his attempt to correct it by substituting a notion of 'eternal God-man-unity or eternal Godmanhood'[3] tends to weaken not only his Christology but also his theology of the Trinity. Nevertheless, the profundity of his insights (and, we might add, the genuinely constructive and unpolemical intentions of Tavard) is shown by the way in which Tavard, by reviving the primitive Christian notion of Jesus as the incarnation of a pre-existing celestial Man, equal to the Father and the Father's perfect image, has suggested that an orthodox post-Chalcedonian Christology might, in fact, be developed along the lines that Tillich has followed. For its own interest I will quote the passage in which Tavard outlines this programme:

> What the Council of Chalcedon, using a Greek vocabulary, called the two natures, divine and human, of Christ, we should call the two humanities of Jesus: the divine Humanity, which is God himself, the eternal Exemplar of all images of God; and the creaturely humanity, in whose shape the divine Humanity appeared on earth at a given moment in history. These two are one—one 'person' in the Chalcedonian language—by way of exemplarity: the creaturely humanity of Jesus is the perfect created likeness of the divine Man. In order to avoid Nestorian implications, we should not speak of Jesus as two men, but as two humanities—divine and human—in one man, the pre-existent divine Man. In order to avoid Monophysite misunderstandings, we should insist on the integrity of the creaturely humanity assumed by the eternal Man, 'in all things like his brethren'. The philosophical difficulty of explaining the co-

[1] Tillich, *Systematic Theology*, II, ch. xiii; cf. Tavard, op. cit., pp. 40f.
[2] Tillich, *The Protestant Era*, *passim*; cf. Tavard, op. cit., pp. 28f.
[3] Tillich, *Systematic Theology*, II, p. 170; cf. Tavard, op. cit., pp. 120f.

existence of two natures in Christ, and the psychological problem raised by the coexistence of a human psyche with a divine knowledge might both be by-passed: the Exemplar itself is, eternally so, divine and yet human, the divine Man. This could conceivably open the door to a solution of the ever-recurrent problem of the knowledge of Christ.[1]

It is perhaps remarkable that neither Tillich nor Tavard shows any sign of acquaintance with the way in which a very similar theme was worked out as long ago as 1878 by Vladimir Soloviev, for an English translation of his *Lectures on Godmanhood* was published in New York as recently as 1944; this is, however, an unimportant point. For our present purposes what is of interest is the fact that Tillich's sustained attempt to express the traditional faith in contemporary terms, while its success seems clearly open to serious doubt, has suggested to his sympathetic critic Tavard the possiblity of a genuine advance in Christological understanding.

II

At this point I may seem to have strayed down a side-turning, and so I have, though I think it has led us to an interesting spot. We shall, in fact, get back to the main path. In the movement of reinterpretation of which we have considered some examples, two chief phases are to be discerned. The first is a belief that the New Testament presentation of Christianity needs to be radically demythologised in accordance with the programme of Bultmann, though this does not seem to be true of Tillich, whose starting-point is not biblical but philosophical.[2] The second is a belief that the necessary reconstruction must be done on the basis of Heideggerian existentialism, though this is not true of van Buren, who strikes out a new line among the demythologisers by taking as his basis the philosophy of the linguistic analysts. And this remark may serve to remind us of a more or less closely linked group of reductionists who are neither New Testament scholars nor existentialists, but professional Anglo-Saxon linguistic philosophers. The best known of these is undoubtedly Professor R. B. Braithwaite, whose Eddington

[1] Tavard, op. cit., pp. 171f.

[2] Thus there are no references to Bultmann in vol. I of the *Systematic Theology*, and only two rather casual ones in vol. II.

Memorial Lecture of 1955 entitled *An Empiricist's View of the Nature of Religious Belief* attracted widespread attention which was unfortunately disappointed by his failure to develop his theme adequately elsewhere or to reply at any length to his critics. Accepting the usual linguistic-empiricist view that, whatever theological statements are, they cannot be factual assertions, he then reinterprets them as announcements of policy-adoption. To declare that one is a Christian is to be taken as a declaration that one is adopting an *agapë*-policied way of life, accompanied by the entertainment of (but not necessarily any belief in) the Christian 'stories'. (It is this last element that distinguishes the professing Christian from the professing Jew or Buddhist.) I have discussed Braithwaite's position at some length in my book *Words and Images*.[1] I shall here only repeat my summary of his conclusion. 'All that [his exposition] leads us to is a form of Christianity without God, without grace and, for all we can tell, without Christ, a religion in which a policy of living for which no ground can be assigned is bolstered up by the psychological encouragement that is provided by entertaining, but not believing, the Christian stories.'[2] Whatever else it may or may not be, this is at least a whole-heartedly reductionist type of Christianity.

A more thorough discussion on substantially the same lines has been given by Mr T. R. Miles in his book *Religion and the Scientific Outlook*. Despite his divergence from Braithwaite on several points (in particular he considers Braithwaite's discussion of the 'stories' to be inadequate and deficient in evidence), he expresses his 'full agreement with Braithwaite over the difficulty in regarding sentences containing the word "God" as straightforward literal truth'.[3] His own programme is summarised in the phrase 'silence qualified by parables', and, while denying that 'the word "God" stands for an extra "paraphysical" entity in addition to ordinary "physical" ones', he claims that his position is not substantially very far from that of any intelligent theologian. The following passage of dialogue, in which the 'Philosopher' stands for Miles himself, is characteristic:

[1] Ch. iv, 'Theism without God'. This title seemed in 1957 a sufficient identification of its theme. Today, it might equally well apply to a discussion of van Buren!

[2] ibid., p. 62.

[3] op. cit., p. 165.

Philosopher: Let us look again at our respective views. God to you is a mystery; to me even the word 'mystery' has an empirical taint, and is misleading. You say 'I do not know' and try to talk; I say 'I do not know' and remain silent. You admit that your talk is not literal; I qualify my silence by telling parables. Is there really all that difference between us?

Theologian: But I claim that what I say is objectively true—true, albeit by analogy, of the actual world. You, it seems, do not.

Philosopher: Precisely. You say your talk is true by analogy of the actual world; I say that mine is literally true in the world of parable.

Theologian: But do you not want to say that your parables are true in the sense of having objective validity?

Philosopher: What does 'objective validity' mean? This is the sort of language that we use when speaking of veridical perceptions in contrast with illusions and hallucinations. Such talk is inapplicable in the case of God. I will have none of it.[1]

Clearly, very much will depend on the kind of relation to reality the language of parable is intended to have. As Miles develops his view on this question, one thing becomes quite plain, that, as he interprets them, the New Testament parables are not about the attitude towards us and dealings with us of a transcendent being named 'God'. He says explicitly:

The appropriate religious policy is one of silence qualified by parables. Instead of 'Do you believe in the existence of God?' we should substitute, 'Do you accept the theistic parable?' This rids us of the temptation to think of God as an 'extra entity'. The questions whether there is such an entity and whether the theistic parable is objectively true can be met only by 'the way of silence'. . . . Parable-assertions are not equivalent either to factual or moral assertions, but factual and moral considerations can influence our choice of parable. Acceptance of the theistic parable involves conversion and a change of outlook.[2]

It is plain that the change of outlook just mentioned can only be a change of outlook upon the world and upon human life.

[1] ibid., pp. 163f.
[2] ibid., p. 179.

This becomes still more evident in the subsequent discussion on 'God and Prayer'. Thus we are told:

> A distinction . . . needs to be made between two varieties of prayer-language, 'pseudo-causal' prayer-language and 'performatory' prayer-language. A standard case of the former is 'O God, please send some rain'; a standard case of the latter is 'Thy will be done'. According to the argument of this book, any prayer-language of the former sort requires to be abandoned [, though not] because the request is an *unworthy* one, whereas the request in the second case is more deserving. The point is rather that 'Thy will be done' is not a request at all. In using these words (and similar ones) we are committing and dedicating ourselves, not trying to persuade an unknown agency to influence the course of nature.[1]

I think any unbiased reader will feel that there is something very arbitrary in reinterpreting the phrase 'Thy will be done' in such a way that 'thy' is not a possessive pronoun, and indeed in a way that is quite inconsistent with the original context of the phrase, which is that of the dominical prayer addressed, in its opening words, to 'Our Father, who art in heaven'.[2] Still less is it consistent with the later occurrence of the phrase in the Agony in the Garden, where it is immediately consequent upon the petition of Jesus (a 'pseudo-causal' prayer if ever there was one), 'O my Father, if it be possible, let this cup pass from me.'[3]

A further example of reinterpretation, and a very revealing one, is given when the prayer in the Anglican Communion Service 'Almighty God, unto whom all hearts be open, all desires known, and from whom no secrets are hid, Cleanse the thoughts of our hearts . . .' is transformed into 'I hereby acknowledge the theistic parable, the parable of one who sees all our inmost thoughts, and I hereby acknowledge my shortcomings and the need for cleansing'. 'Acknowledg[ing] the parable of one who sees all our inmost thoughts' can, presumably, only mean behaving as if there was someone who sees all our inmost thoughts, but I cannot see why we should behave in this way unless we are convinced that there is such a being, and on Miles's view there is no reason to suppose that there is and it is

[1] ibid., p. 186.
[2] Matt. vi. 9.
[3] Matt. xxvi. 39–42.

probably meaningless to enquire whether there is or not. Again, acknowledging the need for cleansing is a very arbitrary interpretation of the petition that the cleansing should be done, for the latter formula implies that there is someone who is capable of doing it, whereas the former carries no such implication and, in the setting of Miles's programme, in fact denies it. It is not, I think, unfair to say that, on Miles's view, petitions in prayer become nothing more than admissions of a predicament for which there is no reason to suppose that there is any remedy. Miles's subsequent reinterpretations of traditional doctrines are very much like those which I shall examine at greater length in my discussion of van Buren. Without pursuing the matter in more detail, it is, I think, legitimate to raise the question whether, if reductionism is to be pushed to these extremes, it would not conduce to clarity if the language of theism and of Christianity were abandoned altogether.

This is hardly the place for an extended examination of Miles's basic philosophical position, though I will give a brief account of it in a footnote.[1] Nor shall I embark upon a defence of the meaningfulness and the truth of the traditional assertions of

[1] The basis of Miles's case is laid down in his irritatingly brief fourth chapter, entitled ' "Absolute" existence'. Starting from the indisputable fact that 'existence' is not a characteristic comparable with properties and attributes, he argues that all sentences involving reference to existence are meaningless, even those asserting the existence of empirical entities. This is indeed a drastic position, even for an empiricist, but empirical entities are alleged to survive, on the ground that other assertions can be made about them than that of their existence. The fact remains, however, that on Miles's view it would seem to be impossible to distinguish significantly between the existence and the non-existence of anything; you can say significantly that the cat is on the mat, but you cannot say significantly whether it is a real or an imaginary cat to which you are referring. I cannot help thinking that, if he had paid some attention to M. Gilson's thesis, expounded in such works as *The Christian Philosophy of St Thomas Aquinas* and *Being and some Philosophers*, that 'existing' (*esse*) is an act, not an attribute, and is therefore expressed in a judgment and not in a concept, the whole course of his subsequent argument might have been different. It is in line with his basic presupposition that he never considers the type of approach which is, in different ways, common to all the writers mentioned in the next sentence of the text above, and according to which the existence of God is somehow manifested to us in and with the existence of finite beings.

There is nothing very new in the proposal to interpret theistic sentences as not being statements about God. Dr John Macquarrie (*The Scope of Demythologising*, pp. 115f) has remarked that Édouard Le Roy, who was one of the leading French modernists at the beginning of the century, proposed to reinterpret 'God is a person' as 'Treat personal values as absolute'.

Christian theism; this task has been undertaken by a number of writers, among whom might be mentioned Dr A. M. Farrer,[1] Dr H. D. Lewis,[2] Dom Mark Pontifex,[3] Mr I. M. Crombie and Mr B. G. Mitchell,[4] and the present author.[5]

A further variant of this attitude is provided by Dr Peter Munz's very interesting book *Problems of Religious Knowledge*. Starting from an analysis of the notion of religious symbolism, he maintains that 'religious knowledge is not extraordinary or supernatural or indirect or allegorical knowledge about this world; but certain and rational knowledge about the religious picture of the world'.[6] And this 'religious picture' of the world is not a 'positive' picture of the kind with which science is concerned; it is a 'symbol' picture. And it is the function of a symbol to *mean* a feeling-state. And the religious function of feeling-states is not to give us knowledge of supernatural realities. It is not epistemological but therapeutic; they bring about *salus*. Somewhat as scientific language implies a relation to *causality*, without talking about it, so religious language implies a relation to *eternity*, without talking about that. And in this context eternity does not mean the mode of existence of God, but a condition of blessedness achievable by man. 'The theologian is interested in descriptions in terms of the concept of eternity, because he knows that the detection of eternity is the only proper therapy for man. . . . The natural scientist's description of nature exhibits the presence of causality and of the uniformity of nature. The theologian's description of the symbol picture exhibits the presence of eternity. This perception of eternity is our greatest consolation and solace. The theologian who helps us to this perception is the great physician.'[7]

Munz's exposition is both subtle and elaborate, and as an account of the psychology of certain religious states it is of the greatest interest. What the theological reader will want to know, however, is whether Dr Munz gives an adequate account of the

[1] *Finite and Infinite.*

[2] *Our Experience of God.* Cf. also Dr Lewis's brilliant essay on 'God and Mystery' in the symposium *Prospect for Metaphysics.*

[3] *The Meaning of Existence.*

[4] Essays in *Faith and Logic* and *New Essays in Philosophical Theology.*

[5] *He Who Is; Existence and Analogy; Words and Images.*

[6] op. cit., p. 39.

[7] ibid., p. 129.

nature of theological discourse, and it must be regretfully said that he does not. A thorough investigation of the epistemological function of the symbol and the image in theology would have been of the greatest use, but clearly Munz does not think that the symbol has any epistemological function whatever; it has an important indefinable relation to a feeling-state, and this feeling-state in turn has a therapeutic value, but it does not give us *knowledge* about anything. Thus Munz writes:

> The element of certainty that is characteristic of religious faith is connected with the symbol picture. *We cling with direct trust to the symbols.* Our faith is concerned with the symbolisation of our feeling-states; it is concerned with what we see and hear; with what we see *sub specie essentiae*. The question as to whether the symbol exhibits one god or many, whether it exhibits a transcendent or an immanent godhead, whether it enjoins asceticism or the practice of worldly activity, must always remain open. At best such questions can be decided hypothetically by speculation. But there can never be a final and definitive answer to them. Our faith is the quality of our perception of the symbol.[1]

Thus, symbols do not enable theology to talk about God; what theology talks about is the symbols. The conclusion to which I find myself led by Munz's fascinating book is that, as an account of the part played by symbols in the more primitive types of religion, his discussion is profound and illuminating; but it ceases to be adequate when he turns to the higher religions, for they are primarily concerned not with feeling but with truth. It does, however, provide us with an extremely interesting further example of what, to adopt Mr Meynell's term, we may call theological reductionism. As our discussion will, I think, have made it clear, starting from widely different standpoints and proceeding by widely divergent paths, Dr Robinson, Dr van Buren, Dr Bultmann, Dr Tillich, Professor Braithwaite, Mr Miles and Dr Munz[2] agree in their conviction of the permanent

[1] ibid., p. 175. (The English words are not italicised in the original.) I might perhaps refer at this point to my *Theology and Images*, which includes a fairly full discussion of an important book which I have not mentioned in the text, Mr A. C. Bridge's *Images of God*.

[2] I have taken Braithwaite, Miles and Munz as typical representatives of the linguistic approach to theology. The whole movement and its repercussions are very fully discussed in Dr Frederick Ferré's very useful book *Language, Logic and God*.

value of the traditional formulas, concepts and images of Christianity, while subjecting them to the most radical reinterpretations. What, we must enquire, is the significance of this remarkable phenomenon?

The key to an answer is, I believe, to be found in the fact that, in their different ways, all these writers agree in an evident determination to abolish altogether, or at least to reduce to a minimum, the supernatural element and emphasis which has characterised Christianity throughout the ages. By 'the supernatural' is meant the whole body of thought and activity which is concerned with man's life as a member of 'another world' than the world that is immediately apprehended by his senses, which sees his life in 'this world' as derived ultimately from that 'other world', and which sees his final destiny as lying in that 'other world' and beyond bodily death. For a Christian theist that 'other world' is the realm of existence of a beneficent Creator, upon whose will 'this world' is dependent for its existence and its preservation and in union with whom his own beatitude will consist. It is not, I think, certain that the 'supranatural' which Tillich rejects is identical with the 'supernatural' as I have just defined it, though there are places where one is tempted to think that this must be so;[1] in Robinson's case the matter seems clearer, though, as we shall see when we come to consider him in more detail, he is a skilful practitioner of the tactics of occupying advanced and indefensible positions and then hastily withdrawing as soon as the counter-attack develops. With van Buren and the others who base their position upon linguistic empiricism the rejection is quite explicit; for to them the whole notion of the supernatural is not merely without a real counterpart but is intrinsically meaningless.

This elimination of the supernatural from Christianity appears to rely upon three main types of argument, which may be found either separately or in various combinations. The first is the philosophical type, based either upon existentialism or upon linguistic empiricism. In both these modes (which have more in common than might be seen on the surface) it has been so thoroughly dealt with by writers whom I have already mentioned that I shall say nothing more about it here, except to express the judgment that, while having failed to substantiate its

[1] Cf. *Systematic Theology*, I, pp. 72 *et al.*

main contentions, it has performed a very useful function in forcing philosophers of theism to re-examine their own arguments and so to acquire a deeper understanding of their own position. The second line of attack derives from the assumption that the discoveries of science have disproved the existence of any supernatural realities or at any rate the possibility of any intervention by them into the natural world. The third line proceeds from New Testament study and alleges that the supernatural element in the Gospels can be proved to have no historical foundation but to be due to the mythopoeic activity of the primitive Church. These last two lines of attack will need careful examination, which I shall undertake to the best of my ability in the latter part of this book. I shall, however, devote the rest of the present chapter to a consideration of the problem with which I began, namely that of the relation between the unchanging revealed datum of the Christian Gospel and the essentially relative, incomplete and changing intellectual frameworks, conceptual systems and verbal formulas in which it finds its expression throughout the history of the Christian Church.

There are two extreme positions which I shall state in order to reject them. The first of these would see some particular verbal formula or body of verbal formulas as expressing the Gospel exhaustively, finally and with complete adequacy for Christians of every epoch, locality, race, culture and individual mental equipment. If the formulas are those of the Bible (or, as is more commonly the case, a few selected texts from the Bible, such as Romans i. 17), we have the typical example of Protestant fundamentalism, but the formulas might equally well be those provided by the decrees of the Ecumenical Councils, the confessional documents of the Reformation, certain widely quoted dicta of fathers, scholastics or reformers, or the famous collection of documents in Denzinger's *Enchiridion*. What characterises this position is not just the acceptance of certain formulas as highly authoritative or even as in practice indispensable and irreformable, but the assumption that, simply as they stand, they are exhaustive and precise statements of dogmatic truth, which are as immediately applicable to all succeeding times and places as they were to the time and place of their first utterance and which can be made use of without any special attention to the particular circumstances that gave rise to them and to the differences between those circumstances and the circumstances of the present day.

At the other extreme is the position which assumes that divine truth is so completely indifferent to the empirical events of the Church's history that its formulation in one particular context is altogether independent of its formulation in any other, and that in consequence the fact that certain formulations have been hammered out in the rough-and-tumble of events is of interest only to historians. In this view, it is really a matter of chance, or at any rate of no significance, that the Christian faith received its classical formulation in the intellectual climate of the Roman Empire rather than in the India of Sankara, the Mexico of the Aztecs or the Japan of the present day. Thus in any time and place the Church's theological task is simply to accommodate the Gospel directly to the thought-forms and verbal conventions of the local and contemporary environment. So, for example, in commending the Gospel to modern Hindus the accumulated body of thought and devotion and liturgical practice which the Church has built up in the course of its history is completely irrelevant and indeed a positive hindrance; the missionary's task is simply to adjust the Gospel message to the thought-forms of modern Hinduism. Similarly, in bringing the Christian religion to present-day technocratic Western society we have simply to adapt the Gospel message to the outlook of modern secularism; this is, of course, the programme of Robinson and van Buren, though van Buren, by his own confession, is not so much concerned to commend the Gospel to those outside the Church as to complete the secularisation of the outlook of those who are within.

Like many pairs of diametrically opposed positions, these have, in spite of their opposition, a good deal in common. In particular, for each of them the systematic and sympathetic study of Christian thought as a living and historical process in a concrete human setting is irrelevant to the theologian. And in this respect it makes little difference whether the Gospel is in every place and time to be proclaimed in the same traditional words or whether it is to be completely 'reinterpreted' and reformulated in agreement with the local and contemporary mental outlook. In the former case there will be virtually no appeal to the critical faculty, in the latter there may be a great deal, but in both cases the Church as an historic entity with a life in space and time will be certainly an irrelevance and probably a nuisance. In other respects, of course, the two positions differ just about as widely as any two positions could. For the former, the time-honoured formulas will be accepted and repeated without any serious attention to the difference between one historical context of thought and life and another; in the fundamentalist variety of this position, of course, the only idiom that is admissible in Christian theology will be that of the Bible, which will be looked upon as self-authenticating and self-interpreting, fathers, councils and the rest counting for nothing. For the latter position, the presentation of the Christian religion in the twentieth century will be entirely unrelated to its presentation in the third or the thirteenth, and the faith as taught in Austin, Texas, will have virtually nothing in common with the faith as taught in Pakistan or New Guinea. Nor will the thought-forms of the Bible, soaked as they are in myth, have more permanent value than those of first-century Greek philosophy. Both will be equally relative and impermanent; all we can hope to do is to bring the intuitions that underlie them into some kind of conformity with the outlook of our own time and culture. In so far as there is anything permanent about the Christian religion it is something that cannot be given any even approximately stable verbal expression; what really matters about 'our' Christianity is that it should be radically contemporary in its outlook and to achieve this end we must be ready to jettison the whole of our Christian inheritance if it is uncongenial to the climate in which we live. All that remains common to the different resulting 'Christianities' is that they are based on some kind of devotion to a Galilean peasant who was crucified under Pontius Pilate, though it is difficult to see how such a complete dehistoricisation as is here involved makes it possible to identify the particular Galilean peasant with the Christ of contemporary experience.

In practice, of course, neither of these positions is likely to be held in an absolutely pure form, for neither is really workable. What we actually find is a number of attempts to adhere to one or other of them as closely as is humanly possible. At the one extreme we have the Barthians (of the primitive observance, for Barth himself is less of a Barthian than he once was), for whom all humanly devised schemes of thought are religiously useless and are branded with the mark of human sin, so that the Church's task in every age consists in the unchanging proclamation of the unchanging Gospel in the unchanging words of the Bible; but a substantially similar attitude is manifested by the type of Anglican who believes that the final expression of authentic Christianity was achieved in the Thirty-nine Articles and the Book of Common Prayer and by the type of Roman Catholic who answers any dogmatic enquiry by producing the appropriate passage from Denzinger. At the other extreme we have the Robinsons and van Burens preaching a secularised Gospel to secularised men, while their opposite numbers in Asia are presumably expected to preach Hinduism to Indians or Confucianism and Taoism to the Chinese under the name of Christianity. Now what I wish to maintain is that each of these positions is an exaggeration of one aspect of the truth, and that the truth itself is very much more complex than either. I cannot hope that my own exposition will be invulnerable to criticism, but I hope that it may be substantially accurate.

To begin, then, I suggest that it must be admitted that there is a necessary distinction to be made between any proposition which is asserted and the form of words in which it is made. This is true even of the most commonplace proposition, as is shown by the fact that it can be asserted in more than one language, or in the same language in more than one way. Thus the same proposition is asserted by the sentence 'Lloyd George knew my father' as by the sentence 'My father was known to Lloyd George'; and the same proposition is asserted by the sentence 'The cat is black' as by the sentence 'Le chat est noir'. But, even in such simple cases as these, there is a certain looseness of fit between the sentences and the propositions which they express, since the structure of reality is much more complex than the structure of language and no two persons use words in entirely identical senses. (It may already have occurred to the reader that 'The cat is black' and 'Le chat est noir' *need not*, in fact, be identical in meaning, since 'cat' in English is of common gender, while 'chat' in the singular in French is masculine.) And if this is true of such everyday objects as cats, fathers and former Prime Ministers, it must *a fortiori* be true of the mysteries of religion and supremely true of God. There is, as is well known, a very real problem as to how it is possible for finite inhabitants of a finite world either to think or to speak of an absolutely transcendent being; the Doctrine of Analogy represents the most determined attempt that has been made to solve it. But I am not maintaining the agnostic position that we cannot think about God or that we cannot intelligibly talk about him; what I am maintaining is that our thoughts about him (or about any of the great Christian mysteries), accurate as they may be up to a point, are bound to be inadequate and that the sentences which we use in order to express these thoughts are bound to be more inadequate still. It will follow, therefore, that even the mighty words and images of the Bible, which all orthodox Christians agree are in some sense of divine provision and not of merely human invention, such words as 'Father', 'covenant', 'ransom' and so on, are inevitably inadequate to express the fullness of the reality which they denote. God is our Father—yes, but not as human fathers, even if his fatherhood is that from which all fatherhood both in earth and in heaven is named. He has made a covenant with his people—yes, but a covenant in which the conditions are laid down entirely by one of the parties. He has ransomed them—yes, but by a price exceeding every other price and, if it is paid to anyone, paid to himself. And the great non-biblical words of classical Christian theology, deriving as they do not from the speech and thought of God's ancient chosen people but from those of pagan Greece and Rome—*hypostasis*, *homoousios*, *theotokos*, *persona*, *sacramentum* and the like—are not these even less adequate to the tasks forced upon them? Yes, indeed, but here there is another point to which we must give heed.

III

The traffic between Christian truth and Greco-Roman or Hellenistic thought is in no sense a one-way traffic; to change the metaphor, the relation between the two is one of cross-fertilisation. Faced with the task of commending to a Greco-Roman world a Gospel of Semitic origin, the Church took up the best words and concepts that she could find at hand and moulded them to her purposes. In doing this she subjected them to a radical transformation and development, but in doing it she also began to understand her own Gospel as she had never understood it before. To the mysterious providence of God, it was pleasing that the eternal Son should become man as a Jew and not as an Ephesian or a Milanese or a Zulu; and if I am asked whether it would not have been as fitting for the Saviour of the world to be born in Java or Mexico as in Palestine, I can only reply that, while anything that God does is fitting, there are presumably many fitting things which God does not do, since even God cannot bring incompatible alternatives into being. And where in this web of possibility and appropriateness these various alternatives lie I cannot even guess. No doubt it would have been very much simpler if God had become man as a Roman rather than as a Semite, or if the transition of Christianity from a Semitic to a Hellenic culture had taken place slowly and gradually instead of in one breathless decade followed by the rapid and brutal extinction of its primordial home. Simpler, no doubt, but not in accordance with the providence of God, to whom it seemed good that the world's salvation should be enacted in one place and become intelligible in another. But even here we must not make the contrast too strong, since the Semitic and Hellenistic cultures had already met and mingled before the Saviour's birth. What confronts us is the spectacle of the divine intervention neither tyrannising over its environment nor vanishing into it, but mastering it by entering into it and transforming it from within. This theme was eloquently expounded by the late Lionel Thornton in his much-neglected book *Revelation and the Modern World*, the first volume of the trilogy bearing the significant title *The Form of the Servant*. The point which I am concerned to make here is that, whether or not, as an abstract possibility, the Incarnation might have occurred in a different place, at a different time and in a different cultural setting, it did in fact occur in Jewry in the time of Augustus Caesar, and the Church which the Incarnate Son left on earth as his body found itself almost immediately transplanted into a Greco-Roman setting. As Gregory Dix pointed out in his *Jew and Greek*, there was a double miracle, first in its transplantation before the home of Judaism was destroyed, and secondly in its survival after it was transplanted. And it is with this concrete fact and not with unrealised hypothetical alternatives that we are concerned.

That there was loss as well as gain in the Hellenising of

Christianity we need not deny. It is notorious that the Christological controversies were complicated by the difficulty which Gentiles had in understanding that in the Bible 'flesh' was a synonym for human nature as a whole and not simply for the material part of it; it is correspondingly fascinating and inspiring to see how the Council of Chalcedon succeeded in stating in the Greek terminology of *physis*, *prosopon* and *hypostasis* that duality of Godhead and manhood in the one Christ which the prologue of St John's Gospel states in Hebrew terms by saying that 'the Word became flesh'. (Not indeed, though this is not always recognised, that the fathers invariably misunderstood the biblical concepts; St Athanasius, for example, was clear that the Bible identified 'man' and 'flesh'.)[1] Again, the need to discountenance a false subordination of the Son to the Father led to the obscuring of that perfectly orthodox type of adoptionism which is expressed in the Acts of the Apostles in such declarations as 'God has made him both Lord and Christ, that Jesus whom ye crucified'.[2] And the insistence upon the sheer equality of the Son with the Father which the Church found itself forced to make (and rightly and inevitably forced to make) against the Arians resulted in a loss of emphasis upon the filial response of the Son to the Father, both in the coinherent life of the Trinity and in the incarnate life of the God-man, though the conservatism of the Roman see maintained the primitive pattern in the central acts of the Liturgy.[3] Nevertheless, intriguing as it no doubt is to speculate upon the course that theology might have taken if it had developed within the climate of its Jewish birth-

[1] Cf. J. N. D. Kelly, *Early Christian Doctrines*, p. 287.

[2] Acts ii. 36.

[3] The Eucharistic canon is, in the West and (normally) in the East as well, addressed to the Father through the Son, though there are to be found Eastern canons addressed to the Son and even to the Blessed Virgin. And the typical form of prayer, as in the Western collects, is directed *to* the Father *through* the Son and *in* the Spirit, the equality of the Persons being expressed in the formula *qui tecum vivit et regnat . . . Deus*. In the East even prayers which begin with an address to the Father tend to end with a trinitarian address 'For thou art a good God and the lover of men and to thee we ascribe glory, Father, Son and Holy Spirit . . .' In both East and West the earlier forms of doxology, 'Glory to the Father through the Son and in the Holy Spirit' and 'Glory to the Father with the Son and together with the Holy Spirit', perforce gave way to the form 'Glory to the Father and to the Son and to the Holy Spirit' in which the equality of the Persons is emphasised with the complete loss of all reference to their mutual relations.

place or if it had leapt out of Judaism not into the Greco-Roman world but into that of Hinduism or of Confucianism, we must, I suggest, accept, as part of the providential ordinance of God, the course that events have actually taken, while making no effort to hide the limitations and aberrations that have accompanied it.[1] For God works not against, but in mysterious collaboration with, human freedom, and even man's errors and sins turn, in the end, to God's glory. That India and China and Africa have contributions to make to the fuller understanding of the Christian faith we must most readily and joyfully insist; the time may indeed be imminent for this great efflorescence of theology to begin. And when it does there is at least one thing of which we can be sure, that these will be contributions which Europe could never have made. Nevertheless, it is not accidental that, in the fullness of time, it was to the Greco-Roman world that the task of giving intellectual formulation to the Christian revelation was first committed. And when the Church comes with the Gospel of Christ to the ancient civilisations of the East, to the peoples of Africa with their youthful promise of glories yet to come, to the secularised technocratic civilisation of the modern Anglo-Saxon

[1] Dr F. W. Beare has put the question: 'Is it rash to suggest that the Christian doctrine of the Church is a kind of fusion of the Hebrew conception of the People of God with this Hellenistic vision of mankind united in a single community of heart and mind, animated by the one spirit which is also the spirit of the universe itself?' ('New Testament Christianity and the Hellenistic World', in *The Communication of the Gospel in New Testament Times*, p. 67.) And no less determinedly biblical a theologian than Dr C. H. Dodd has written:

> The work that the Hellenistic theologians did was an example to theologians of every period. They sought an expression for the fundamental truths of the Gospel in terms which would give them relevance to the large questions which in that age were being asked about God, man and the universe. We in turn have the task of giving them relevance to the large questions which are being asked by men of our time. But if theology seeks an accommodation with temporary fashions of thought by cutting loose from its firm foundations in *kerygma* and testimonies, as it has sometimes done, it declines into insignificance, and has in fact nothing to say to the world which the world may not learn elsewhere. The challenge of a new period with its peculiar problems should force us back to the pit from whence we were digged and the rock from whence we were hewn. (*According to the Scriptures*, p. 138.)

Cf. Gregory Dix's assertion, in his unjustly neglected work *Jew and Greek*: 'The Jewish-Christian Church formulated neither the doctrine of the Trinity, nor that of the Incarnation, for it could not think metaphysically. But it made them necessary.' (Pp. 27f.)

world or to the militantly atheistic Marxist nations of the Soviet Union and of China, it can only come with that Gospel in the form which it has taken as a result of the Church's actual history. This is what makes the present situation so perilously exciting. This is why it confronts the theologian or the evangelist with such demands upon both his prudence and his courage. For, first, it is imperative that what he offers to his contemporaries is the authentic Christian revelation and not some superficially more attractive substitute for it. Secondly, while readily admitting that the form in which he presents it is inevitably conditioned by the particularities and relativities of the history—basically that of Greco-Roman culture—through which the Church has passed in these first two millennia of its life, he must never deny the permanent value of much that it has come to learn in the course of that history; to pretend that Augustine, Bernard and Aquinas, Athanasius and Basil and Palamas have nothing of importance to offer to the future Christianity of Africa and Asia would be to wrap in a napkin the talents that God has given and bury them deep in the earth; it would be to keep our riches for our own enjoyment and to refuse, through cowardice if not through selfishness, to share them with those who might make far better use of them than we have made. But thirdly, we must be ready to find that much in our European heritage will seem strange and unattractive to our Asian and African fellow Christians and we must be equally ready to find them expressing their Christian commitment in ways that seem strange and unattractive to us. Lastly we must be prepared for the most surprising and far-reaching developments of both thought and practice if and when Christianity really takes root in Asian and African soil. This will no doubt bring with it great opportunities for good and evil alike; there is no place for romanticism in the matter, and Asian and African Christianity may be expected to produce their own heresies, which will be no less dangerous to the Church and the Gospel than those which European Christianity produced for itself. Prophecy is always a tempting activity, for in all probability one will be dead before one's prophecies have been disproved by events; it is also a dangerous one, for false prophecies can induce disastrous policies. It may, of course, happen that in the immediate future Asia and Africa will show themselves impervious or hostile to Christianity and that the Church, instead of entering upon a glorious period of expansion and efflorescence, may find itself frustrated, rejected and persecuted, as indeed it is in many parts of the world today. Nevertheless, we have no right to acquiesce in this assumption, and if we are to commend the Christian way of life and thought to cultures which as yet have not received it there are three principles that we must unfailingly bear in mind. First, we must be quite clear, to use the words of Pope John which I have placed at the head of this chapter, about the distinction between the substance of the ancient doctrine and its formulation; there must be no compromise about the former, in loyalty to our Lord and in charity to his children. Secondly, while resisting all temptations to impose permanently upon others those formulations of the doctrine and its practical expressions that are the product of our own particular cultural setting, we must be ready and anxious to share with them the blessings which we have received in the course of our Christian history. And thirdly, we must encourage and assist new formulations and expressions which we could never have produced for ourselves, but from which, when others have produced them, we may profit no less than they. For we are not concerned simply with the adaptation of the theoretical scheme to the requirements of a novel situation, but with the integration of fresh men and women and fresh cultures into the historic Body of Christ. And we must be quite clear that there are not a European Christianity, an Asian Christianity and an African Christianity; there is one Christianity, within which European, Asian and African cultures may find fulfilment in their several modes of expression and may share with one another the gifts that God has given to each. Nor, we may add, are there, strictly speaking, a first-century, a thirteenth-century and a twentieth-century Christianity, convenient as it may sometimes be to use these expressions; there is one Christianity to which each age may make its special contribution for succeeding ages to inherit. It may well be that at this stage in history the Church is on the brink of a transformation of thought and life not less radical than that which took place in the middle of the first century when it was transformed from a Semitic to a Hellenic religion. But the two processes will be different in important respects. In the first place, the primitive Jewish

Christianity, while it inherited an extremely elaborate conceptual and imaginal outlook from later Judaism,[1] had hardly begun to formulate systematically its own faith; whereas Christianity as we know it today has appropriated and moulded to its needs the whole apparatus of classical thought. To assess the gains and losses of this process is indeed a colossal task, and Christian theologians are far from agreement about it. To some (Dr Nygren's *Agape and Eros* will provide one example and Dr Subilia's *Problem of Catholicism* another) the whole story from St John to Luther is that of a progressive contamination of the Gospel by paganism; to others the philosophy of the Greco-Roman civilisation was the divinely provided conceptual framework in which alone Christianity could achieve an adequate intellectual expression. At what precise point between these two extremes the truth lies is not easy to determine, nor is it necessary for our present purpose; I am concerned only to emphasise that in the concrete form in which it has come to us, and which of necessity provides the starting-point for any further re-expression, Christian theology is a product of European civilisation. This is as much a fact as the fact that the divine Logos became man as a Jew. And while there will be important parallels between the transplanting of primitive Jewish Christianity into a Hellenic setting and the transplanting of twentieth-century Christianity into an Asian or African setting, there will also be important differences. A second point which must be observed is that, since Jewish Christianity became virtually extinct as soon as the transplanting had taken place, Hellenic Christianity had a virtually clear field in which to develop. The discipline, which would have been both invigorating and restraining, of the parallel but mutually enriching development of a Jewish and a Hellenic Christian theological tradition side by side never had a chance. With all its inner differentiation, which was indeed vast, Christian theology achieved its classical formulation upon the basis of Greco-Roman thought. Even the contrast within this tradition in its later developments between the Greek East and the Latin West lost most of its power of cross-fertilisation as a result of the destruction of the African bridge-church and the later schism between Rome and Constantinople; and one can only speculate what might have resulted if the great scholastic

[1] Cf. J. Daniélou, *The Theology of Jewish Christianity*, *passim*.

synthesis of the West had come into really fruitful and constructive discourse with the Eastern hesychast tradition which culminated in the fourteenth century with the work of St Gregory Palamas. In the modern world no such segregation is possible and, unless the whole tradition of Christian thought and practice which we have inherited is to become as extinct as the primitive Jewish Christianity and the Christianity of North Africa after the seventh century (though this is a possibility which we cannot exclude under the providence of God), we must look forward to a theological future in which, without any abandonment of the great achievements of the existing theological tradition of Christendom, new and unpredictable riches may be drawn from the treasury of God's household when it is explored by the minds of men whose way of thought is radically different from ours. The task has indeed begun, and it will no doubt come as a surprise to many that some of its most enthusiastic proponents are scholars of the Roman Catholic obedience. The penetrating and inspiring books of Professor Zaehner,[1] Dom Aelred Graham's intriguing work *Zen Christianity*,[2] various articles by the late Fr Victor White and by Bernard Kelly,[3] and the earlier work of Louis Massignon and Joseph Maréchal bear witness to this. But these writers, for all their learning and sympathetic understanding, are themselves Europeans;[4] the real work remains to be done by Christians who have received their own intellectual formation in the cultures concerned. If this should happen on a large scale the results may indeed be surprising.[5]

Two further remarks must be made, though I cannot here discuss their implications. (1) There will, of course, be a notable difference between the case of Asia, which possesses highly developed systems of philosophy as old as, or older than, those of

[1] *Mysticism Sacred and Profane; At Sundry Times; The Convergent Spirit.*

[2] Cf. also the article 'The Ecumenical Approach to Hinduism' in *Search*, May 1964, by Dom Bede Griffiths.

[3] *Dominican Studies*, 1954.

[4] An exception must be made for the extremely interesting monograph *The Quintessence of Hinduism*, by the Indian priest Fr H. O. Mascarenhas; there are no doubt others.

[5] Hans Küng raises the question explicitly: 'Does Christian theology absolutely have to be bound up with Aristotelianism, or can it, fundamentally, be equally well developed with the aid of a Vedantic philosophy or a Bantu philosophy?' (*The Living Church*, pp. 380f.)

Europe, and that of Africa, where, in spite of the existence of elaborate social and religious patterns, indigenous thought of a philosophical type is practically absent. (2) Christianity is not the only outlook upon life which Europe has brought to bear upon the peoples of Africa and Asia; the sheer secularism, which has in effect superseded Christianity as the attitude to life of the greater number of civilised Europeans and Americans, has made a far greater impact than has Christianity, and an impact which, in spite of the material blessings which it has brought in its train, as for example in the fields of agriculture and medicine, has been largely destructive of the native patterns of religion and culture. Nor, as Mr Oliver Fielding Clarke[1] has impressed on us, must we forget the ever-present attractions of Marxism, with its promise of an earthly beatitude.

IV

In this book I am concerned with the comparatively limited task of considering some of the programmes, and indeed one particular type of programme, which are offered us today for reinterpreting the Christian faith in our own local situation, but it seems to me to be essential to see that task in the wider setting of the Church's confrontation of the contemporary world as a whole and not just in the setting of our Western technocratic culture. I am, therefore, not making a cheap debating-point when I endorse, in a sense different from that which he intended, Dr Robinson's suggestion that the charge to which his exposition exposes itself is not that of being too radical but that of not being radical enough. Before examining his celebrated little book *Honest to God* I shall analyse in detail the much more systematic work of Dr van Buren of which he has spoken in such warm terms of praise, *The Secular Meaning of the Gospel*. I shall then attempt to deal constructively with the main issues that are raised by the general approach which these two works exemplify. I shall do my best to treat the various arguments involved on their merits from a purely rational standpoint. But since there is a widespread assumption that, in comparison with the alleged narrowness and sterility of traditional Christian theology, this new approach is noteworthy for its breadth of vision and its

[1] *For Christ's Sake*, pt. II.

fruitfulness, I must now express my conviction that the precise opposite is the case. What most characterises it, I suggest, is its provincialism. In order to conform to the alleged demands of twentieth-century secularised man, it is ready to discard the accumulated wisdom of the Christian centuries and to ignore the profound insights, and indeed the existence, of the great Asian religions which yet await baptism into Christ. It is, however, against this vast background, at once intimidating and invigorating, of the Church's concern with mankind in its totality that I see the admittedly restricted undertaking to which I am here committed. This must be my excuse for the sketchy, and no doubt amateurish, remarks of the last few pages. Anxious as I am that the Christian doctrine should be presented to contemporary civilised Englishmen and Americans in language that they will recognise as both intelligible and relevant, I am more anxious that what is presented to them shall be in fact the Christian doctrine and not some substitute for it, and I am very conscious that if we take as normative the thought-forms of such a very specialised and secularised group as this we may render ourselves unintelligible to a much wider and less secularised body of men and women. But before I conclude this chapter there is one central problem on which I must touch.

I have said that, while formulations of Christian doctrine may and should legitimately differ, its substance must be preserved. This raises the immense theme of what is often called the development of doctrine but might, I think, better be called the development of doctrinal formulations and implications. The special aspect of it with which I am concerned here is this; granted that the formulations may legitimately differ, how can we specify and recognise the substance? Clearly, not by laying down some unalterable form of words, for this would be simply an additional formulation. How, then, is the theologian to maintain his loyalty to the revealed Gospel, while at the same time making every effort to express it in terms intelligible to its hearers and to help them to see its implications for their particular circumstances and situations? It is, I suggest, by forming a deliberate habit of loyal submission to Christian tradition, while at the same time bringing to bear upon it all the critical and interpretative gifts which God has given him. And, although the theologian's task is clearly an intellectual one, in the sense that he is concerned with understanding and expressing *truth*, its successful performance (as far as that is possible) does not depend primarily upon his personal mental agility but upon his union with God who is the Truth itself. Theology is thus in its essence a function of the Church as the Body of Christ, and the theologian is a man to whom the exercise of that function has been specially committed. Thus, without any suggestion of paradox, M. Gilson has remarked that the ideal theologian needs two intellectual qualities whose combination in the same mind is rather rare: a perfect intellectual modesty and an almost reckless intellectual audacity;[1] and Fr Charles Davis has well commented that, while the combination which is urged seems impossible, it becomes feasible if the audacity is referred to the work of understanding and the modesty to the claim of certitude.[2] I will develop this point by making some quotations from the Inaugural Lecture on Theology and History which I delivered at King's College, London, in 1962.

> I do not think it that it is necessary for either the individual theologian or for the general body of theologians at any epoch to know all the answers to all the questions or even to know which are the questions to which the final and irrefutable answers have been found. The theologian's motto should *not* be 'It all depends on me'. He is not committed to 'beginning all over again'; rather he is 'in a great tradition'. He should neither be a victim of the over-confidence which is convinced that it has given the Christian religion the ultimate and definitive form nor be haunted by the *Angst* which fears that the whole structure of Christian thought may be without solid rational foundations. He is part of something which is greater than himself; he is the heir of the Christian ages. He may indeed hope that he will be able to make his own contribution to the great body of Christian thought within which his own thinking is set. He may at times have a painful suspicion that the tradition, as it has been presented to him, is, in this or the other respect, distorted, unbalanced, stunted, fossilised, forgetful of its own past achievements or insensitive to the needs and demands of the contemporary world. If so, he will, with that combination of intellectual audacity and intellectual modesty which we have seen to be so desirable and at the same time so

[1] *Reason and Revelation in the Middle Ages*, p. 71.
[2] *Theology and the University*, p. 123.

> difficult to acquire, make his own contribution to the common inheritance and leave it to others to estimate its value. . . . It will not matter very much if the theologian is sometimes wrong, as long as he is not convinced that he is always right. What, I would maintain, he must and can be convinced of is the truth of the great Christian tradition, even when he is in the humiliating position of not being sure that he or anyone else has yet adequately understood its content or seen it in its true proportions.

It is this last sentence that, paradoxical as it may sound, gives, as I believe, the key to our present problem. To continue:

> Thus, as I see it, the task of the Christian theologian is that of theologising within the great historical tradition; *theologizandum est in fide*. Even when he feels constrained to criticise adversely the contemporary expressions of the tradition, he will be conscious that he is bringing out from the depths of the tradition its latent and hitherto unrecognised contents; he is acting as its organ and its exponent. He will also offer his own contribution for it to digest and assimilate if it can. Like the good householder he will bring out of his treasure things new and old. But he will have no other Gospel than that which he has received.[1]

The bearings of this upon our present problem may be more clearly seen if I add that, while all formulations of Christian truth, even the most authoritative, are of necessity expressed in human words and interpreted by the discursive activity of human minds, and thus share in the inevitable imprecision and incompleteness of all our finite speech and thought, the truth itself (the 'substance of the doctrine' as distinct from its 'formulation') exists in its fullness in the mind of Christ, not as a set of propositions explored by the discursive reason but as one totally apprehended object of the intellect, possessed in all its fullness in one supreme contemplative act. It is because the Church, of which the theologian is a member and an agent, is Christ's body that the formulations are genuine, though partial and inadequate, projections on to the plane of the temporal existence of the Church militant, of the unformulated substance of Christian truth held in the mind of him who is Truth itself. It is in this way that I would solve the problem of the relation between the immutable substance of Christian doctrine and the

[1] *Theology and History*, pp. 16–17.

mutability and unfinished character of its verbal expression. I would add that, so far from leaving us wallowing in a morass of theological relativism, the recognition of the essential incompleteness of the formulations should provide us with the strongest incentive to cleave to the truth which, however imperfectly, they express and preserve us from being led into error by ignoring their limitations. Finally, I would remark that the view which I have been expounding has no connection whatever with the view which one used so frequently to hear asserted, that revelation is given in acts and not in propositions. In one sense this seems to me to be a truism, and in another to be obviously false; but in any case it is not what we have been concerned with here.

CHAPTER TWO

THE SECULARISATION OF CHRISTIANITY

Il faut être absolument moderne.—Rimbaud.

I

WHATEVER ITS OTHER merits may be, Dr J. A. T. Robinson's best-selling paper-back volume *Honest to God* has at any rate attracted attention to a movement in present-day theology which, while it has not perhaps the monopoly of enlightened and constructive thought with which some of its more fervent exponents have credited it, may be more wide-spread than has been commonly recognised in English-speaking religious circles. It is difficult to describe it in a few words, since, as in other theological movements, there are considerable differences of opinion among its leaders on many important questions. Its main features may nevertheless be indicated by the three adjectives 'secularist', 'demythologising' and 'existentialist'; their precise meaning, in so far as their meaning can be said to be precise, will, I hope, appear in the sequel. A further difficulty arises from the fact that many of its spokesmen write in an idiom which, whether deliberately or not, is at best obscure and at worst self-contradictory. I shall therefore begin my discussion by making a detailed examination of a book which has come out from the Episcopal Theological Seminary of Austin, Texas, which Dr Robinson has himself described as being one of the most exciting and disturbing that he has read[1] and which has what seems to me to be the even greater merit of extreme lucidity. Furthermore its very recent date has enabled its author to consider and criticise the earlier manifestations of the movement, so that in discussing his views it will be possible to a large

[1] *The Honest to God Debate*, p. 250.

degree to form a judgment on its general drift and achievements. This book is the work by Dr Paul M. van Buren entitled *The Secular Meaning of the Gospel*; its author's special angle of approach is shown by the additional phrase: 'based on an analysis of its language'.

Dr van Buren opens his preface by confessing that in our time there is considerable confusion about the nature of both the Christian Gospel and secularism. Rather surprisingly, he takes 'secularism' as 'a loose designation of the reaction to the Idealism of the last century'. He goes on to say that 'both modern so-called Biblical theology and modern so-called analytic philosophy are responses to secularism'.[1] Here the word 'response' would seem to be capable of either a positive or a negative connotation, for, however secularism is understood, biblical theology would seem to be a reaction against it and analytic philosophy on the whole one of its allies. However, as the argument proceeds, secularism does not seem to be understood in a narrowly philosophical sense, as the above description would suggest, for the main argument is introduced by a definitely non-philosophical quotation from Dietrich Bonhoeffer which Dr Robinson has already made famous:

> Honesty demands that we recognise that we must live in the world as if there were no God. . . . God himself drives us to this realisation.—God makes us know that we must live as men who can get along without him. . . . We stand continually in the presence of the God who makes us live in the world without the God-hypothesis.

It would be perhaps unfair to Bonhoeffer to take *au pied de la lettre* words written from a Nazi prison camp under conditions of grave physical and emotional distress; the spiritual experience of feeling forsaken by God has been common to many of the greatest saints and can claim even more august authority in the Fourth Word from the Cross. However, as van Buren goes on to point out, Bonhoeffer put forward his assertion as a serious theological reply to the weakness of the traditional Liberal Protestant theology of the past century, and those who have made use of it, including van Buren, have certainly interpreted it as such. It can therefore hardly be unfair to these latter

[1] op. cit., p. xiii.

persons to point out what extraordinary statements are made in this passage. In the first place, it would seem to be obvious that honesty can demand that a man should live in the world as if there were no God only if he were convinced that there was no God or at any rate were doubtful whether there was a God or not; to believe that there was a God and then to live as if one believed that there was not, whatever else it might be called, could hardly be called honest. And the subsequent assertion that 'God himself drives us to this realisation' certainly implies belief that there is a God, even though it also implies that God is forcing us to live in accordance with a lie. 'God makes us know that we must live as men who can get along without him' might just be taken as meaning that God tells us that we must at times live without any consciousness of his presence, but the further assertion that 'we stand continually in the presence of the God who makes us *live in the world without the God-hypothesis*' certainly seems to imply that we must plan our whole lives without any reference to God, and this is undoubtedly the sense in which it is understood by those who have quoted it most exuberantly and not least by van Buren. For he is emphatic that he is not concerned with the question how the Christian can preach the Gospel to modern secular man and help him to become a Christian, but with the question how modern man *within the Church* can retain a radically secularist outlook and yet be in some sense, and indeed in the truest sense, a Christian.

Whether van Buren has failed to see this or merely looks upon it as irrelevant, it is a clear consequence of his basic assumption that, if he is right, conversion to Christianity, while it involves a moral reorientation, has no intellectual implications whatever; the anti-intellectualism which, rightly or wrongly, has often been attributed to the traditional German Protestantism from which van Buren seems to draw his chief inspiration could hardly go farther than this. It is the basic dogma of his system that, in order to be a twentieth-century Christian, a Christian must adopt whole-heartedly the intellectual outlook of other twentieth-century men; it never occurs to him that he might be expected to adopt the outlook that throughout the ages has been common to other Christians. Furthermore, what is taken as normative for twentieth-century man is the common outlook of members of our industrialised technological Western civilisation.

It is not at all clear what van Buren thinks should be the outlook of a Christian in Asia or Africa whose native culture has not yet been destroyed by ours. Should he first secularise himself to come into line with us, or should he accommodate his Christianity to his own inherited beliefs in pantheism, reincarnation, witchcraft and so on? But perhaps the question simply does not arise, for van Buren repudiates all concern of the Church with apologetics and evangelism and limits its task to the production of the correct secularist attitude in its own members. 'The meaning of that claim now', he writes, referring to the phrase 'claiming the world for Christ', 'is simply that the whole world may be seen with the Christian's perspective. He need not expect the world to understand itself as he understands it. Since he has acquired this perspective in connection with a freedom which is contagious, he should be content to let this contagion work its own way in the world.'[1] We shall see later what these words 'perspective' and 'contagious' mean; they hold a very central place in van Buren's system. For the moment it is sufficient to notice that, at the very starting-point of his exposition, he explicitly denies that the Gospel has any distinctive intellectual content and demands that Christians should simply adopt the secularist Godless outlook of the world around them. Mr Harry Blamires, in a superb work of Christian apologetics, has written, under the significant heading 'The Surrender to Secularism', the following words:

> There is no longer a Christian mind. It is a commonplace that the mind of modern man has been secularised. For instance, it has been deprived of any orientation towards the supernatural. Tragic as this fact is, it would not be so desperately tragic had the Christian mind held out against the secular drift. But unfortunately the Christian mind has succumbed to the secular drift with a degree of weakness and nervelessness unmatched in Christian history. It is difficult to do justice in words to the complete loss of intellectual morale in the twentieth-century Church.[2]

But I doubt whether even Mr Blamires expected to find capitulation to secularism adopted as his guiding principle by a professional exponent of Christian theology.

[1] ibid., p. 191.
[2] *The Christian Mind*, p. 3.

It is interesting to notice that van Buren makes no attempt to discover the causes for the secularisation of the outlook of modern industrialised man. Had he done so, he might have been led to question whether a Christian ought either to capitulate to it or acquiesce in it. His own reason for defending a Godless system is, as we shall see, derived from a somewhat uncritical acceptance of the doctrines of a vociferous but already weakening school of Anglo-Saxon philosophers, but one can hardly believe, even in these days of the Third Programme, that this, any more than Copernican astronomy or Darwinian biology, is the *direct* cause of the unbelief of the contemporary ton-up boy, stockbroker or shop assistant. I would suggest that the main cause is the continual impact upon the senses of a technocratic culture in which all the emphasis falls upon what man can do with things and hardly any upon what they really are, but this is not the place to argue the point. In any case, I should maintain that to attribute absolute value to the secular, as van Buren does, is in ıact to degrade it and that it is only in its due relatioin to the transcendent God who has created it that the secular can find its fulfilment. It is very noticeable that, in spite of all his talk about the secular, van Buren has no *theology of the secular*; all he is concerned with is the *secularising of theology*. He has nothing to correspond to Jacques Maritain's splendid notion of a theocentric humanism[1] or to Pierre Teilhard de Chardin's magnificent vision of the function of the scientist and the technician as the transformation of the created world in accordance with the purposes of God.[2] Nor does he pay any attention to the apologetic for supernatural religion which has been so originally and impressively developed, from a purely scientific and empirical standpoint, by the distinguished French biologist M. Rémy Chauvin in his striking work *God of the Scientist, God of the Experiment*. And the whole notion of Christian sociology, as manifested, for example, in the Christian social movement which took its inspiration from F. D. Maurice, becomes simply irrelevant, if not indeed pernicious. In the task of giving Christian men a secularised understanding of the Gospel, the task of giving secularised men a Christian understanding of their world is abandoned. For, let us repeat, van Buren is not concerned

[1] *True Humanism* (*L'humanisme intégral*).
[2] *Le Milieu divin.*

with the validation of the dim awareness of God that even secularised man in some degree preserves; he is concerned to secularise the religion of Christians. 'Bultmann and Ogden', he writes, 'are asking how the Christian can preach the Gospel to secular modern man so that he will be able to hear, understand, and become a Christian. They are interested in the "modern man" who is outside the church. Our question has to do with the "modern man" who is inside the church, more or less, and who is wondering what he is doing there.'[1] Van Buren might do well to heed Père Bouyer's reminder that a too facile adaptation of religion to the contemporary situation defeats its own purpose[2] and Fr Karl Rahner's equally timely observation that the apparent atrophy of the religious sense today may well be only a passing phenomenon.[3]

As I have already mentioned, van Buren finds the guiding principle for the secularisation of Christianity in the philosophical school which is commonly known as linguistic analysis. However, before entering upon this task he turns aside to consider the movement in biblical interpretation which was initiated by Dr Rudolf Bultmann and of which the key-word is 'demythologising' (*Entmythologisierung*). The history of this movement has been admirably related by Dr R. H. Fuller in his little book *The New Testament in Current Study*, while the controversy to which it has given rise in the land of its birth can be studied in the two volumes of essays published in English under the title *Kerygma and Myth*, the former of which contains a penetrating critique by Dr A. M. Farrer. Bultmann's programme falls into two parts. In the first it is asserted that the biblical presentation of the Gospel is given in mythological terms which are unintelligible and unacceptable to modern man, who does not believe in a three-storey universe, divine intervention or a world of spirits; hence the need for demythologising the Gospel. In the second stage, when the demythologising has been done, man's religion is restored to him in the existential act of faith, which is evoked from him by the proclamation of the Gospel, the *kerygma*. 'Faith is dependent upon the event of Jesus Christ, his appearance in history, his words and death. Although, accord-

[1] op. cit., p. 11.
[2] *Rite and Man*, p. 61.
[3] *Mission and Grace*, I, p. 53.

ing to Bultmann, an existentialist analysis of man can discover something of man's problem, and even define what an authentic existence would be, the kerygma alone offers man the possibility of this new existence, and the kerygma is grounded in the event of Christ.'[1] Thus, while Bultmann is ready to jettison the historicity of almost the whole Gospel story and especially its miraculous and supernatural elements, he accepts the fact of the crucifixion, and the existence of Jesus as a historic person is essential to his system in order to give it some anchorage in the world of which we who believe are part. Some of Bultmann's followers have gone even farther than he has; thus, for example, Dr Fritz Buri, not content with demythologising the Gospel, wants to dekerygmatise it as well. And even of Bultmann's own position it has been said that it identifies redemption not with Christ dying on the cross but with Dr Bultmann entering the pulpit on Sunday morning.[2] Van Buren observes that Bultmann has, in fact, been attacked from two opposite positions. On the one hand, the conservative critics, of whom the most distinguished is the famous biblical theologian Dr Karl Barth, accuse Bultmann of evacuating the Gospel in order to make it acceptable to modern man. On the other hand the radicals, such as Buri and Dr Schubert M. Ogden, accuse him of retaining a mythological element by tying the Gospel to the figure of the historic Jesus and so making the Gospel still unacceptable. In van Buren's words:

> Bultmann's critics from both sides agree on the existence of a serious inconsistency in his proposal. Bultmann says, on the one hand, that faith must be interpreted exhaustively as the realisation of man's original possibility of 'authentic existence' as this is conceived by 'an appropriate philosophical analysis'. On the other hand, he insists that faith can only be realised because of the event of Jesus of Nazareth. Barth objects that the first thesis threatens the second; Ogden objects that the second negates the first.[3]

Van Buren himself accepts neither Barth's position nor Ogden's. Roughly speaking, we might say that he rejects Barth because Barth wants to keep both God and Christ and that he rejects

[1] van Buren, op. cit., p. 6.
[2] Cf. Fuller, op. cit., p. 73.
[3] van Buren op. cit., p. 10.

Ogden because Ogden wants to keep neither, whereas he himself (and this is where the logical analysts come in) wants to keep Christ and get rid of God. To put it this way, however, is not really fair to Ogden, who is not nearly so anxious to get rid of God as van Buren is. The real weakness of Ogden from van Buren's point of view is that, in spite of his assertion that Jesus is the decisive manifestation of God's love, 'as Ogden reads the New Testament, the apostolic claim that God is revealed "only in Jesus Christ" means not that God can be found, or faith realised, only in him, but that the God made known in Jesus Christ is the only one there is: the God who is to be found everywhere. The logical conclusion would be that Christian faith is not dependent on the event of Jesus Christ.'[1] But both Bultmann and Ogden differ from van Buren in the fact that they are concerned with the problem of preaching the faith to modern man; van Buren, as we have seen, is concerned only with secularising the faith of Christians. He is thoroughly frank about this and has no illusions about the practical results:

> To develop an interpretation of the Gospel on the basis of certain empirical attitudes [he writes] . . . hardly serves an apologetic interest in making the Gospel understandable or more available to contemporary 'unbelievers'. It can only serve the purpose of faith seeking understanding. If other 'believers' find that they too are struck by and committed to that which the author finds compelling in 'secularism', they may also find this study helpful in seeking understanding. . . . This is a conversation 'from faith to faith'.[2]

II

Passing from his introductory remarks, van Buren begins his main exposition by giving a brief account of the development of Christology from the New Testament to the Council of Chalcedon. The Logos-Christology, he tells us, was developed in order to defend Christians from the charge of worshipping a man. 'When they were charged with blasphemy for worshipping Jesus, they answered that their Lord Jesus Christ was not merely a man, but the eternal and universal Logos of God from which

[1] ibid., p. 11.
[2] ibid., p. 20.

all order and rationality was derived.'[1] This was, in the Bultmannite sense, a 'mythological' notion, though it served its purpose at the time. Even in the hands of Justin, so van Buren assures us, the Logos-doctrine, while professing to accept the manhood of Jesus, set him apart from other men,[2] and this tendency was accentuated by growing conviction of the Alexandrian thinkers that the Logos must be thought of as almost, and in the upshot as fully, equal to God. So we come to the final answer that the hypostasis of the Logos, having already a divine 'nature', took on a human 'nature', too. 'These two "natures" were united "inseparably, indivisibly, unchanged, and unconfused", according to the formula of Chalcedon, specifically in the hypostasis of the Logos.'[3]

Remarking in passing that in recent years the Chalcedonian formulation has been defended by a biblical theologian of no lesser stature than that of Karl Barth, van Buren next discusses what he describes as the Problem of Biblical and Patristic Categories. 'Considered from a modern perspective', he tells us (whatever that rather question-begging phrase may mean), 'orthodox patristic Christology did not do justice to the manhood of Jesus of Nazareth.'[4] He refuses to accept that the insistence of the orthodox Fathers on the completeness of Christ's manhood is in any way adequate. 'Christians have hesitated to say that Jesus was "only a man", even if a man whose existence was grounded quite particularly in the existence and act of God the Word.'[5] This is a revealing sentence, for it shows that, for van Buren, to deny that Jesus is *only* a man is to deny that he is a man in any real sense of the words. The common formula that Jesus is fully man and also fully God would seem to van Buren self-contradictory, or, indeed, simply meaningless, for, as we shall see when we go on to consider his general philosophical position, van Buren's adherence to an extreme form of linguistic empiricism makes it impossible for him to accept as factual assertions any statements in which the word 'God' occurs. Thus, when he goes on to tell us what kind of Christological statements he thinks the Fathers ought to have made, it is not because he

[1] ibid., p. 25.
[2] ibid., pp. 25, 39.
[3] ibid., p. 31.
[4] ibid., p. 38.
[5] ibid., p. 40.

thinks the proposed amendments express better than the commonly accepted formulas the true metaphysical status of Jesus Christ, but because he thinks they can be more easily replaced by the purely empirical assertions which are all that his secularist outlook allows him to make. He tells us, for example, that 'the Greek fathers tended to neglect history, as is evident in their tendency to focus, not on the incarnation as an event, but on *incarnatedness* as a condition'.[1] This is, I think, quite untrue of St Athanasius and only superficially true of Chalcedon, but even were it fully true of both the fact would remain that van Buren would reject the notion of incarnation as an event, no less emphatically than that of incarnatedness as a condition, if the event was asserted to be an event in the history of the Divine Word; the only history which he would accept is the history of the human life of Jesus of Nazareth. Again he writes:

> If [the Fathers] had been more consistent in saying that God is unknown apart from his self-revelation and that we must begin with Jesus Christ in order to know anything about God at all, they might have been able to begin with the cross as the event of self-revelation of a God who is quite able to take suffering to himself and whose glory is so great that he can also humble himself. Had this been done, the course of the development of classical Christology would have been quite different.[2]

This may well be the case, but the alternative course would have been equally unsuccessful in meeting the demands which van Buren has to make about the necessary features of an acceptable language of theological discourse. We may also notice here that, for all his strivings to be contemporary and secular, van Buren's attitude lands him in complete denial not only of all forms of natural theology but also of any genuine religious experience outside the strictly Christian sphere. For his insistence, which, as we shall see, is quite fundamental for him, that statements which appear to be about God can be accepted only if they can be reinterpreted as statements (not necessarily the *same* statements) about Jesus inevitably leads to this conclusion. Here, I am, however, anticipating.

It is interesting at this point to note that van Buren's attitude

[1] ibid., p. 41.
[2] ibid., p. 42.

of reserve applies to the biblical no less than the patristic theologians.

> There can be little doubt [he writes] that the thought and categories of the Fathers are quite different from ours. The Ritschlian thesis, however, asserts that the thought world of the Fathers is also far from that of the New Testament. The wide acceptance of this judgment, and of the assumption that we can more easily understand the thought of the biblical writers than that of the Fathers, has contributed to the rise of modern 'biblical theology'. Whether biblical theology does in fact understand the thought world of the Bible better than did the Fathers is perhaps a judgment best left to history.[1]

And he makes reference in a footnote to the devastating criticism which Dr James Barr has applied to the writings of some of the most distinguished of contemporary biblical theologians in his book *The Semantics of Biblical Language*; he might well have added to this Dr Barr's other book *Biblical Words for Time*. Nevertheless van Buren remarks, apparently with approval, that 'biblical theology has given modern theology a fresh appreciation of the distinctive thought world of the Bible and of the categories which were central for the biblical authors', and he lists 'the centrality of the Covenant, the highly dynamic, historical character of the event of God's self-revelation, the importance of man's obedience as the proper response of man in God's covenant' as 'biblical categories which played only a minor part in the development of patristic Christology'.[2]

In accordance with this attitude of qualified approval of the biblical theologians van Buren proceeds to expound what he describes as 'a Christology of "Call" and "Response" '. (The reader may find himself puzzled by the difficulty of reconciling this with van Buren's radical linguistic empiricism if he has failed to notice the footnote on page 18 in which van Buren remarks that, while he believes this particular interpretation of Christology to be his own, it represents not his present position but that which he held before he had read Wittgenstein's *Philosophical Investigations*.) In the Old Testament context, he tells us (and he is so determined to place his Christology in this

[1] ibid., pp. 44f.
[2] ibid., p. 45.

context that he proposes to speak of 'Yahweh' rather than of 'God'), the Christological passages of the New Testament speak not of the incarnation of the divine Logos but of the perfect 'response' of Jesus to the 'call' of Yahweh. 'The election of Jesus of Nazareth to be supremely the man who lived for the sake of other men was Yahweh's primary decision, which began to be realised in the creation of the world and then in the calling of Israel.' On these lines—and we need not at the moment enquire about the accuracy of this interpretation or its relation to the subsequent patristic Christology—it is clearly possible to secularise Jesus, but the problem of secularising Yahweh, even when we have decided not to call him 'God', is more difficult. Van Buren asserts that 'it is an abstraction to conceive of Yahweh in any other way than as the one who has made himself known through his covenant with Jesus for the sake of the world' and introduces the notion of Yahweh's 'decision'. 'It was possible to identify Yahweh with his decision because the New Testament writers conceived of God always in relation to the decision enacted in Jesus of Nazareth.'[1] The obvious reflection that a decision involves someone who decides is thus set aside, but at the cost of hypostatising the decision itself, and this does not seem to be the sort of thing that an empiricist of such a radical type as van Buren ought to do. However, he now asserts that

> an intention became an action; a plan was enacted. To ask whether the plan exists apart from its enactment, or whether it has been transformed into its enactment, indicates that one is thinking of a plan or word as a quasi-physical substance. [This in itself seems odd, for nobody 'enacts' a 'substance'. But to continue—] It is simply a plan, and its enactment is simply what results when the plan is realised.[2]

'To summarise this idea in naïve terms', we are told, 'Yahweh determined in his heart of hearts upon having his faithful son, Jesus, and through him a faithful creation. . . .' But, if we are to avoid these naïve terms, we shall want to know whose is the plan? If we say merely that it is Jesus' own plan, we are falling into a tautology, and in addition it will be difficult to know what we are to make of the notion of Jesus' 'obedience', which is

[1] ibid., pp. 51f.
[2] ibid., p. 52.

another of the biblical categories. However, 'the apostolic witnesses made no attempt to account for Jesus' obedience. Rather, they stood in awe before this obedience, which was authenticated for them by the Easter event.'[1]

How far van Buren himself is convinced by this reinterpretation of the traditional Christology is, as we have seen, open to doubt; it certainly seems to be inconsistent with what he has to say later on. He himself concludes this part of his discussion with the assertion that 'although such an interpretation may be called "orthodox", it is still, from the point of view of the theological "left", sadly mythological in form, if not in content',[2] but, although he goes on to state the objections of the 'theological left' he does not here commit himself to membership of it. On the other hand, he does say that 'when we compare this interpretation with that of the Fathers, we find that it meets the problems which led the Fathers to their conclusions', and it may be useful to quote the main sentences of the passage in which he summarises this interpretation:

> The patristic Logos or Eternal Son has been interpreted as Yahweh's purpose, the expression of his very self, and it meets the problem posed by Arianism. The Fathers wanted to say 'God of God' and in our own way we have said the same. They said that Jesus Christ was 'very man', and we have secured this side of the matter in another way: we have conceived of the fulness or perfection of man as residing not in the fact that all of his 'parts' are there, but in his historical existence and social relationships. . . . He was truly man in that he was as involved in life, as mixed up in politics, as much in the middle of human hate and love, friendship and enmity, as it is possible for man to be, and he was like this in fulfilling his calling to be present for others. . . .
>
> So entirely is he to be understood from the perspective of Easter, so fully is his life to be seen as a life of obedience to a divine election, that, like the New Testament, the believer cannot speak of a Jesus of Nazareth who might have existed independently of Yahweh's purpose. This man, moreover, though fully man and in no sense 'more than a man', is not to be confused with other men. He stood apart from them for the very reason of his solidarity with them: he was the one man who

[1] ibid., p. 53.
[2] ibid., p. 55.

> truly existed for others. His calling was to be the one for the many, whereas the calling of all other men is to let him be that for them: the way, the truth, and the life. He stands apart from all the others also in that he was obedient to his calling, whereas they are not obedient to theirs, or they only learn obedience by relying solely on the obedience of him whom they know and confess as Lord and Saviour.[1]

This is indeed a moving passage and, even if he felt that much needed to be added to it, any Christian could well agree with its positive assertions. We have seen, however, that for van Buren in his present phase the position which it states is not radical enough in its demythologising. He therefore goes on to consider the criticisms which have been made of it from the 'theological left'.

To many English readers the position which has just been outlined will seem a fairly revolutionary one and it will come to them as something of a surprise when they discover that for van Buren it is definitely conservative and is insufficiently 'contemporary'. As representatives of the 'left' he takes Bultmann and Ogden, and because Ogden is even farther to the left than Bultmann he starts from the analysis of Bultmann's position which is given by Ogden in his book *Christ Without Myth.* For both Bultmann and Ogden the basic problem which confronts modern man in understanding the New Testament lies in his inability to accept the mythological world-picture in which the New Testament message is clothed. ' "A mythological world-picture" is one in which (1) the non-objective reality that man experiences as the ground and limit of himself and his world is "objectified" and thus presented as but another part of the objective world; (2) the origin and goal of the world as a whole, as well as certain happenings within it, are referred to non-natural, yet "objective" causes; (3) the resulting complex of ideas comprising the picture takes the form of a double history.'[2] The required demythologising thus involves a great deal more than merely the abandonment of the view of a three-storey universe or of belief in demonic possession; what is required is nothing less than a rejection of all belief in a transcendent order of reality. This does not mean, however, that the mythology is

[1] ibid., p. 53f.
[2] Ogden, op. cit., p. 27, quoted by van Buren, op. cit., p. 58.

simply to be rejected; it is to be reformulated as a description of the religious experience of the Christian. 'Myth is . . . not simply to be eliminated; it must be interpreted as an expression of man's existential self-understanding.'[1] Thus, according to Ogden, for Bultmann the whole content of the Christian faith is reduced to one assertion: 'I henceforth understand myself no longer in terms of my past, but solely in terms of the future that is here and now disclosed to me as grace in my encounter with the Church's proclamation.' 'The very nature of the New Testament witness and of faith, therefore, demands an existentialist interpretation. To treat the New Testament as a source of information, and faith as assent to what is said, is to misunderstand the character of the document.'[2]

Behind all this there lies Bultmann's commitment to the existentialist philosophy of Martin Heidegger, a mode of thought which to most English readers is extremely unfamiliar and, as anyone who has tried to cope with *Being and Time* will readily admit, extraordinarily hard to understand. It is, nevertheless, integral to Bultmann's whole system, and no Dominican has ever thrown himself into the arms of St Thomas Aquinas with the fervour with which Bultmann has committed himself to Heidegger. Bultmann is, however, not only a Heideggerian but also a Christian, and he is emphatic that the existential act by which a Christian achieves his freedom can only be an act of faith in Jesus Christ. Thus van Buren summarises Bultmann's doctrine of salvation in the following words:

> Man cannot free himself; he must be set free, and this can happen only because God has already given himself for us in Jesus Christ. This saving act of God, however, is not in the distant past, for the liberating event takes place when a man responds to the word of the cross by deciding to understand himself as crucified and dead to his own past and open solely to the future offered to him in that word. The issue of this self-understanding was posed for the disciples by their confrontation with Jesus and his message, and again by the crucifixion. The 'objective fact' connected with Easter was their response of faith to God's gracious offer of this new possibility of authentic existence.[3]

[1] van Buren, op. cit., p. 59.
[2] ibid., p. 60.
[3] ibid., p. 61.

In Bultmann's own words, 'the salvation event is nowhere present except in the proclaiming, accosting, demanding and promising word of preaching'.[1]

As van Buren points out, Bultmann, in his anxiety to be both an existentialist and a Christian, is forced to maintain two incompatible theses. As Ogden states them they are:

(1) *The existentialist thesis:* Christian faith is to be interpreted exhaustively and without remainder as man's original possibility of authentic historical (*geschichtlich*) existence as this is more or less adequately clarified and conceptualised by an appropriate philosophical analysis.

(2) *The Christian thesis:* Christian faith is actually realisable, or is a 'possibility in fact' only because of the particular historical (*historisch*) event of Jesus of Nazareth, which is the originative event of the Church and its distinctive word and sacraments. Conscious as they are of the incompatibility of these two theses, Bultmann's critics have felt bound to choose between them. Those of the 'theological right' accept the second and deny the first; those of the 'left' accept the first and deny the second. Ogden, who is very much a man of the left, adopts the latter alternative, while modifying Bultmann's second thesis in order to make it consistent with the first. Thus for him the two theses are restated as follows:

(1) Christian faith is to be interpreted exhaustively and without remainder as man's original possibility of authentic existence as this is clarified and conceptualised by an appropriate philosophical analysis.

(2) Christian faith is always a 'possibility in fact' because of the unconditioned gift and demand of God's love, which is the ever-present ground and end of all created things; the decisive manifestation of this divine love, however, is the event of Jesus of Nazareth, which fulfils and corrects all other manifestations and is the originative event of the Church and its distinctive word and sacraments.

Thus, in Ogden's restatement, the omission of the words 'historical' and 'more or less' from the first principle, expresses, as van Buren remarks, Ogden's conviction that Christian faith is simply that real possibility for every man of authentic existence

[1] *Theology of the New Testament*, I, p. 302, cit. R. H. Fuller, *The New Testament in Current Study*, p. 73.

which we find in the system of Heidegger; in spite of the adjective 'Christian' it has no necessary connection with the particular human being Jesus of Nazareth. And the change of 'only' to 'always' in the second principle underlines this shift of position. In van Buren's words, 'the particular, historical prerequisite for faith, which is the event of Jesus of Nazareth, has been replaced by a universal and omnipresent prerequisite or cause'.[1] The precise bearing of the words 'decisive' and 'fulfilling and correcting' are somewhat obscure, but it is clear that Jesus is seen as providing one example, though it may be a unique one and is certainly one that has, in fact, been of tremendous historical significance, of something that can equally well occur independently of him.

Having stated the alternative to Bultmann's position which is offered by Ogden, van Buren finds Ogden's position itself open to no less than five objections. The first three condemn it as being insufficiently 'modern', in the sense of empirical and secular, in spite of its deliberate attempt to keep up to date. The last two condemn it as failing to do full justice to the Gospel in its historical aspect. They can be briefly summarised as follows:

(1) The talk in which both Bultmann and Ogden indulge about 'experienced non-objective reality' is meaningless when judged by strictly empirical criteria. For it clearly does not signify either the things or the persons which our senses perceive and does, in fact, seem to mean what less up-to-date people have meant by 'God'. In fact, as we have seen, in his second thesis Ogden speaks of 'God's love' as 'the ever-present ground and end of all created things' and this is far too metaphysical a phrase for a radical empiricist. What would count as an experience of such a ground and end?

(2) Van Buren's second objection follows from the first. It consists of the assertion that analogical speech about God is meaningless, though any speech about God would have to be analogical. Therefore in speaking about God, Bultmann and Ogden are using words without meaning. I shall have more to say about this later on, but it may be well to observe that this denial of the possibility of analogical speech is made by van Buren quite dogmatically, without reference to the considerable mass of writing in recent years which has been produced in its

[1] op. cit., p. 63.

defence. He quotes in his support an essay by Ronald Hepburn, though not Hepburn's full-scale work *Christianity and Paradox*; and he fails to notice that there are a number of philosophical theologians who would consider Bultmann's doctrine of mythological discourse to be highly vulnerable without rejecting analogical discourse in general.

(3) The third objection is that 'while Bultmann says there are only two kinds of statements: those which offer objective information about the world or phenomena in it, and those which are existential, which call the hearer to a decision about his understanding of himself', the typical statements of the New Testament are mixed, and their empirical aspect cannot be ignored.[1] As examples van Buren gives such typical texts as 'The Word became flesh and dwelt among us', 'God was in Christ reconciling the world to himself' and 'You have died, and your life is hid with Christ in God' (John i. 14; 2 Cor. v. 19; Col. iii. 3). While admitting that 'there are . . . serious difficulties in taking the "objective" side of the Gospel as straightforward empirical assertions', he maintains that 'the problem may not be avoided by focusing exclusively on the existential side of the Gospel'[1] and he reserves his own answer to the later part of his study.

(4) Van Buren now objects, from the other wing, that Ogden displaces the historical event of Jesus of Nazareth by the existential response of the believer. As an example he gives Ogden's description of the cross as an 'eschatological event' and points out that the New Testament never speaks of the cross in this way. 'That is the language of the contemporary existentialist-theological position, not that of the authors of the New Testament. Whatever else may be said about the cross, it was two pieces of wood joined together and used for the execution of Jesus of Nazareth at a certain place and time, most definitely in the past. It cannot, for many obvious reasons, become present at all, least of all in words, unless the madness of metaphysics is truly upon us in considering this problem.'[2] While admitting that the cross may be 'a significant event which leads us to see ourselves and the world in a certain way', van Buren insists that 'it is an event of the past in any case'.[3] 'Of course more is said

[1] ibid., p. 68.
[2] ibid., pp. 69f.
[3] ibid., p. 71.

than merely that a certain man had died at a certain time, but not less.'[1]

(5) The final objection is that the 'theological left' circumvents Easter; the resurrection plays no central part in Ogden's reconstruction. For him, the Easter faith of the primitive Church was in reality 'its way of responding to the ministry of the historical Jesus'.[2] In Ogden's view, 'the only final condition for sharing in authentic life that the New Testament lays down is a condition that can be formulated in complete abstraction from the event Jesus of Nazareth and all that it specifically imports'.[3] As van Buren somewhat cuttingly remarks: 'Feeling free to dispense with the resurrection and to understand faith apart from Easter, Ogden ends by dispensing with Jesus himself. This conclusion scarcely meets his own demand that any restatement of the Gospel should comprehend the major dimensions of that Gospel.'[4]

Having stated his five objections to the Bultmann-Ogden programme, van Buren ends his discussion of it by subjecting the two theses and the two principles by which Ogden reworded them to a careful analysis. The word 'original' in Bultmann's first thesis, he points out, can hardly be meant empirically; neither Bultmann nor Ogden appears to be referring to the earliest specimen of *homo sapiens*. Its association with 'Christian faith' makes it plain that it refers to the status of the 'believer', and this the thesis makes clear is nothing other than the 'authentic existence' defined by Heidegger.

> The final commitment of the left-wing existential-theological position, therefore, is to the freedom of man as it has been defined by Heidegger. Heidegger is as essential to a theology resting on this thesis as Aristotle is to Thomism. For Ogden (and to some extent for Bultmann), the first thesis turns out to make a particular philosophy and its analysis of human existence into the final norm for faith.[5]

Bultmann's second thesis asserts that Christian faith is actually realisable '*only because*' of the event of Jesus of Nazareth. Van

[1] ibid., p. 72.
[2] Ogden, op. cit., p. 88, quoted by van Buren, op. cit., p. 72.
[3] Ogden, op. cit., p. 143, quoted by van Buren, op. cit., p. 73.
[4] op. cit., p. 73.
[5] op. cit., p. 75.

Buren comments that this appears to be a statement of empirical causality, but is nothing of the kind. It is not an empirical generalisation based upon an examination of all the Christians there have ever been, which has led to the discovery that their authentic existence as free men was caused by the fact that there once was a man named Jesus. 'Bultmann seems rather to say that faith is in fact a response to Jesus and his message, a response logically dependent on Jesus. If "faith" means the authentic existence of those who stand in a relationship to the message of Jesus, then the use of the restrictive word "only" is redundant but intelligible. . . . But', van Buren retorts, 'if Bultmann really means that Jesus of Nazareth is essential to Christian faith, or to authentic existence, that presents a conflict with the first thesis.'[1] Bultmann thus appears to have two norms: (1) Jesus and the New Testament, (2) Heidegger. Ogden has, of course, seen this, and that is why he has modified the second thesis. No more than Bultmann is he willing to take the thesis as a mere recommendation of the Christian faith. He tries to keep its empirical character while removing the narrowness of Bultmann's reference to Christ, as expressed in the words 'only because', and he therefore substitutes for it, as the only prerequisite of faith, 'the ever-present ground and end of all created things'. Then he reintroduces Jesus Christ in the words 'decisive' and 'fulfils and corrects', but this, as van Buren aptly observes, makes his conclusion hardly less restrictive than Bultmann's. His attempt to improve on Bultmann is therefore judged as a failure.

Van Buren now considers the two principles which Ogden laid down for his attempt. The first principle is that 'the demand for demythologising that arises with necessity from the situation of modern man must be accepted without condition'.[2] Van Buren points out that the 'necessity' to which Ogden refers is, by his own avowal, the necessity of communicating the Gospel to those who are at present unbelievers. This is not, however, the task in which van Buren is interested. His picture is of 'the Christian, himself a secular man, who realises that the juxtaposition of his faith, expressed in traditional terms, and his ordinary way of thinking, causes a spiritual schizophrenia'.[3] The

[1] op. cit., p. 75.
[2] Ogden, op. cit., p. 127, quoted by van Buren, op. cit., p. 77.
[3] op. cit., p. 77.

point is clearly an interesting one, but I do not think that the difference between the way in which Bultmann and Ogden have set about their task and the way in which van Buren has set about his seems to be very obviously connected with this difference of aim, since all of them, as they see it, are trying to express the Gospel in the idiom of modern secularised man.

Ogden's second principle is that 'the sole norm of every legitimate theological assertion is the revealed word of God declared in Jesus Christ, expressed in Holy Scripture, and made concretely present in the proclamation of the church through its word and sacrament'.[1] Van Buren makes the very pertinent comment that for the modern man a term such as 'the word of God' will simply seem to be begging the question:

> Since Ogden has said that when he talks about 'God' he is actually talking about man, perhaps his 'word of God' is really a human word, one that is 'declared' in Jesus, 'expressed' in the Bible and 'present' in the preaching of the church. If Ogden's variation on Bultmann's two theses conforms to this norm, this 'word' is a self-understanding available to every man and conforming to Heidegger's analysis of existence. It is Heidegger who gives the final definition of Ogden's 'norm'.[2]

Van Buren's conclusion, thus, is that neither Bultmann's two theses nor Ogden's modification of them measure up to the demands of a radically empirical outlook adjusted to the situation of modern secularised man. Ogden, as an uncompromising Heideggerian existentialist, protests against the Christological interest of Bultmann, with its localised and particularised identification of the Gospel with the event of Jesus of Nazareth, and wants to substitute Theology (talk about God) for Christology (talk about Jesus). Unfortunately, talk about God, the transcendent non-empirical ground and end of all things, is just what the modern man, as van Buren understands him, cannot do anything with. 'If the choice is between "God", however subtly hidden in oblique language, and the man Jesus of Nazareth, the empirically-minded secular "believer" can only choose the latter, for he does not know what to do with Theology. Analogical as well as literal language about God makes no sense

[1] Ogden, op. cit., p. 138, quoted by van Buren, op. cit., p. 78.
[2] op. cit., pp. 78f.

to him.'[1] We seem, in fact, to be on the horns of a dilemma. If modern man is the Heideggerian secularist that van Buren believes him to be, then the Heideggerian in him will revolt against the particularity of a religion centred in Jesus and the secularist in him will revolt against the transcendentalism of a religion centred in God. The theological 'right' will seem irrelevant on the latter of these counts and the theological 'left' will seem irrelevant on the former, while traditional pre-Bultmannite theology will seem irrelevant on both. Van Buren, however, tries to find a way out of this impasse by reconsidering the language of the New Testament concerning Jesus. I have already remarked upon the fact that van Buren was led to make a complete reconstruction of his outlook on the nature of Christianity by his reading of Wittgenstein's *Philosophical Investigations*. Now Wittgenstein, although he became a somewhat enigmatic figure in his later years, tended more and more to be captivated by the problems of linguistics; it is therefore hardly surprising that van Buren initiates his own investigation by an analysis of theological language.

III

As a preliminary to this investigation, he remarks that 'religion' for Bonhoeffer, and indeed for Bultmann as well, consists of appealing to God as a means of explaining, justifying, or otherwise 'filling in the picture' of the world or human affairs. 'The religionless posture, on the other hand, is that of "coming to terms with reality apart from God" or without use of the God-hypothesis', and he alleges that 'contemporary theologians from Barth to Ogden are agreed that Christianity does not conform to this definition of religion. Religion', he continues, 'they would say, is man's use of God to solve some human problem, whereas the Gospel proclaims God's unexpected use of man for his own purposes; this distinction lies behind Bonhoeffer's search for a "nonreligious" interpretation of biblical concepts.'[2] The sweeping character of this passage shows how limited is the range within which van Buren allows his thought to move; 'contemporary theologians' for him means Protestant theologians, and one particular school of Protestant theologians at that, though it

[1] op. cit., p. 79.
[2] ibid., p. 82.

is a school that is influential and vociferous. He recognises, however, that all these theologians continue to speak of God, even though some of them try to do this in a 'worldly' way. 'The solution proposed by existentialist theologians consists of eliminating all "objectification" of God in thought and word, but since Bultmann also objects to using the word "God" simply as a symbol for human experience, the word "God" appears to refer to nothing at all. The "nonobjective" use of the word "God" allows of no verification and is therefore meaningless.'[1] And it is here that van Buren links up with the logical analysts, or rather with that extreme school among them which denies all factual character to statements which, from their grammatical form, appear to be assertions about a being called 'God'. 'The empiricist in us finds the heart of the difficulty not in what is said about God, but in the very talking about God at all. We do not know "what" God is, and we cannot understand how the word "God" is being used.'[2] I have commented on this linguistic empiricism at an earlier stage of my discussion.[3] Here it is important only to comment on the fact that there has been produced in recent years a very large body of argument against this position to which van Buren makes no reference whatever. He speaks with high approval of Professor A. G. N. Flew, Mr T. R. Miles and Professor R. B. Braithwaite, all of whom in their different ways deny the factual character of sentences which have the word 'God' as their subject. He expresses appreciation of Mr R. M. Hare's interpretation of theological utterances as 'expressions of a "blik", an orientation, a commitment to see the world in a certain way, and a way of life following inevitably upon this orientation'.[4] He claims in his support Professor I. T. Ramsey in a way which certainly does not do justice to the realistic theism which lies behind the Nolloth Professor's interest in the peculiar structure of theological discourse and the odd behaviour of theological words. But he ignores completely Dr A. M. Farrer's great work *Finite and Infinite*, the late W. G. de Burgh's book *The Life of Reason*, Dom Illtyd Trethowan's *Essay in Christian Philosophy* and the monu-

[1] ibid., p. 83.
[2] ibid., p. 84.
[3] Cf. ch. i *supra*.
[4] ibid., p. 87.

mental works of M. Jacques Maritain and M. Étienne Gilson. It is possible that Professor H. D. Lewis's masterly work *Our Experience of God* and the same writer's brilliant essay on 'God and Mystery' in the volume *Prospect for Metaphysics* were not available to Dr van Buren at the time when he was writing his book, but the reader should at least be warned that there is a great deal more to be said in support of a theistic metaphysic than van Buren recognises.

However, van Buren makes it quite plain that, while he is glad to follow Molière's maxim *Il m'est permis de reprendre mon bien où je le trouve*, his real reason for refusing all factual character to theological statements has nothing to do with linguistic analysis and indeed has no rational basis whatever. In a remarkably frank passage he writes as follows:

> We reject the cognitive approach to theological language, however, not primarily because it is logically puzzling, but because of certain theological commitments out of which this study has arisen. That approach builds its case on a natural sense of the divine, on natural religion and a natural revelation. The history of theology, seen from the perspective of modern kerygmatic theology, suggests that this is a road leading into the wilderness. Within the Protestant tradition, that road has been clearly charted and firmly marked with a 'dead-end' sign by the work of Karl Barth, and we see no reason to ignore the warning.[1]

Again:

> The cognitive approach to faith-statements presented by some linguistic analysts leads into the old inner contradiction of earlier forms of natural theology. It begins by speaking of a divine being of whom it *cannot* be said that this is the God of grace, the God who finds man wandering into idolatry with every conception he forms of the divine, the God who comes and makes himself known to man, not through, but in spite of, man's natural conceptions of the divine. Either the 'God' of which Christians have tried to speak is the God of grace and *self*-revelation, or he is the neutral 'it' of natural theology.[2]

The last sentence is quite astounding, coming as it does from a writer who has just denied the cognitive character of theological

[1] ibid., p. 98.
[2] ibid., p. 98.

language altogether. If the position for which van Buren is contending is sound, the 'God' of which Christians have tried to speak cannot be the God of grace and self-revelation, for when they try to speak of God they do not succeed in speaking of anyone at all. Dr Farrer pointed out many years ago that the problem of speaking about God cannot be evaded by denying the validity of natural theology. 'There is a superstition among revelationists', he wrote, 'that by declaring themselves independent of any proof of God by analogy from the finite world, they have escaped the necessity of considering the analogy or relation of the finite to the infinite altogether. They are completely mistaken; for all their statements about God must be expressed and plainly are expressed in language drawn from the finite world. . . . For the revelation has to be thought about to be received, and can be thought about only by the aid of words or finite images; and these cannot signify of God unless the appropriate "mode of signification" functions in our minds.'[1] If the cognitive attitude to theological language is rejected, all assertions about God must vanish, even those that purport to speak of the God of revelation, and they are indeed in worse case even than those of natural theology. For the latter claim at least to say something about the empirical realm, since they assert that God is its creator, while the statements of the pure revelationist claim to speak about God in total disconnection from all natural human experience. Van Buren is indeed speaking truly when he says that 'to follow the cognitive approach to religious language would contradict our point of departure'. He goes on, however, to assert that 'it [*sc.* the cognitive approach] tends to mark off a certain area of experience as "religious", and it argues for a religious way of knowing, in contrast to other (secular?) ways of knowing'.[2] And here we must distinguish. Traditional natural theology certainly asserts that there is a valid way of apprehending the world which enables one to see it as the creature of a transcendent self-existent being, and traditional Catholic theology has held that this knowledge of God is enhanced and supplemented by a further 'way of knowing' which is due to God's revelation of himself. It is, on the other hand, traditional Protestant theology that has claimed that God

[1] *Finite and Infinite*, pp. 2f.
[2] op. cit., p. 99.

is known by a revelation which has no relationship with man's natural apprehension of the world in which he lives and that he is known in no other way. This is indeed to mark off a certain area of experience as 'religious' and to argue for a religious way of knowing in contrast to other and secular ways of knowing. Van Buren's non-cognitive view of religious language demolishes the God of grace and revelation just as thoroughly as the God of natural theology. And, in fact, in the subsequent development of his argument the God of grace and revelation finds no place whatever. It is, therefore, I think, safe to discard the passage which we have just been considering as a bit of vestigial traditional Protestantism which is due to van Buren having been incompletely secularised. There can, however, be no doubt about the extent of his ambition for secularisation. Take, for example, the following statement:

> Simple literal theism is wrong and qualified literal theism is meaningless. The first of these assertions is another way of making Bultmann's point that myth is no longer tenable; the idea of the empirical intervention of a supernatural 'God' in the world of men has been ruled out by the influence of modern science on our thinking. In making such statements, we reveal our own commitments to modern science, and we would only add that modern thought tends to grant the validity of the findings of the natural sciences.[1]

This passage is extremely revealing as indicating the grounds on which van Buren takes up his position. He does not say that the idea of the empirical intervention of a supernatural 'God' has been shown by modern science to be false; it has merely been 'ruled out by the influence of modern science on our thinking'. And this is simply a statement about the influence of modern science upon the psychological make-up of certain not very clearly specified persons, of whom van Buren is presumably one. The 'commitment to modern science' which he reveals as 'our own' seems to be merely a capitulation to the secularist atmosphere of a world dominated by scientific technology. In view of the large amount of writing that has appeared in recent years on the subject of the relations between science and theology, much of which has shown no tendency to abandon the

[1] op. cit., p. 100.

traditional doctrines of Christian theology,[1] van Buren's statements are, to put it mildly, sweeping. Nevertheless, he alleges, the language of faith has a meaning; it has a function which may be clarified by linguistic analysis. And it 'has meaning when it is taken to refer to the Christian way of life; it is not a set of cosmological assertions'.[2]

When van Buren goes on to outline the method of theological reconstruction which he proposes to follow, he is even more explicit:

> The analyses of theological language constitute a clarification which shows us where problems may be dissolved and where the real problems of the language of faith lie. This clarification has been accomplished by a frankly empirical method which reflects the thinking of an industrialised, scientific age. It has taken certain empirical attitudes characteristic of modern thought seriously and accepted them without qualification.[3]

(The two concluding words of this passage should be noted.) Summing up the analyses of theological language which have been undertaken along this line, van Buren writes:

> They even emphasise the empirical, human, historical and ethical side of the Gospel at the expense of its divine, cosmological, transhistorical, and supernatural elements. Christologically speaking, these interpretations imply holding to the humanity of Christ, to the man Jesus of Nazareth, and letting the issue of his divinity fall where it may.[4]

And, although he describes this last statement as an exaggeration, it is very difficult to admit that it is an exaggeration of his own position, for he goes on to say: 'Today, we cannot even understand the Nietzschian cry that "God is dead!" for if it were so, how could we know? No, the problem now is that the *word* "God" is dead.'[5]

Van Buren admits that the examples which he quoted from

[1] Cf., e.g., Sir Edmund Whittaker, *Space and Spirit*; W. G. Pollard, *Physicist and Christian*; J. D. Lambert, *Science and Sanctity*; P. Teilhard de Chardin, *Le Milieu Divin*; E. L. Mascall, *Christian Theology and Natural Science*.

[2] op. cit., p. 101.

[3] ibid., pp. 101f.

[4] ibid., p. 102.

[5] ibid., p. 103.

the writings of Hare, Miles, Braithwaite and Ramsey of attempts to apply the methods of linguistic analysis to the interpretation of the language of faith do not provide him with all that he needs for his own task, though he thinks that they furnish some valuable suggestions and even that a short section in one of Ramsey's books gives a hint of what the desired interpretation of the Gospel might be. He points out very pertinently that the linguistic philosophers when they have given their attention to theological discourse have almost always restricted themselves to the classical statements of natural theology and that they have shown no interest in the revolution in theology which has been manifested in the biblical scholars of the last half-century. This is an important point, but it might equally well have been pointed out that they have paid equally little attention to the classical statements of dogmatic theology. It is true that they have frequently written as if the only relevant theological statements were 'There is a God', 'God loves us as a Father loves his children' (Flew's favourite example) and the like. They have, however, not only neglected such biblical formulas as 'Jesus is Lord', 'Your life is hid with Christ in God' and 'No man cometh to the Father but by me', but also such formulas of credal and dogmatic theology as 'Begotten of his Father before all worlds', 'Three Persons in one substance' and 'Conversion of the whole substance of the bread into the substance of the body of Christ', statements which are, if anything, more remote from the idiom of ordinary speech than those of the New Testament. It is, however, the language of the Bible that van Buren is chiefly concerned to reinterpret, and he applies himself to this task with an unqualified acceptance of the verification principle in the form that the meaning of a word is its use in its context. Thus he maintains that any attempt to interpret the language of faith outside its context will be misleading. The words 'Jesus is Lord', for example, will depend for their meaning on the context in which they are uttered, and since they may be used in more than one context they may not always have the same meaning. Clearly there is an important point here. There is a story about a patient in a hospital who was reduced to a state of extreme apprehensiveness on observing against his name the formula 'Ter die', words which have a different significance in the context of Latin and in that of uneducated English. I do not think, however, that van Buren sufficiently recognises that a word in many cases derives its meaning from its use in some context which is recognised as normative and archetypal, and frequently with the assistance of a good deal of added explanatory exposition, and that when it is transferred to a different context it may not simply change its meaning in conformity to the new context, but may in fact also (and perhaps much more) modify the meaning of the context by the associations which it brings with it and with which it is already loaded. He also appears to draw rather questionable inferences from the fact, upon which he has previously remarked with reference to the writings of Ramsey and Dr William Poteat, namely the odd logical character of the word 'I'. 'The fact that the Christian creed begins with this odd word should warn us to expect the whole series of creedal declarations to be odd.'[1] I cannot see that this follows. There are, of course, certain odd features about the use of the word 'I' in certain contexts to which modern writers have drawn attention. I may say 'Queen Anne is dead' without evoking comment, but I shall seem to be speaking very strangely if I say 'I am dead'. 'He promises to keep the rules of the Hogsnorton Pig Club' is a merely descriptive statement, whereas 'I promise to keep the rules of the Hogsnorton Pig Club' is a performatory statement by which I may be committing myself to serious obligations, though it may be added that it fails in addition to be descriptive (if it does fail) only because it is not usually necessary for me to say that I am performing actions that I am in fact quite obviously performing. There are, however, plenty of statements beginning with the word 'I', perhaps the great bulk of such statements, which have nothing odd about them: 'I was in Aberystwyth last week' is as straightforward a statement as 'Macpherson was in Aberystwyth last week'. Van Buren does, indeed, point out that at the beginning of the creeds the odd word 'I' is followed by another 'logical oddity', namely the word 'believe', which, as he says, 'points to the language of discernment and commitment', but it is hard to see that this justifies his further assertion that 'Christians should beware, for example, of a question about "the historic facts of the Virgin Birth and other articles in the Creed" '.[2] For while it is true that, in their original

[1] ibid., p. 105.
[2] ibid., p. 105.

context as baptismal professions of faith (to which, rather strangely van Buren does not seem to refer), the Creeds were very emphatic expressions of commitment to a way of life, they were also clearly expressions of belief in certain propositions about the nature of God and his relation to the world and about certain alleged events in the life of the Incarnate Son. It would have been somewhat to the point if van Buren had commented on the fact that when, by their adoption as formularies of faith by the great Councils, the Church transferred the Creeds from their original context as baptismal professions of faith into a new context as tests of orthodoxy, the opening 'I believe' was replaced by the plural form 'We believe', and, although the word 'we' is itself 'logically odd', it is not logically odd in the same way as the word 'I'. This does not, however, imply that in either context the creeds were not meant to state facts as well as to express commitments, and it is quite clear that it was only because the facts were believed in that the commitment was expected to be made.

Van Buren makes the very relevant comment that, 'for the sake of clarity, believers should make clear when and how they are using odd words. If "God" is not a word which refers to something, they should be careful not to use it in a way that suggests that it does. If they are talking about a "blik" rather than about "how things are", they should say so.'[1] ('Blik' is a word coined by Hare to signify a fundamental attitude, an orientation, a commitment to see the world in a certain way, in contrast to a factual assertion.) I very heartily agree, but it is, I think, van Buren and those who share his general outlook who are the worst offenders in this respect. For they do not, so far as I can see, propose, as did some of the old-fashioned liberal theologians, to discard the creeds and the traditional theological formulations, but only to reinterpret them in a highly sophisticated and unobvious way. Unless the words 'I believe . . .' are changed to 'I have the following blik . . .' or some equivalent form of words, the ordinary believer will certainly go on supposing, like his Christian predecessors, that, whatever function they may have in addition, the Creeds are assertions about the nature of God, his relation to the world and his dealings with mankind.

[1] ibid., pp. 105f.

It is only fair to say that van Buren adds, that, although he shares certain empirical attitudes with the linguistic analysts, he has not said how far these take him or to what degree they are shared. The quotations which I have previously made, nevertheless suggest that they take him a very long way and that they are shared pretty whole-heartedly. This is, however, still to be seen in the light of the reconstruction which he proceeds to make.

IV

The starting-point of this reconstruction is the recognition that Christianity is an historical religion, that is to say that it has something to do with a particular man who lived and died in Palestine at a particular time. This leads him to consider what is meant by the words 'historical' and 'history', and he follows R. G. Collingwood in defining 'history' as an answering of questions about human action in the past.[1] This, of course, rules out of 'history' any alleged action of God, though it does not prove that such action cannot occur or has not occurred; it will merely have to be called by some other name than 'history'. Van Buren instances Erich Frank as describing the advent of Christ, as Christians have understood it, not by the term 'history' but by the term 'history of salvation' (the famous German *Heilsgeschichte*). Similarly Bultmann is quoted as saying that, if a man wants to see the 'meaning in history', he must not look around himself into 'universal history' (i.e. Collingwood's 'history' *tout court*) but into his 'personal history'. Van Buren dislikes both Frank's and Bultmann's distinctions between two kinds of history and wishes to identify 'history' with 'the profane history of this world'. This is more than a merely verbal difference; it is due to van Buren's determination to restrict his consideration of Jesus and his work to their purely empirical aspects. 'We indicate', he says, 'our uneasiness with Frank's and Bultmann's distinctions by saying that we prefer to speak of Jesus having a place in "secular" history', though he tries to guard himself from the accusation that he is begging the question by a verbal dodge, by adding the rather vague qualification that 'this intentionally indefinite statement again suggests something of the "open texture" of our use of the word "secular", as well as

[1] op. cit., p. 110.

something about our use of the word "history" '.[1] Thus 'meaning in history' has for van Buren no objective character: it 'refers to the attitude of the viewer or speaker. It points to *the way in which he sees* history. . . . Logically, to find "meaning in history" is to have a "blik": an intention to behave in a certain way (in our examples, as a loyal American citizen or as a loyal Communist), connected with the "entertainment" of certain stories (the Gettysburg Address, or the Communist Manifesto).'[2] Van Buren's radical linguisticism is made evident when he says: 'The meaning in history . . . cannot (logically) lie "in" history itself, as Bultmann uses these words. But it is misleading to say that it lies "in" man or in his "personal history". The expression "meaning in history" belongs to the language-game of reading or hearing history and discerning it in a way which leads to a new commitment.'[3] This 'discernment' does not, of course, consist in *observing* some character of, or factor in, history which had not been observed before; if it did, the 'meaning' would lie 'in' history and would not be due to a 'blik'. The question thus arises how ought one to acquire the appropriate blik and what makes it appropriate?

Van Buren notes that for Collingwood the appropriate activity of the historian is to enter sympathetically into his subject and to seek to share the subject's experiences, but he sees that if the subject is Jesus of Nazareth we are faced with difficulties, since all the attempts to pursue 'the quest of the historical Jesus' have failed, and this not only because of the radical difference between Jesus' outlook and ours but also because the available documents are ill adapted for such an approach. 'Modern study of the Gospels', writes van Buren, 'has made it clear that the point of view not only of the evangelists but also of the early preaching of the Church on which their work was based was radically coloured by faith in the resurrection of Jesus. The earliest memories and reports of Jesus' life and words seem to have been shaped by the impact of the Easter event and the Easter faith.'[4] It would, we must note, be foreign to van Buren's whole position to enquire whether the Easter faith itself may

[1] ibid., pp. 111f.
[2] ibid., p. 113.
[3] ibid., p. 114.
[4] ibid., p. 115.

have been due to the actual occurrence of certain supernatural events within human history; by definition no such events could be part of 'history'. Therefore van Buren feels bound to continue: 'The evangelists were not asking questions; they wrote with the conviction that the proclamation on which their writings were based was an answer, not an inquiry. They did not reach an answer by weighing the evidence'—in flagrant contradiction of the emphatic declaration with which St Luke begins his Gospel. And it seems relevant to remark that even if the evangelists were giving an answer and not asking a question, their answer must have been an answer to some question and we should like to know what. In fact, van Buren himself has to admit that their subject was the action of 'God' and that 'their avowed purpose, however much it had to do with saying something about man, was to make known something about the one they called "God" '; and, if van Buren has to put 'God' in inverted commas in order to safeguard his radical empiricism, the evangelists certainly did not. As he himself says, 'they did not try to "enter sympathetically" into the mind of Jesus'. Nor does van Buren try to enter sympathetically into the minds of those who do:

> Our interest in this study is not in the historical problems of such a quest of the historical Jesus . . . but in the function of the language of the New Testament kerygma, for even if we form a picture of the historical Jesus, a faith based on this picture would be different from the faith of the apostles. . . . According to the New Testament, Christian faith first arose in connection with the event of Easter and afterwards in the context of the proclamation of that event.[1]

And two consequences follow in virtue of van Buren's secularist empiricism. The first is that this Easter event cannot be something of a supernatural character that happened to Jesus, but only the unexplained and inexplicable appearance of a new blik in the minds of his disciples; the second is that it is nevertheless fundamentally related to the man Jesus whom they had known in the days when he was alive, though it would be contrary to all empirical and secularist principles to suppose that he is now any different from any other dead man. Van Buren does

[1] ibid., p. 116.

not put the matter quite as bluntly as this, but it is clearly implied in such sentences as the following:

> Easter was the turning-point in the way the disciples *looked at and spoke of* Jesus; from that time, they *saw him and spoke of him* in a new way. . . . The one of whom the disciples *spoke in a new way* beginning on Easter was the man whom they had known by the name of Jesus, a man of Nazareth whose brothers, sisters, and parents were known.[1]

Van Buren is forced to admit that the primitive Christians looked upon their own experience in a less subjective and more unsophisticated way than this and that there was something rather odd about the 'Easter event'. Nevertheless his standpoint is unchanged:

> Without denying the peculiar relationship of faith to the event of Easter, a subject to which we shall return, let us see what we can say about the history of Jesus as a man. What we include and what we exclude, already suggested by speaking of 'the history of Jesus as a man', will indicate yet more clearly the categorical commitments on the basis of which this study is made and the meaning of the word 'secular' in its title.[2]

It would be possible to construct an interpretation of the Christian religion for which the existence of Jesus as an historical figure was both doubtful and irrelevant, for which the 'Easter experience', as something that could be reproduced by an appropriate technique in the minds of men and women today, was all-important but for which Jesus was merely the central figure in a myth which had been invented in order to provide this experience with appropriate imagery. This, however, as we have seen, is not van Buren's way. In accordance with his radical secularism he eliminates from the figure of Jesus every supernatural element, just as he has already eliminated, in accordance with his linguistic positivism, every reference to God, but Jesus, as a concrete human being, he will not let go. Thus he tells us that 'there is no reasonable doubt among contemporary Western-trained historians that there was a man named Jesus, a Jew who lived, taught, and died in Palestine during the first third of the first century A.D., and who has been ever since the

[1] ibid., pp. 116f (italics added).
[2] ibid., p. 117.

centre of concern of the Christian religion', though, following in the footsteps of Barth and Bultmann the line initiated by Schweitzer, he maintains that 'a few of the major themes of his preaching, the general location of his activity, and the place and date of his execution at the hands of the Roman authorities are about all that the historian can discover'.

> All the rest [he continues]—from legends of his birth, through stories concerning his relationship with his disciples, to details of his arrest and execution—has come to us through the preaching of the early Christian congregations. This material was not intended to be documentary evidence of historical or biographical 'facts'. It was a story in the service of the Easter kerygma.[1]

We shall have later on to examine the presuppositions that underlie such an interpretation of the Gospels as this. We may, however, remark that, apart from one or two very slight possible references to Jesus in the writings of contemporary historians, the facts about Jesus that van Buren is prepared to take as historical, no less than those that he dismisses as mythical, alike come to us through the preaching of the early Christian congregations. Van Buren may, of course, for reasons of his own maintain that this material is not reliable documentary evidence of the historical or biographical facts, but to say that it was not *intended* to be such is to fly in the face of such plain statements as the opening words of St Luke's Gospel. And to suggest that the primitive Church deliberately embroidered the simple human life of Jesus with a mass of mythical and largely miraculous material in order to convince either itself or outsiders of the authenticity of a purely psychological 'Easter experience' is to attribute to the first generation of Christians a degree of conscious sophistication for which there is really no evidence.

Van Buren remarks that Barth and Bultmann have quite different reasons for rejoicing at this minimisation of the historical element in the Gospels. Bultmann likes it because he is interested essentially in kerygma, the proclamation, itself; Barth likes it because for him all that matters is the witness of the apostles to the fact that God has raised Jesus from the dead. And, while Bultmann is not prepared to accept the Gospel story

[1] ibid., pp. 117f.

as historical, since he suspects the motives of those who produced it, Barth is prepared by and large to accept it, although he is not very much interested in it, because it rests on the testimony of the same persons as those who witnessed to the resurrection. Van Buren also points out that, while the old-fashioned attempt of the nineteenth-century liberal Protestants to write straightforward biographies of Jesus collapsed under the onslaught of Schweitzer, there has recently come into being a post-Bultmannite 'New Quest of the Historical Jesus', which, while recognising that all the reports concerning Jesus were coloured and often shaped by the Easter faith, or were even produced by it, so that any attempt to write an ordered biography of Jesus is doomed to frustration, nevertheless believes that it is possible to obtain from the documents a reliable picture of the kind of person that Jesus was from the various fragments which have gone to make up the Gospel tradition.[1] Not that they have all produced the same picture:

[1] Cf., e.g., J. M. Robinson, *A New Quest of the Historical Jesus*; R. H. Fuller, *The New Testament in Current Study*, ch. iii. It may be useful to reflect on the following remarks of Dr R. M. Grant on theories about an original, authentic, pure Christianity which was later distorted by various secondary factors:

> Such theories have a long history within, and on the edge of, the Christian Church. Marcion, for example, held that the pure gospel of Jesus was distorted by his disciples, who modified it severely when they presented it to Jews; and similar notions are often latent in the work of modern scholars. Since fashions change, the contrasts developed by one generation often differ from those emphasised by the previous one; but it can be shown that underlying a good deal of study supposedly analytical in nature there is a very simple set of antitheses which are supposed to be self-evident. In previous times it was customary to contrast Jesus with Paul, or the Jesus of history with the Christ of faith, or the synoptic gospels with the Fourth Gospel. Alternatively, faith or grace could be contrasted with works, moralism, sacraments, doctrines and creeds, and the 'New Testament teaching' could be found in Paul but not in James, Matthew, or the synoptic gospels in general. For a time there were those who believed that the essential 'kerygma' could be emphasised at the expense of the less significant 'didache', though the fairly obvious fact that in early Christianity 'gospel' included both preaching and teaching lessens the force of this contrast. More recently it has been fashionable to compare the authentic Hebrew elements in the New Testament with the less satisfactory elements which can be called 'late Jewish' or 'Greek'.
>
> The chief difficulty with these antitheses is that they are not historical. They arise out of the needs of modern writers to pick and choose among the various elements in the New Testament and Christian synthesis, and when they are used as instruments of analysis they

> One [E. Fuchs] has focused on the conduct of Jesus, a man who acted neither as prophet nor as teacher, but as a man who dared to act in God's place and as God's son; another [G. Ebeling] has focused on the question of what issue was posed for men by their coming into contact with Jesus, concluding that the issue was that of faith; another [G. Bornkamm] has emphasised the immediacy and authority with which Jesus confronted each person and situation, acting in sovereign freedom from the past.[1]

Given the presuppositions of the investigators, they would indeed seem to have set themselves a hazardous task, and there is more than a suspicion that they have severally found in Jesus the characteristics that have interested them. Van Buren, however, who finds it easy to be uncritical where the supernatural is not concerned, sums all these up under the embracing concept of 'freedom'. Jesus 'stands out as a remarkably free man in the records of remembered parable, saying, or incident, and in the way in which the early Christian community spoke of him'.

> In describing him with the word 'free', however, we would allow that word to take on new connotations from the glimpses of him in the fragments which make up the record. . . . If we would define Jesus by his freedom, however, we must emphasise its positive character. He was free from anxiety and the need to establish his own identity, but he was above all free for his neighbour. . . . A story like that of his washing his disciples' feet, for which the historical sources are uncertain, illustrates the impression Jesus made on men. The story represents a response to one who could have done this sort of thing, and we can find the basis for such a response in any number of more reliable fragments of the tradition. He was, apparently, a man free to give himself to others, whoever they were. He lived thus, and he was put to death for being this kind of man in the midst of fearful and defensive men.[2]

---

become substitutes for thought. They are created by laying emphasis on certain distinctive, or seemingly distinctive, features in the various documents and by neglecting equally important resemblances. . . . The world in which Christianity arose was not characterised by the contrasts which some scholars have imagined to exist. (*Historical Introduction to the New Testament*, pp. 81f.)

[1] van Buren, op. cit., p. 121.
[2] ibid., pp. 121, 123.

Whether this last sentence provides an adequate statement of the reason for his condemnation and how far it is tenable without accepting a good deal more of the Gospel material than van Buren is ready to accept, and whether its significance in the kerygma does not involve a less naturalistic understanding of Jesus than van Buren will tolerate, needs further investigation. Van Buren is at any rate perfectly frank about his reason for choosing 'freedom' as his key-concept:

> Others have used other terms, like 'faith'. We prefer the word 'freedom' to the word 'faith' in part because it does not lead us so easily onto the slippery ground of the nonempirical. . . . It might be argued that Jesus was 'free' because 'he trusted in the God of love'. The statement, 'He trusted in the God of love', is related in the language of Christian faith to such statements as, 'He loved men' and 'He was willing to die'. It appears to have 'cash value' in the realm of human conduct. Generally speaking, Christians have tended to say that freedom from fear and freedom to love one's neighbour count for the validity of one's making this assertion. He who said he trusted in God, but was afraid of failure or death and was unloving, would be misusing language. Freedom, in this sense, therefore, is not the consequence of faith. It is its logical meaning.[1]

The conclusion of this argument seems questionable. The First Epistle of St John certainly says that love of God implies love of one's neighbour, and presumably love of God includes trust in God. But it does not follow that the two loves are identical, and there are many people who would claim to love their neighbour without loving (or even believing in) God. And indeed van Buren would appear by his radical secularism to be one of these people. It would, however, require an even more drastic expurgation of the Gospels than even van Buren is prepared to undertake to maintain that *Jesus* did not believe in God. And this is no doubt why van Buren tries to reinterpret all statements that appear to express Jesus' belief in God in terms of Jesus' freedom to serve men, in spite of the implausibility of this interpretation.

Nevertheless, as we saw very early on in this discussion, while van Buren does not believe in God, he does very sincerely believe in Jesus, and he is quite clear that 'a historical knowledge of

[1] ibid., pp. 123f.

Jesus . . . is not faith'.[1] He explicitly recognises that his previous assertion that 'Christian faith and its expression in the kerygma is related to Jesus' is not enough, without a further definition of this relationship. Merely witnessing Jesus as an historical figure, whether with one's own eyes or in the proclamation of the Church, would not produce faith in the sense of a reproduction in oneself of Jesus's own freedom, for his disciples witnessed him with their own eyes before his passion and yet they all forsook him and fled. 'The historical Jesus did not elicit faith, in the sense of the response of the early Christian. . . . We conclude, therefore, that Christian faith was not, and is not, a direct result of seeing Jesus as a historical figure. . . . Jesus did not cause his disciples to share in his freedom. In this sense we can say that faith is not based on history.' 'There were no Christians before Easter.'[2] Between Jesus and faith there stands the event of Easter. Here van Buren tells us there lies the essential paradox of Christianity:

> We arrive at a seeming contradiction when we try to investigate the relationship of faith (or the believer himself) to the historical Jesus. This paradox is a consequence of the event of Easter, which stands between Jesus and the believer, as indeed it stands between Jesus and the New Testament witness to him. . . . Faith is not based simply on a picture of the historical Jesus, but the historical Jesus is indispensable for faith. In order to achieve greater clarity here, we must turn to the event of Easter and the peculiar problems of the language which was used to speak of what happened.[3]

It is one of the merits of van Buren's exposition that, however anxious he is to maintain that his secularised version of the Gospel is in essence the view of the New Testament writers, he is honest enough to recognise that the New Testament writers did not share his secularist outlook and were therefore not troubled by his problems. He is, however, led unconsciously to assume that, if their knowledge of the facts had been as accurate as he believes his own to be, they would have adopted a secularist interpretation of them. The earliest extant written tradition, he tells, is simply that of various 'appearances' of Jesus to disciples

[1] ibid.
[2] ibid., p. 125.
[3] ibid., p. 126.

after his death, as recorded in 1 Cor. xv. 3–7. 'The more developed (and presumably later) tradition'[1] found in the Gospels, tells in addition of the empty tomb. We must observe that in place of the neutral adjective 'ampler', we are presented, without argument, with the loaded and question-begging expressions 'developed' and 'presumably later'. Neither tradition, we are rightly reminded, describes the actual rising from the dead. However, even the second tradition, that of the empty tomb, van Buren tells us, raises difficulties if we speak of Easter as a 'fact'. We might imagine that this difficulty was going to be concerned with problems raised by the linguistic empiricism to which van Buren has committed himself, but this is not so. It is a scientific difficulty. 'Because of the influence of the natural sciences, especially biology, on our thinking today, we can no more silence the questions concerning the changes in cells at death which spring to our minds when we read the Easter story of the Gospels than we can deny that we live in the twentieth century.'[2] Now, it is true that there are great problems about the resurrection if we assume that it was a purely natural process, and it is a dogma of van Buren's faith that if it took place it could be nothing else. But that a supernatural transformation of the body of Jesus is not inconsistent with a genuinely natural antecedent death is indicated by the fact that those Catholic scholars who have investigated the authenticity of the Holy Shroud of Turin have taken for granted the physical processes that would normally take place after death in a hastily embalmed body. It may also be relevant to remark that the distinguished French biologist M. Rémy Chauvin, who adopts an almost defiantly empirical approach to the relationship between science and religion, has no difficulty in believing in the miraculous.[3] There are, of course, interesting questions that can be asked about the nature of the transformation which our Lord's body underwent in his resurrection, and if we know anything about physics and biology we are quite likely to ask them. But, since we are concerned with an occurrence which is *ex hypothesi* unique in certain relevant respects, we are most unlikely to be able to give confident answers to them. Van Buren's remarks

[1] ibid., p. 127.
[2] ibid., p. 127.
[3] *God of the Scientists*, pp. 80f.

about biology and the twentieth century are nothing more than rhetoric or, at best, are simply empirical statements about his own psychology. The first century knew as well as the twentieth that dead bodies do not naturally come to life again, and no amount of twentieth-century knowledge about natural processes can tell us what may happen by supernatural means.

Now, van Buren is correct when he goes on to say that belief in the resurrection is not just belief in resuscitation, and that belief in resuscitation would not be the same as Christian faith. This does not imply, however, that belief in the resurrection does not include belief in resuscitation, even if it involves not mere restoration to life but a unique transformation as well. Van Buren finds fault with Professor I. T. Ramsey for asserting that the resurrection is 'an "object of sense" and more' and accuses Ramsey of wanting to have it both ways by arguing that acceptance of the 'fact' is included in Easter faith; for him, this conclusion 'endangers our whole understanding of the Gospel of Easter by insisting that it is *also* an assertion concerning a body'.[1] Nevertheless, his refusal to take the tradition at its face value involves him in a view of the resurrection that is not only, as he admits, paradoxical but in effect unintelligible. Here is his account:

> We can say that Jesus died and was buried, and that the disciples were then discouraged and disappointed men. That was the situation before Easter. Assuming that Jesus' predictions of his resurrection are a later tradition read back into the record after the fact (an assumption based on a consensus of historical scholarship today), there is nothing in the pre-Easter situation which points towards Easter itself.

(We may notice the odd logic of the last sentence, which is tantamount to saying that if we remove the evidence for something no evidence for it will remain; we might also enquire how universal is the consensus to which he appeals and to what extent it is based on the question-begging assumption that Jesus could not have foretold his resurrection. But to continue:)

> There is no ground for assuming that the disciples expected anything more to happen. On the other side of Easter, we can say that the disciples were changed men. They apparently

[1] op. cit., p. 128, note.

> found themselves caught up into something like the freedom of Jesus himself, having become men who were free to face even death without fear. Whatever it was that lay in between, and which might account for this change, is not open to our historical investigation. The evident is insufficient. All we can say is that something happened.[1]

However, if all that van Buren can say is 'Something happened', he has to admit that this is not all that the New Testament says. 'The older tradition indicates this "something" with the words "he appeared".' But 'is this to be explained psychologically, or by myth, or in the language of space and time?' Van Buren supposes that Peter's earliest announcement of this occurrence was in the form 'The Lord appeared to me'. 'The use of the passive, "He appeared to me", rather than the active, "I saw him", suggests the "objective" character of the image "on the mirror of the mind": as we have noted the appearance was unexpected.'[2] We are not told why van Buren thinks that the passive form of words was, in fact, used by Peter in his earlier announcement, but the question is unimportant, for the next stage in the argument assumes, quite reasonably, that their meaning is identical, and it proceeds, in fact, from the form 'I saw him'. And it is based on some very questionable linguistic analysis.

'I saw him', we are told, is a statement of sense-content and therefore cannot be verified by common-sense or empirical means. 'A sense-content statement is about what "I saw", not about what is "there for everyone to see". Only "I" can record what was "on the mirror of my mind".' And 'the way to verify a statement of sense-content is to see if the words and actions of the person who makes the statement conform to it. . . . Peter's statement of sense-content, which identifies the one he saw with a man who had lived a certain kind of life, is verified by Peter's subsequent life.'[3]

I can only say that this argument seems to me to be highly implausible. Admittedly I may feel a certain incredulity if someone professes to have seen a highly unlikely object. If a friend says to me 'I saw Adolf Hitler yesterday in King's Road,

[1] ibid., p. 128.
[2] ibid., p. 129.
[3] ibid., pp. 129f.

Chelsea', I shall hesitate to believe him. But this is because I have grounds for supposing Hitler to be dead, and not because of the logical oddity of statements beginning with 'I'; I shall feel equally incredulous if my friend says 'The Mayor of Westminster saw Adolf Hitler yesterday in King's Road, Chelsea', or even simply 'Adolf Hitler was yesterday in King's Road, Chelsea'. If I know that my friend is normally truthful I shall first suppose that he was joking, failing that I shall suppose that he was mistaken, and if all else fails I may be forced reluctantly to the conviction that Hitler is not dead after all. It is certainly not true that 'the way to verify a statement of sense-content is to see if the words and actions of the person who makes the statement conform to it', if by this is meant that his subsequent behaviour is what it would be if he believed the statement to be true. All that this behaviour could verify is that he believed his statement to be true; whether it was true in fact I could only judge by my antecedent reasons for believing that my friend is neither untruthful nor subject to delusions. In any case, I suspect that van Buren has fallen into an ambiguity in his use of the term 'sense-content'. He seems to hold that in 'I saw Jesus', 'Jesus' is merely the name of a sense-datum, and there are strong (though not perhaps conclusive) reasons for thinking that no sense-datum can be sensed by more than one person and that nobody can be mistaken in believing that he is sensing a particular sense-datum.[1] 'Jesus' is, however, the name not of a sense-datum but of an object. It is perfectly possible for more than one person to perceive the same object and for a person to be mistaken in believing that he has seen a particular object. It is here that the experience of other percipients is not only possible but important from the point of view of verification: 'He was seen', wrote St Paul, 'of Cephas, then of the twelve; after that he was seen of above five hundred brethren at once; . . . after that he was seen of James; then of all the Apostles' (1 Cor. xv. 5–7).

Van Buren seems to have dimly apprehended the point at issue when he goes on to say that we may suppose, on the basis of the evidence, that Peter's hypothetical statement 'I saw Jesus'

[1] Thus he says that if I say 'I saw John was in the station yesterday' when in fact John was somewhere else, although I should have been wrong in inferring 'John was in the station yesterday', I should not be mistaken in my original assertion.

was followed by a second assertion 'Jesus is risen'. Here again he seems to have got quite unnecessarily involved in problems of linguistic analysis. First of all he says that the evidence indicates that the apostles did not intend to assert a physical resuscitation of the dead Jesus. His evidence for this is (*a*) that the 'risen body' was not like the earthly body, (*b*) that, although it bore the marks of the crucifixion, the disciples had some difficulty in recognising the 'risen Jesus', and (*c*) that if he ate with them, according to some accounts, he also appeared and disappeared in a most unbodily fashion, according to others. This would, however, suggest not that the apostles did not intend to assert a physical resuscitation but that, to use Professor Ramsey's idiom, they intended to assert a physical resurrection *and more*. This is, however, preliminary to van Buren's main point, which is that the statement 'Jesus is risen' is linguistically odd because it juxtaposes words from two dissimilar language-games. 'Jesus' is a proper name and it would be improper to use the word 'is' of anyone who had died. This is surely not true. It would, of course, be improper to use the word 'is' of somebody or something that no longer exists; it is linguistically improper to say in 1964, '1665 is a very unhealthy year for Londoners'. But it is only improper to use the word 'is' of someone who has died if someone who has died no longer exists, and this impropriety will be not a linguistic but a factual one. However, van Buren goes on to assert that 'in this case [sc., 'Jesus is risen'], "is" forms part of a verb which had its logical placing in Jewish eschatology, in the hope and its expression of a future given by "God". The word "risen" was at home in the context of such phrases as "Kingdom of God" and "a new heaven and a new earth", which were used to point to the end and goal of all existence. The assertion "Jesus is risen" takes the name of a historical man and says that he was of the realm of "the end".' This seems to be quite extraordinarily perverse. It is, of course, perfectly true that the primitive Church believed that in Jesus the Kingdom of God had come and God's ultimate purposes were in principle realised. But to say that when the apostle Peter said 'Jesus is risen' he meant 'Jesus is no longer alive, but before he died he was of the realm of "the end" ' seems, to say the least, unlikely. It should also be observed that to rule out the normally understood meaning of 'Jesus is risen' on linguistic grounds is in effect to claim to prove the impossibility of a physical occurrence by pure logic, and this is not at all the sort of thing that a modern empiricist is supposed to do.

Nevertheless, given the interpretation which van Buren adopts, we need not be surprised that he writes as follows:

> We have no means of knowing what would count for or against the declaration that Jesus is risen, and granting our empirical attitudes, we would say that it is not an empirical assertion, whatever else it may be. . . . The statement 'Jesus is risen' therefore does not signify a movement from a sense-content statement, 'He appeared to me', to an empirical assertion. It is a movement to an 'end-word' statement, which is verified by the conduct of the man who uses it. . . . It seems appropriate to say that a situation of discernment occurred for Peter and the other disciples on Easter, in which, against the background of their memory of Jesus, they suddenly saw Jesus in a new and unexpected way. . . . The experience of Peter and the others on Easter was certainly their own 'subjective' experience. But it was an experience of Jesus and his freedom in a way which was quite new for them. They may still have been attracted by their memory of Jesus. But on Easter they found themselves beginning to share in this freedom, and this had not happened to them before. We might say that, on Easter, the freedom of Jesus began to be *contagious*.[1]

The cavalier way in which van Buren retains the classical phraseology of Christianity while entirely changing its meaning is seen by the following examples which he gives in order to amplify the statements just quoted. (We must remember in examining them that, partly on secularist 'twentieth-century' grounds and partly on linguistic grounds, van Buren holds that there is no transcendent being to whom the name 'God' applies and that neither Jesus nor anyone else survives his physical death.)

> In saying that *God* raised up Jesus, the disciples indicated that what had happened to them was fundamental to their life and thought: Jesus as the liberator had become the point from which they saw the world and lived in it. In saying that Jesus was Lord over the whole world, they indicated that their perspective covered the totality of life, the world, and history,

[1] ibid., pp. 131ff.

as well as their understanding of themselves and other men. . . . The emphasis of the later tradition on the bodily aspect of the risen Jesus underscored that it was the same Jesus of Nazareth who was now seen in a new way and whose freedom defined the freedom of the apostles.

Finally, van Buren summarises his interpretation in the following passage which I quote in full:

Jesus of Nazareth was a free man in his own life, who attracted followers and created enemies according to the dynamics of personality and in a manner comparable to the effect of other liberated persons in history upon people about them. He died as a result of the threat that such a free man poses for insecure and bound men. His disciples were left no less insecure and frightened. Two days later, Peter, and then other disciples, had an experience of which Jesus was the sense-content. They experienced a discernment-situation in which Jesus the free man whom they had known, themselves, and indeed the whole world, were seen in a quite new way. From that moment, the disciples began to possess something of the freedom of Jesus. His freedom began to be 'contagious'. For the disciples, therefore, the story of Jesus could not be told simply as the story of a free man who had died. Because of the new way in which the disciples saw him and because of what had happened to them, the story had to include the event of Easter. In telling the story of Jesus of Nazareth, therefore, they told it as the story of the free man who had set them free. This was the story which they proclaimed as the Gospel for all men.[1]

V

Having produced his completely secularised version of the Christian Gospel, van Buren devotes the concluding chapters of his book to the formidable task of arguing that, in spite of all appearances, this version is identical in all essentials with the teaching of the New Testament and with the historic faith of Christendom, and that only minor and unimportant differences result from his rejection of the idea of a transcendent deity and his denial that Jesus survived his crucifixion. Before embarking on this hazardous voyage, however, he has perforce to attend to the point with which the last quotation concluded, that the

[1] ibid., pp. 133–4.

mysterious and paradoxical 'Easter event' was not simply experienced by the apostles and their associates on the first Easter day, but was proclaimed by them as something which was to be reproduced in the lives of succeeding generations of men and women who had nothing to rely upon except their testimony. 'The apostles proclaimed the Gospel to others, and some of their hearers responded positively. Those who became Christians in this way understood themselves as sharing with the apostles in a freedom defined by the freedom of Jesus of Nazareth and in a new perspective upon life and the world. This experience has been traditionally called conversion. . . . Although the language of conversion differs from the language of those involved in the Easter event, they function in a remarkably similar manner. The difference between the two lies in the fact that the believers' expression of faith depends logically and historically upon that of the apostles.'[1]

It is of central importance to stress the force of the words 'logically and historically' in the passage just quoted. The naïve believer may all too easily take van Buren as meaning that Jesus, the risen Saviour, as a living agent, has done for later Christians what he did on Easter Day for the apostles. Such an understanding would, however, be entirely inconsistent with the empiricist position to which van Buren has committed himself. From the moment when he died on the cross, Jesus, as a living agent, could do nothing for anybody, for by his death he ceased to exist. Whatever the mysterious Easter experience was—and it does not seem open to van Buren to understand it as anything but a psychological upheaval of shattering intensity—it was not an experience whose object was Jesus himself. And the only way in which it could be reproduced in the lives of later Christians was by the immediate or transmitted testimony of the apostles: hence the phrase 'logically and historically'. It is this and this only that makes the later experiences Christian experiences at all; for there have been other free men than Jesus in history. 'There is no empirical ground . . . for the Christian's saying that something of this sort could not happen to a disciple of Socrates. Reading the history of Socrates might conceivably have a liberating effect on a person, who might say that he shared in the freedom of the philosopher. . . . He would be "in

[1] ibid., pp. 136–7.

Socrates", let us say, not "in Christ".'[1] And, as we shall see, van Buren finds it very difficult to give any reason for the unique salvific character of the Christian message; it simply depends on a 'blik'.

The point just made must be driven home even at the risk of wearying the reader, for it is only too easy to forget that, for van Buren, it can only be the spoken or written story about Jesus, and not Jesus himself that saves men and sets them free. Hence the emphasis which he lays on preaching. 'The Gospel', we are told, 'is not merely about a free man; it is the good news of a free man who has set other men free, first proclaimed by those to whom this has happened. And it has happened again and again during nineteen centuries that, *in the context of hearing this apostolic proclamation*, men have been liberated.' This might be the language of old-fashioned evangelicalism, until we see how it continues: 'Their response, which the New Testament calls "faith", consists in acknowledging that this has happened by accepting the liberator, Jesus of Nazareth'—not as the living Lord who saves them by his present action, but—'as the man who *defines for them what it means to be a man* and as the *point of orientation* for their lives. They are "in Christ" ', but this is simply 'to say that *their understanding* of themselves and their lives and all things is determined by *their understanding* of Jesus', not that their lives are determined by Jesus himself. 'They are a "new creation" in that this *orientation* to the whole world is new for them.'[2]

Van Buren does, of course, recognise that Christians, as contrasted with Socratists or Buddhists, attribute this transformation of orientation uniquely to the story of Jesus and not of anyone else. This he sees as implied by the linguistically improper attribution to Jesus by the early Church of terms such as 'God' and 'Lord'. It thus 'expressed a particular *perspective* upon life and history' and 'this universal perspective had its *norm* in the history of Jesus of Nazareth and Easter'.[3] How this 'norm' is to be given its content appears to be left rather vague in view of van Buren's acceptance of the depredations of the Bultmannites upon the Gospel story; perhaps 'the history which the post-Easter church read back into the life of Jesus' would

[1] ibid., pp. 138f.
[2] ibid., p. 138 (italics added).
[3] ibid., p. 140 (italics added).

express his meaning rather better than 'the history of Jesus' in this description of the norm. And here van Buren, in order to establish the uniqueness of Christianity, asserts that Christian faith, in contrast to all other faiths, is not *chosen* by the believer, but *grasps* him. 'This perspective cannot be held as one point of view among many. It is not a logical conclusion to a chain of reasoning. Of either of these a man might say, "This is the position which I chose". [But do we in fact say that we 'choose' the conclusion of a logical deduction?] The language of faith, by referring to a transcendent element, indicates that something has happened to the believer, rather than that he has done something.' Nevertheless, 'The new discernment and its accompanying commitment to a way of life is experienced as a response. This perspective arises in connection with *hearing* the Gospel concerning Jesus of Nazareth and it *looks back* to him continually as *its historical point of orientation*. To affirm the Gospel is *to express this historical perspective*.'[1] Once again we have the looking back upon a figure and events that no longer exist or occur. The point is even more plain in the following sentence:

> The man who says, 'Jesus is Lord', is saying that the history of Jesus and of what happened on Easter has exercised a liberating effect upon him, and that he has been so grasped by it that it has become the historical norm of his perspective upon life.[2]

It is not 'Jesus' and 'what happened on Easter' that have had this liberating effect on the believer, but 'the *history* of Jesus' and the *history* of 'what happened on Easter', and this history has done all that a mere history can do; it has provided the historical norm of the man's perspective, that is to say something in the past to which he can look back in order to get guidance and encouragement. Thus 'he sees not only his own *history* but the *history* of all men in the light of the one *history* of Jesus of Nazareth'.[3] 'The "blik" of the Christian finds its adequate expression in the Gospel . . . and it is related always, if sometimes indirectly [this phrase raises questions which need more attention than they receive], to the history of Jesus of Nazareth. This is why we call this perspective *historical*.'[4] But, anyhow,

[1] ibid., pp. 140f (italics added).
[2] ibid., p. 141.
[3] ibid., p. 142 (italics added).
[4] ibid., p. 143.

'Easter faith depended on the disciples' memory of Jesus, and Christian faith requires minimal [how minimal, we wonder?] acquaintance with the Gospel narratives'.[1]

After this, it is somewhat surprising to find that van Buren is not satisfied with the position of Professor R. B. Braithwaite, for whom Christian statements are simply announcements of intention to pursue an agapeistically policied way of life, while entertaining, without necessarily believing, the Christian stories;[2] he finds this deficient in the elements of 'discernment' and 'commitment'. I am not sure that this is, in fact, fair to Braithwaite, for whom Christian profession, as distinct from the mere utterance of Christian statements, certainly involves commitment to a marked degree. Van Buren expresses his dissatisfaction by saying that the freedom which characterises the Christian way of life is 'caught' from Jesus and is 'contagious'. I find this medical metaphor, which van Buren uses more than once, very puzzling, for, since in his view Jesus no longer exists, it is difficult to see how we can catch anything from him. The metaphor seems quite inappropriate to a view according to which the past history of Jesus provides a norm for our perspective. Van Buren seems to be on sounder ground in saying that Braithwaite does not do justice to the historical aspect of the Gospel, though this is a criticism from which he himself is hardly immune. But when he says that Braithwaite has 'completely neglected' the peculiar 'story' of Easter, it might be replied that he has only neglected it in not explicitly mentioning it. He would certainly include it in the Christian stories, though he would not perhaps make it, as van Buren does, the essential though paradoxical source of all Christian faith.

It is at this point that van Buren feels obliged to face the accusation that such an interpretation of the Christian faith as he has given is not really Christian at all. As he admits, 'the word "God" has been avoided', but this is only 'because it equivocates and misleads. . . . An interpretation of the language of the Gospel which does not necessitate assertions concerning "the nature and activities of a supposed personal creator" . . . involves discarding some of the traditional lan-

[1] ibid., p. 144.

[2] I have discussed Braithwaite's position at length in chapter iii of my book *Words and Images*.

guage of Christianity, no matter how much other ages have revered this language.'[1] Now, it cannot be denied that the New Testament writers, and Jesus himself, certainly believed that there was someone whom they denoted by the name 'God', and this involves van Buren in the difficult task of providing equivalents for the New Testament language which will come up to his empirical requirements. Recognising that both the terms 'God' and 'Father' raise the same difficulties, he takes one of the easier texts for his purpose as normative of the rest: 'He who has seen me has seen the Father' (John xiv. 9). 'We have no idea what would count for or against the assertion that in seeing Jesus one had seen the Father. Unless we knew already the meaning of the word "Father", how could we verify or falsify this claim?' However, 'if this passage is understood as a recommendation to turn away from asking about the Father and to ask about Jesus of Nazareth instead, its meaning becomes clear'.[2] In other words, what Jesus meant, in spite of the fact that he himself *believed* (as is evident in many other passages in the Gospels, especially those in which he addressed the Father in prayer) in the existence of a transempirical entity named 'Father', what he was *telling* his hearers to do was to concentrate instead upon himself. Van Buren has to admit that the following sentence, 'The words that I say to you I do not speak on my own authority; but the Father who dwells in me does his works', would seem to run clean counter to the interpretation he has just given: 'Undoubtedly Jesus believed he was obeying some "one" whom he called "Father" ', but 'the verification principle precludes taking this assertion of cosmological obedience as a straightforward empirical proposition', and the somewhat shaky assertion is made that 'the Gospel of John, as well as the logic of language, forces us to silence before all questions concerning that "one" '.[3] After this quite heroic piece of reinterpretation van Buren feels able to face what he admits is the even more difficult passage of St Paul: 'In Christ God was reconciling the world to himself' (2 Cor. v. 19). As he says, this is very definitely a 'God-statement'. However, since 'he who asserts that the history of Jesus was a normative history of reconciliation means that he is committed to the *sort* of

[1] ibid., pp. 145f.
[2] ibid., p. 147.
[3] ibid., p. 148.

reconciliation revealed in that history',[1] this can be taken as an equivalent. And so we go on. 'He died for our sins' means that his death is to be regarded as the measure of the freedom for which he set other men free. However—and this is of fundamental importance—the liberation which is involved did not in any sense take place when Jesus died; it would be grossly unempirical to suggest that the liberation of a man who did not come into existence until after Jesus ceased to exist could have taken place when Jesus died on the cross. By a skilful and uncriticised use of the metaphor of 'contagion' it is said that this freedom became contagious for the first disciples in the Easter event and that later generations have caught it from one another, but each man can only say that he 'became free at the time when he acquired his new perspective'. However, since the man has discerned that the primary source of this contagion was the Jesus who, although he no longer exists, did exist once, the man can say that it was Jesus who set him free, since 'it belongs to the language of a discernment-situation that we speak of that situation as containing already ("objectively"), prior to its becoming the occasion of a discernment, what was only "seen" at a later time'.[2] But this is only how we 'speak of' it; it is not how it really is. We may recall the song which was *called* 'Ways and Means' but which really *was* 'A-sitting on a Gate', and there is indeed a somewhat looking-glass character about van Buren's whole method of reinterpretation; like a mirror-image the transformed statement has perhaps the same empirical façade as its original (though even that might be doubted), but it has none of the substance of the original.

Finally, after giving us these examples of his technique, van Buren states two principles of interpretation which, in his theory, roughly correspond to those which were previously given in connection with the theories of Bultmann and Ogden. They are as follows:

(1) Statements of faith are to be interpreted, by means of the modified verification principle, as statements which express, describe, or commend a particular way of seeing the world, other men, and oneself, and the way of life appropriate to such a perspective.

[1] ibid., p. 149.
[2] ibid., p. 153.

(2) The norm of the Christian perspective is the series of events to which the New Testament documents testify, centring in the life, death, and resurrection of Jesus of Nazareth.[1]

The first principle is alleged to meet the demand of the theological 'left' to accept modern criticism of ancient ways of thinking; the second is alleged to meet the demand of the theological 'right' for the centrality of Christology.

At this point it is, I think, desirable to draw attention to a logical difficulty which may well be fatal to van Buren's whole technique of reinterpretation. That technique consists of substituting for a traditional 'non-empirical' statement, e.g. 'He who has seen me has seen the Father', an empirical statement which is alleged to have the same practical implications, e.g. 'Take me as the key to your understanding and living of life.' Now, provided the non-empirical statement is taken as meaningful, even if it is in fact believed to be false, the procedure proposed is at least a possible one, even if it is a somewhat unnatural one. I mean by this that a man might say, 'Although I do not believe that there is in fact a God, I can see that if there were a God certain practical consequences would follow, and, since I approve of those practical consequences and propose to live in accordance with them, I shall express this fact by saying that (of course in a "Pickwickian" and not a literal sense) I believe in God. What I mean by believing in God is doing good to other people [or whatever it may be].' If, however, the form of words 'There is a God' is not merely false but is strictly meaningless, the transition to the practical consequences cannot be made; for it is ridiculous to ask what would be the consequences if a meaningless expression were true. And it is fundamental to van Buren's position that this is the case. In one place he seems indeed to recognise this, when he writes: 'We have no idea what would count for or against the assertion that in seeing Jesus one had seen the Father. Unless we knew already the meaning of the word "Father", how could we verify or falsify this claim?' Nevertheless, as we have seen, he goes on to say: 'But if this passage is understood as a recommendation to turn away from asking about the Father and to ask about Jesus of Nazareth instead, its meaning becomes clear.' No doubt it does, but in asking us to make this substitution van Buren is either (1) con-

[1] ibid., p. 156.

tradicting his immediately prior allegation that nothing could count for or against the original statement or (2) abandoning his fundamental dogma that only empirically verifiable statements are meaningful or (3) substituting a statement which is meaningful for one which is meaningless under cover of expressing the true meaning of the meaningless statement. There is, I suggest, a simple explanation of this curious procedure, but it is a psychological and not a logical one. Van Buren is, in fact, trying to be two incompatible things, a radical linguistic empiricist and an evangelical Christian. If he were merely trying to be a radical linguistic empiricist he would simply formulate a set of ethical principles and fortify them by whatever 'blik' appealed to him; if this 'blik' happened to be one of admiration for the character of Jesus, well and good, but there would be no need to maintain that these principles and this 'blik' could, by some tortuous process of 'reinterpretation', be looked upon as equivalent to a large number of meaningless formulas which abound in the New Testament. Because he is, however, also anxious to be an evangelical Christian he hangs on to the meaningless New Testament formulas at any cost. He has therefore to set up some sort of correspondence between the empirical assertions and policy-announcements which are allowed by the linguistic empiricist half of him and the old-fashioned biblical texts which are demanded by the evangelical half. The correspondence, therefore, is extremely arbitrary, and it involves putting a ludicrously forced interpretation on some of the texts and conveniently ignoring many others. All this does great credit to van Buren's heart but little to his logic. As the sort of philosopher that he is, he is not only unable to believe, but even to assign a meaning to saying, that there is a God and that Jesus survived his crucifixion; as the sort of religious man that he is he wants to recognise that Jesus has set him free and to imitate Jesus' attitude of obedience to God. The only way to reconcile these two aspirations is by reducing the effect of Jesus upon men who live after him to an indescribable 'Easter experience' of liberation which appears to be induced partly by a kind of psychological 'contagion' and partly by the preaching and reading of the New Testament. But a religion for which belief in God is meaningless and for which Jesus is no longer in existence has little claim to be regarded as even a highly modernised version of traditional

Christianity. This will become even clearer when we see how van Buren 'reinterprets' the traditional formulas of Christian theology. In the meantime it will be well to emphasise how completely unintelligible and inexplicable, on van Buren's own principles, becomes the 'Easter experience' on which, for him, everything depends.[1] If there really existed either a transcendent God or a risen and living Christ, it might be ascribed to his activity. But since, on van Buren's view, there is neither, it becomes simply an odd psychological upheaval which occurs to some people and whose aetiology is entirely mysterious. No doubt a Freudian or Jungian psychologist would be ready to explain it as some kind of uprush from the unconscious, but this would discredit rather than confirm its validity as a desirable attitude to life. In default of this, it is nothing but an inexplicable blik, having neither any assignable cause or any rational justification. And this is an unsatisfactory position for an empiricist to find himself in.

VI

The tension between the traditional formulas and the reinterpretations of them which van Buren offers approaches breaking-

[1] The following words of Dr Alan Richardson are very relevant (and it should be noted that, while van Buren bases his rejection of the supernatural on linguistic rather than on existentialist philosophy, his *theological* attitude is authentically 'existentialist'):

> The weakness of the existentialist theology is that it has given no rationally convincing account of the origin of the Church and its faith on the assumption that the resurrection of Christ was not an historical event. It dissociates the Christian faith from historical testimony to its actual origin and nature, and it attempts to remain 'scientific' while giving existentialist interpretations of the meaning of faith as a substitute for historical explanation. . . . The problem becomes all the more insoluble in view of the assertion of the Bultmann school that neither Jesus nor his disciples had believed during his earthly life that he was the Messiah or the Son of Man. If there was no prior faith in Jesus' divinity to create the belief in the resurrection, and if there was no historical resurrection to create the faith of the Church, we are left with faith—an undeniable historical reality, Bornkamm's 'last fact' accessible to historians—hanging in the air, to be explained by existentialist analysis rather than historically. (*History, Sacred and Profane*, p. 209.)

These words will apply with equal force to the position of Dr John Knox, discussed in chapter v *infra*.

point, if it does not pass beyond it, when he passes from the language of the Bible to that of historic Christian theology. While any cosmological character of the classical assertions is rejected, 'responsibility to the history of Christian thought may be acknowledged by inquiring whether our interpretation is faithful to the intention of Chalcedonian Christology, remembering that, here again, fidelity to intention demands transformation of language. . . . Re-examination can, however, show that since the Christology of Chalcedon, in its time and in its own way, may be judged faithful to the intention of the New Testament message, our own interpretation, in its own way, may be shown to be faithful not only to the intention of the apostles but also to the intention of the Chalcedonian decision.'[1] The somewhat uneasy phrases 'in its time' and 'in its own way' may suggest that the fidelity in question will turn out to be rather a qualified one, reminiscent of Ernest Dowson's 'I have been faithful to thee, Cynara! *in my fashion*'; and there can be little doubt that if the Chalcedonian fathers had been offered van Buren's restatements as reinterpretations 'faithful to their intention' they would have felt that there were more dangerous heresies to be dealt with than those of Nestorius and Eutyches. We must now see what the offered interpretations are.

At the Council of Nicaea, the Church, rejecting the teaching of Arius, defined that the Word or *Logos* of God, which was incarnate in Jesus of Nazareth, was nothing less than God himself. For van Buren, this is to be interpreted as meaning that the Christian perspective is neither derivative nor in need of further support. Traditional Christian doctrine has held not only the doctrine of the 'economic' but also of the 'essential' Trinity (i.e. that God is triune not only in his relations to the created world, but also in his own inner life); this becomes the assertion that faith is not a provisional 'opinion', open to revision, but an irrevocable 'blik'. The assertion that the Logos is 'eternal' becomes the assertion that when a man became a believer it was not the world that changed, but his perspective on it. The formula 'The eternal Son, without ceasing to be God, became flesh' must be taken as meaning that the 'discernment' which takes place in the 'Easter experience' and the freedom which results can be satisfactorily described only in terms of

[1] ibid., p. 158.

'contagion' from the freedom of Jesus, so that the Christian will be 'liable' to use 'final' words, expressing wonder, awe and worship, in relation to him. 'Very man' means that Jesus was a real historical figure; this is a fairly easy transposition, as the original phrase was in the empirical realm. 'Jesus, as true man, was like us in all things except sin'; this is more difficult, for 'to what extent this obedience or "sinlessness" was recognised before Easter is a matter for conjecture, for the records were written after Easter, and they look back upon Jesus' history in the light of that event'.[1] Still, 'like us in all things' points to the fact that Jesus was a man. 'Without sin' points to his freedom. And in acknowledging him as 'sinless' we are 'committed to understanding all other men in the light of Jesus, and not vice versa'.[2]

Van Buren's reinterpretation of the doctrine of the virginal conception of Jesus must be dealt with rather more fully. Historically considered, he looks upon it as unfounded and undesirable. Understood 'factually' the nativity stories must be rejected, for 'such an interpretation would indeed threaten the doctrine of the full manhood of Jesus specified in the Christology of Chalcedon'. Nevertheless, 'considered as the language of thanksgiving, awe, and joy over the fact of the coming into being of this man, the nativity stories of Matthew and Luke are appropriate and appealing'. So 'the story of the babe born in total poverty and weakness may be an occasion for the deepening or renewal of the Christian perspective, a sign pointing to the life of freedom in the midst of fearful men which ended on the cross.'[3]

I shall leave until a later stage in this book the question of the historicity of the narratives in question. Here I shall merely comment on the peculiar logic that appears to underlie van Buren's argument. The literal truth of the virginal conception and the other miraculous elements in the narratives would, we are told, threaten the doctrine of the full manhood of Jesus as taught at Chalcedon. Chalcedon certainly did not think so, but it is difficult to see why the appeal to Chalcedon should be made here, unless it is simply for reasons of prestige, since Chalcedon

[1] ibid., p. 163.
[2] ibid., p. 164.
[3] ibid., p. 165.

believed that the full manhood of Jesus was entirely compatible with his full and literal Godhead, and in this van Buren holds Chalcedon was totally mistaken. If Chalcedon's view about the Godhead has to be transformed beyond recognition, why should we naïvely accept its view about the manhood? Furthermore, if we are, with van Buren, to hold that a literal acceptance of the miraculous stories is incompatible with the true nature of Jesus, it is difficult to see how any devotion, other than a grossly misdirected and superstitious one, can be fostered by dwelling upon them, with no matter how much thanksgiving, awe and joy. What will be deepened or renewed by this process will hardly be the Christian perspective as van Buren conceives it, but far more probably that very understanding of the Incarnation which he rejects as unempirical, unsecular and unmodern. If I were myself a van-Burenite, the last thing I should want to encourage would be meditation upon the nativity stories in Matthew and Luke. But to continue.

Classical Christology has said that the human nature of Jesus had no independent existence, considered apart from that of the incarnate Word, in which it was, to use the technical term, 'enhypostatic'. This means, for the modern empirical Christian, two things: first, that the free man Jesus has no compelling interest for the believer apart from the consequences of Easter, and secondly, that the Christian can only conceive of Jesus as a man whose freedom has become contagious. The unity of the two natures in Jesus means that the freedom which Jesus himself had and the freedom which the disciples caught by contagion on Easter cannot, in the Christian perspective, be separated. Again, Chalcedon asserted that the two natures remained unchanged and unconfused by their union in the person of the Logos. This is translated into the assertion that the history of Jesus is a piece of quite ordinary human history and must not be confused with the perspective to which, through its contagious character, it has given rise. 'When an ordinary situation becomes an occasion of discernment for a man, the change lies in the viewing, in what now becomes clear, in the light breaking; it is not an empirical change in the situation. The change is logically and historically significant, however; it marks the difference between faith and unbelief.'[1]

[1] ibid., p. 167.

Like his reinterpretation of the language of the New Testament, van Buren's reinterpretation of the language of Chalcedon might well be described as heroic, and indeed with even more justification. One is, in fact, left wondering why anyone who thought that the language needed such drastic renovation should think it was worth while retaining at all. There comes a point at which a building becomes so antiquated and decrepit that modernisation becomes both uneconomic and inefficient; if it is worth preserving, it is only as a museum piece. And I doubt whether the ordinary secularised modern man, who has not van Buren's professional interest in Christian theology, will, if he is converted to van Buren's general outlook on the Christian religion, see van Buren's attempt at the moral rehabilitation of Chalcedon as anything else than sentimental and romantic. Van Buren is indeed forced to admit that he has 'found no simple correspondence between patristic christological terms and those of [his] own interpretation', though he maintains that they have a 'logical equivalence'.[1] (One is sometimes led to wonder at his use of the words 'logical' and 'logic'.) What he means by this, he explains, is that he has placed the doctrine of Christ's human nature in the context of language appropriate to the history of a free man; this, he says, was relatively straightforward. The doctrine of Christ's divine nature, he admits, involves him in a more complex 'logic'; but still he has placed it in the context of language appropriate to a freedom which has been contagious, and to the historical perspective which arises from a discernment-situation. This, he surprisingly says, oversimplifies the picture (some may feel rather that it overcomplicates it); since Jesus' freedom was already contagious before its story was written down, and those who told it were already liberated and had acquired the perspective of faith. 'The function of the language of Christology is to define this historical perspective and to indicate its roots in the history of Jesus of Nazareth and in the proclamation of the Gospel of Easter.'[2] It is notable how central to van Buren's position are the concepts of freedom, contagion, disclosure and perspective; it is unfortunate that he never seems to recognise the large element of metaphor which is involved in his use of these terms or to ask himself whether they do not lose

[1] ibid., p. 168.
[2] ibid., p. 169.

much of their empirical character when he transposes them from their normal uses into the context of theology.

Van Buren rounds off his reinterpretation of Chalcedon by enquiring how far it is likely to satisfy the demands of his theological contemporaries. The theological 'right' are assured that Christology precedes soteriology, that 'that which is decisive for man has happened already long before man becomes aware of it and assents to it in faith'.[1] 'Both the language of history, which refers to the past, and the language of a historical perspective freshly gained, support the "objective" emphasis of conservative theology.'[2] And this is no doubt expected to console the 'right' for a deficiency which is not at this point mentioned, namely that for the last nineteen hundred years Jesus has not existed.

The theological 'left' receive a very different assurance, that the position commended is thoroughly in line with modern thought and indeed even more so than that of many thinkers who usually pass for radicals. The substitution for 'God' of such phrases as 'our ultimate concern', 'transcendent reality' or even 'the ground and end of all things' does not go far enough, for though they masquerade as empirical name-tags they lead us back into the ancient thought from which we were trying to extricate ourselves or, worse still, they are condemned by the criterion of linguistic analysis. So, although they are not mentioned here, Tillich and J. A. T. Robinson are thoroughly out of date, as are Bultmann and even Ogden, though the issues with which the last two are concerned are alleged to be faced more satisfactorily than they themselves faced them. And the five points on which, at an early stage in the discussion, Ogden was condemned as inadequate are now confronted with van Buren's alternatives. (1) Van Buren has not had to use the non-empirical phrase 'experienced non-objective reality' or anything like it, but has spoken instead of 'situations of discernment' and 'contagious freedom'. (2) He has therefore not had to cope with the problem of speaking analogically about God, for he has not spoken about God at all. (3) Though this is not explicitly stated, van Buren presumably holds that his view avoids the sharp distinction of New-Testament statements into empirical and existential, with no mixed types, for which he had condemned

[1] ibid., p. 169.
[2] ibid., p. 170.

Ogden and Bultmann. (4) Jesus of Nazareth is central to Christianity for van Buren, and so is (5) the Easter event, whereas both are peripheral, if not indeed irrelevant, for Ogden. In fact, we are left with the odd result that, for Ogden, Jesus and the Easter event, even if they were real, would be unimportant, while for van Buren they are of central importance, but are no longer, in any normal sense of the word, real.

The final stage in van Buren's exposition consists in specifying the substitutes which he offers for the main notions and doctrines of traditional theology. They can be stated quite simply, and the reader must decide for himself how far, if at all, they are sufficient. The traditional doctrine of *Revelation* held that the 'truths of revelation' cannot be discovered by reason alone and yet are susceptible of rational analysis and are logical in structure; the parallel to this is the fact that it is not logically or psychologically necessary that the record of Jesus and of Easter should become an occasion of 'discernment', but once the blik has been acquired hard thinking is needed to see its implications for the life of the individual who has acquired it. *Predestination* in its classical form held that God chose some men only; in Barth it holds that God, in choosing one man only for the sake of all men, has chosen all men. The modern equivalent of this, though it is not clearly stated, appears to be that the most important thing about a man is simply his manhood. *Creation* of the world by God is replaced by the Christian's affirmative attitude to the world and his refusal to allow anything except the biblical history centring in the history of Jesus to determine his orientation. *Providence*—the Christian's assertion that nothing can separate him from the love of God in Christ—becomes an assertion of the strength of the grasp that the Christian's perspective has on him. *Sin* becomes a denial of the idea that man is to be measured by the norm of Jesus. Pelagianism ignores the fact that, in the historical perspective of the Christian, freedom has come as a result of the Gospel of Easter. *Justification* becomes the fact that the believer no longer feels the need to 'prove' himself to himself or to anyone else. *Sanctification* is simply love for one's neighbour. The *Church*, as the Body of Christ, means simply that Christians have an historical perspective in common and that the freedom of Jesus has been contagious through Christians. *Baptism* represents the change which Christians have felt between their past bondage and their present liberty. *Preaching* may be an occasion for renewing and deepening the hearer's historical perspective, if he is a Christian; if he is not, it may become the occasion of a discernment that leads him to hold this perspective. It has expository and exhortative functions, too. The *Lord's Supper* is 'celebrated to provide an opportunity for the believer to "see" more clearly the basis of his "blik" and be "renewed" in his faith.'[1] The *Real Presence* means that the Lord's Supper has been and can again become a discernment-situation. *Prayer* cannot be thought of as addressing God, for there is no God to address; 'the meaning of intercessory prayer is its use: it begins in reflection on the situation in the light of the Christian perspective and leads to appropriate action'.[2] 'Thanksgiving and adoration express [the Christian's] joy and wonder before the fact that the world is and he is, and that his historical perspective gives him a way of understanding both himself and the world.'[3] But there is, of course, no one for him to thank or adore. Finally *the Church's Mission*, or rather the mission of the Christian is simply to be a man, as this is defined by Jesus.

The contemporary meaning of 'claiming the world for Christ' cannot be a return to medieval metaphysics and the confusion of the power of the Church with the contagious power of the freedom of Jesus. The meaning of that claim now is simply that the whole world may be seen with the Christian's perspective. He need not ask nor expect the world to understand itself as he understands it. Since he has acquired this perspective in connection with a freedom which is contagious, he should be content to let this contagion work its own way in the world, without his taking thought for the morrow, especially the morrow of the Church.[4] This is given by van Buren as his reason for questioning the concern of Bultmann and Ogden with evangelism; he endorses, in contrast, Barth's assertion that theology is done by the Church, takes place in the Church, and is for the Church. This takes us back to a feature of van Buren's position which we noted at the start of our investigation, that, in spite of his concern with expressing the Gospel in terms of the secularised thought of

[1] ibid., p. 187.
[2] ibid., p. 189.
[3] ibid., p. 190.
[4] ibid., p. 191.

the modern man, he is not in the least interested in commending the Gospel to the modern man who is at present outside the Church, but only with secularising its understanding by the Christian man who is already inside. For he holds that, unless this is done, the Christian will not be able to relate his life to the world in which he lives and of which he is part. For van Buren there is no question of Christianising the secular mind, but only of secularising the Christian mind. In a book to which I have already referred in terms of high praise Mr Harry Blamires has affirmed that there is no longer a Christian mind; if this is really true, van Buren's work is unnecessary, for his end has been already achieved.

I shall give reasons later on in this book for believing that modern science and historical study,[1] unless they are adopted one-sidedly and uncritically, in no way demand the radical secularisation of the Christian faith and its traditional beliefs and notions which van Buren so enthusiastically undertakes. At the moment I shall simply point out that the reinterpretation which he offers leaves us with an extraordinarily etiolated and deviscerated substitute for the rich and fertile organism of traditional Christianity. If we compare, for example, his flimsy and spectral statement of the nature of the Lord's Supper with all that the Eucharist has meant through the ages to the Body of Christ, as it is set before us, for example, in the magnificent treatises of Dix and Jungmann, or if we compare his account of prayer as reflection upon the situation in the light of the Christian perspective with the tremendous descriptions given by St John of the Cross or St Teresa of Avila of the adventures of the Christian soul in its deepening knowledge of the Divine Lover, we cannot but feel that, whether or not the interpretation which van Buren offers us is mandatory for present-day man, it is a very much impoverished version of the Christian religion. And, indeed, in his concluding chapter, which is simply entitled 'Secular Christianity', van Buren's confidence in his own position seems to waver. 'We have', he says (rather surprisingly, if we reflect on the details of his argument), 'neither urged that this path be taken nor denied that there are alternatives.' Considering the revolutionary nature of his programme, he seems to

[1] I have dealt fairly extensively with the impact of contemporary philosophy in my book *Words and Images*.

be extraordinarily detached about it. 'When we say that contemporary thought is secular,' he writes, 'we are calling attention to certain characteristics of the way we think and speak today. We have not argued that ours is a better or worse mode of thought than that of ancient times.'[1] He has, however, very clearly argued that it is the only mode that can survive the scrutiny of the logical analysts, which he takes at its face value and of which he accepts all the claims. Any idea that historic Christianity might itself be the criterion by which contemporary modes of secular thought should be judged, and their deficiencies exposed and corrected, never seems to have entered his head. What remains of the traditional faith, and this is a deeply moving feature of van Buren's position which sets it in contrast with that of Ogden, is a deep devotion to the figure of Jesus of Nazareth and a firm conviction of his uniqueness and centrality in human history, even though this goes with a belief that Jesus has not existed for the last nineteen hundred years and that the God to whom he prayed and whose will he believed himself to be obeying has never existed at all. But when van Buren writes, somewhat wistfully, that 'the fact that the language of our interpretation of Jesus and Easter is different from that of Paul does not preclude the possibility that our meaning and Paul's may be the same',[2] the only adequate comment would seem to be that it all depends on what you mean by 'meaning'.

Finally, I must comment, however briefly, on the amazingly naïve confidence which van Buren appears to have in the permanence of the linguistic-analytical doctrine of philosophy. It has been a frequent trait in Christian theologians down the ages to commit themselves whole-heartedly to the fashionable philosophies of their day, while passing severe judgments on their predecessors for adopting precisely the same attitude. How close the Alexandrian apologists sailed to the wind of gnosticism is a commonplace among church historians, and the Platonising or neo-Platonising of the Fathers has been a constant source of sorrow to biblical theologians, equalled only by their laments over the Aristotelianising of the medievals. Even such a great theologian as Charles Gore, while condemning the Roman doctrine of transubstantiation as 'a verbal incumbrance due to an

[1] ibid., p. 193.
[2] ibid., p. 199.

inopportune intrusion into church doctrine of a temporary phase of metaphysics',[1] substituted for it a doctrine explicitly based on a 'modern philosophy', assumed to be incorrigible and immortal, which was in fact a contemporary version of Kantian idealism. Van Buren clearly is in no different case. So difficult is it, even for the Christian theologian, to resist the temptation to be in the fashion. One need, however, only study the impressive collection of papers by contemporary philosophers which has been assembled by Professor H. D. Lewis and published under the title *Clarity is not Enough* in order to see that the citadel of linguistic analysis is already crumbling from within.[2]

[1] *The Body of Christ*, p. 120.

[2] Mr Don Cupitt, in a short but very discerning article in *Theology* (LXVII (1964), pp. 343ff.), entitled 'What is the Gospel?' which he was provoked to write by reading van Buren, has raised bluntly the question whether the Gospel is about God or about Jesus. Most people, he correctly remarks, will say it is about both, but he adds that this unity has now been sundered: 'There has for long been a distinction between theocentric and Christocentric emphases in Christian doctrine; but it is now widening into a distinction between theistic and non-theistic interpretations of the Gospel message.' Christian atheism is now a live issue. 'It is now a real question whether the Gospel is basically about God or about Jesus.'

Traditional theology, as Cupitt illustrates from general liturgical usage, sees the Gospel as about *God*: 'about God as Jesus shows him to be, about God as known in Jesus, but nevertheless, about God'. On the other hand, there has now appeared a 'Christian atheism', which may take either the 'practical' form, which is at least agnostic about God, or the 'speculative' form, which holds that ' "God" has been a harmful and is now a meaningless notion'. For this Christian atheism, the Gospel is simply about *Jesus*; God does not come into it.

Cupitt's contribution is to see this issue as related both to post-Kantian logic and to the problem of natural theology. If we say 'Jesus is like God', he asks, are we making a synthetic or an analytic statement? That is to say, are we taking 'God' as a word of whose meaning we have at least some limited knowledge apart from what we see in Jesus or are we defining it simply to denote what we do see in Jesus?

Traditional theology, with its insistence that the Gospel is about God, implies that 'we have some knowledge of God before the Gospel. It cannot be *merely* "knowledge" *that* he exists, because to know that something exists is not to know anything unless it is known *what* exists. The Gospel states that it is the holy God in whom we already believed, whom ignorantly we worshipped, whose true nature is now finally declared in Jesus.' St Paul, both in Romans and in Acts, asserts that Gentiles as well as Jews have this knowledge. 'And so, if we say that Jesus is from God, manifests God, or is God, we are making a synthetic assertion.' On the other hand, 'if someone holds that we have no knowledge of God apart from Jesus, and also holds that it is revealed that Jesus is like God, then nothing can tell either for or against this alleged revelation except the authority of the revealer. Since the revealer is said to be the very God to whom the proposition first introduces us we run here into a most awkward circularity.' And, Cupitt adds, we do not solve the difficulty by introducing the word 'self-authenticating'.

He goes on to point out that, in contrast to traditional theology, this 'neo-orthodox' theology is marked by a fundamental instability. When this is recognised we can choose between two ways. We can either say that Jesus is related to God 'synthetically', and this will reopen the whole question of natural theology. Or we may say that Jesus is related to God 'analytically', and this will lead us into either practical or speculative Christian atheism. Many Protestant associations, Cupitt remarks, have been content to state their belief as simply 'Jesus Christ as God and Saviour', but they did not expect the new development in which 'one now often meets Christians who hold that we need not, cannot, or must not speak of God any longer. Jesus is all of God that we can or need to know.'

Cupitt's own position is firmly on the side of traditional theology, with its conviction that we can have some knowledge of God prior to the Gospel; this he maintains was the position not only of the apologists but also (whatever the 'neo-orthodox' may say) of St Paul. 'The Gospel, in short, *must* presuppose a natural theology.' Here, I believe, he is entirely right. It is, however, ironical to reflect that the extreme revelationism of the Barthians, for whom God was everything and man was nothing, should have led to the Christian atheism for which the man Jesus is everything and God is nothing, in spite of the difficulty which Cupitt remarks, that Jesus himself both believed in and prayed to God his Father.

CHAPTER THREE

EMOTION RECOLLECTED IN TRANQUILLITY

A Reconsideration of *Honest to God*

Voici le temps des assassins.—Rimbaud.

I

NOW THAT THE tumult and the shouting have to some extent died, though the captains and the kings have certainly not departed, the time would seem ripe for a careful and sympathetic reassessment of the Bishop of Woolwich's famous little book *Honest to God*. In making this reconsideration I shall do my best to be fair to its author and not to exploit accidental obscurities of style and infelicities of phrasing. For if Dr Robinson has, in fact, certain things of importance to tell us which we did not know before, it is far more desirable that we should find out what these are than that we should find fault with his method of telling us about them. On the other hand, just because these things are of such vital importance, it is all the more necessary for us first of all to make quite sure what it is that he is trying to tell us and then to do our best to decide whether it is true or false. And this may involve us in minute examination of his statements, in a way which to many people will seem to be finicky and fault-finding. It will also necessitate the rejection of two contentions that have been urged by some of Dr Robinson's supporters, namely that a book written for the general public ought not to be submitted to the detailed scrutiny that would be proper to the examination of a work of technical scholarship in a learned journal, and that, because the deep mysteries of religion are, of their very nature, profound and obscure, we may legitimately indulge in obscurity in our discussion of them. For, in the first place, it is even more of a duty to avoid vagueness and ambiguity in a popular work than in a learned treatise, since the readers, being less skilled in the subject, are less able to correct for themselves any mistakes into which the writer may have fallen. Popular theological writing is one of the most difficult of all forms of communication, and its practitioner needs to be careful and self-critical to a degree; like marriage, it is not by any to be enterprised, nor taken in hand, unadvisedly, lightly, or wantonly, like brute beasts that have no understanding, but reverently, discreetly, advisedly, soberly and in the fear of God; I can vividly remember how impressed I was many years ago by the extreme trouble which that great Christian apologist the late Dorothy Sayers took in her popular writings on religion to ensure that what she was trying to express in a contemporary idiom was the authentic teaching of Christianity and that the technique which she had worked out was neither ambiguous nor misleading. And, secondly, the very fact that the Christian mysteries in their profundity outstrip our finite powers of comprehension makes it all the more important for us to express the limited grasp which we have of them with all the clarity and accuracy at our command, while fully recognising how very imperfect and partial our grasp of them is. No two Christian writers, I suppose, have been as conscious of the unfathomable mystery of God as were St Thomas Aquinas and St John of the Cross and so anxious to stress the inadequacy of even our most augustly authenticated concepts and images of him; but none have been so conscientious in their efforts to avoid imprecision and incoherence in their writing about him. Of all subjects, theology is that in which it is most important not to be slipshod. God indeed moves in a mysterious way his wonders to perform, but in this respect the theologian is not called to imitate him. I shall therefore make no excuse for scrutinising Robinson's arguments with the utmost care, in order to discover what he wishes to tell us and to decide, if we can, whether it is true or false.

On reading the Preface[1] to *Honest to God* it is not difficult to see, in broad general terms, the nature of the problem with which Robinson is exercised; it is that of making the Christian

[1] Pp. 7–10. *Honest to God* is a short book and it should not be necessary to give detailed page references to the passages quoted. I shall simply give the page numbers of each chapter as we come to it.

religion intelligible and acceptable to twentieth-century civilised men and women. Remarking that it belongs to the office of a bishop in the Church to be a guardian and defender of its doctrine, he goes on to assert that the discharge of this burden can seldom have demanded greater depth of divinity and quality of discernment. 'I suspect', he affirms, in a somewhat verbose passage, 'that we stand on the brink of a period in which it is going to become increasingly difficult to know what the true defence of Christian truth requires.' '*True* defence of Christian *truth*' is itself an odd phrase, but I imagine that *effective* defence of Christian truth is what is meant. The reasons for this suspicion we are not told, but, whether or not the defence is, as Robinson prophesies, going to become progressively more difficult, we need not deny that it is difficult enough at the present time. His reaction to this situation is, however, puzzling. For, after paying a handsome compliment to what he describes as 'the indispensable vocation' of those who give themselves to the task of the firm reiteration, in fresh and intelligent contemporary language, of 'the faith once delivered to the saints', he goes on to assert that he believes 'we are being called, over the years ahead, to far more than a restating of traditional orthodoxy in modern terms'. It is difficult to see what this could involve except the substitution of a new religion for Christianity, especially as he goes on to judge that 'a much more radical recasting . . . is demanded, in the process of which the most fundamental categories of our theology—of God, of the supernatural, and of religion itself—must go into the melting'. The reason which is given for this programme is that 'there is a growing gulf between the traditional orthodox supernaturalism in which our Faith has been framed and the categories which the "lay" world (for want of a better term) finds meaningful today', and moreover that this gap does not merely divide Christians from pagans but leaves many Christians on the same side as the pagans themselves. Indeed, Robinson confesses that the line of division runs right through the middle of himself, although as time goes on he finds that there is less and less of himself to the right (which I take to mean the traditionalist) side of it. Now, one possible explanation of this would be that the outlook of what Robinson calls the 'lay' world has become radically unchristian and that he himself has been dangerously influenced by it. This I believe to be in fact the case, though I would not go so far as Mr Alasdair MacIntyre in his article in *Encounter*[1] and say that 'what is striking about Dr Robinson's book is first and foremost that he is an atheist'. What I think becomes more and more clear as one reads his book is that he is a very unclear thinker and that his heart is where his head ought to be. At any rate, the possibility of the explanation which I have just given seems never to have occurred to him. Restatement of the faith once delivered to the saints, however fresh, intelligent and contemporary the language in which it might be expressed, has already been rejected as insufficiently radical to meet the situation. One might be pardoned for supposing that Robinson had despaired of trying to convert the world to Christianity and had decided instead to try to convert Christianity to the world. And this is what, as far as I can see, he would be committing himself to doing if he saw the full implication of his words. However, he almost immediately contradicts himself, for, after admitting that in listening to a broadcast discussion between a Christian and a humanist most of his sympathies are often on the humanist's side, he says: 'This is not in the least because my faith or commitment is in doubt, but because I share instinctively with him his inability to accept the scheme of thought and mould of religion within which alone that Faith is being offered to him.' He amplifies this by pleading for the recognition of 'those who believe their share in the total apologetic task of the Church to be a radical questioning of the established "religious frame" '. If this is so—if all that is wrong is the 'scheme of thought' or the 'religious frame' and not the Faith itself—then what is called for would seem to be just that firm reiteration, in fresh and intelligent contemporary language, of the faith once delivered which Robinson began by declaring to be insufficient. The matter is complicated by his further avowal that 'with a large part of himself' he finds the traditional framework of metaphysics and morals entirely acceptable. This peculiar state in which it is possible to hold contradictory positions with different parts of the mind seems to me to be either irrelevant or morbid. For if it merely means that Dr Robinson feels emotionally attracted to the two positions it is fully understandable, but of no great importance to those of us who are primarily interested not in Robinson's emotional state

[1] Reprinted in shortened form in *The Honest to God Debate*, pp. 215ff.

but in the truth or falsehood of the Christian religion; but if it means that Robinson believes contradictory propositions with different parts of his mind it reveals a situation which is alarming.

What I think Robinson has in fact failed to see is the importance of discriminating between the essential Christian Gospel and the forms in which it may be expressed at any particular epoch, difficult as it may be to draw the line with absolute precision. The consequence is that, in his warm-hearted desire to claim all good men as his brothers, he allows his sense of truth and falsehood to be smothered. 'Among one's intelligent non-Christian friends', he writes, 'one discovers many who are nearer to the Kingdom of heaven than they themselves can credit.' Who is expected to be surprised by this, except a certain type of extreme Calvinist? Certainly nobody in the Catholic tradition, for which *Facienti quod in se est Deus non denegat gratiam* is an accepted principle. But he continues as follows: 'For while they imagine they have rejected the Gospel, they have in fact largely been put off by a particular way of thinking about the world which quite legitimately they find incredible.' And all we can say about this is that it may be true in some cases, but is unlikely to be true in many and is certainly not true in all. There may be, as Robinson tells us, many among his friends who really accept the Gospel but imagine they have rejected it, and whose odd state of mind is due to their having been put off by a particular way of thinking about the world which they rightly find incredible, but if this is so he would seem to have missed a golden opportunity of enlightening them. But I strongly suspect that many of them are thoroughly good men who know pretty clearly what the Christian faith is and quite honestly believe that it is false. It is quite illegitimate to redefine Christianity in order to include within it all men of good will, though we shall see later on that this is what Robinson's programme in fact amounts to. And I am sure that there are few things which are more likely to infuriate an intelligent man than to tell him that he really believes in Christianity (or in anything else) when he is quite convinced that he doesn't. Robinson is not the first Christian apologist to distinguish between what people believe 'with the top of their minds' from what they believe 'in the bottom of their hearts' and to claim as Christians many people who think that they are not; the late John Baillie was a striking example of this.[1] The diagnosis and the deduction from it need, however, to be made with the greatest circumspection, and Robinson seems to be far too casual in making them. He is, in fact, so anxious to claim as a Christian anyone who, in spite of his professions of atheism or agnosticism, evidences a serious and generous attitude to life, that he is ready to atheise or agnosticise the Christian faith to almost any extent to bring the professing unbeliever within it. This is, I think, the explanation of the rhetorical assertion 'As for the images of God, whether metal or mental, I am prepared to be an agnostic with the agnostics, even an atheist with the atheists',[2] an assertion which does not, in fact, appear to be compatible with many of his utterances elsewhere in the book. However, if we are really to get to grips with contemporary unbelief, we must take it very much more seriously than this. Its causes are many and various, and, although it is perfectly true that one of them is the attachment of many Christians to obsolete imagery and concepts, there is very much more to it than this. It is not simply implicit Christianity, and if we assume that it is we shall almost inevitably find ourselves compelled to give to the word 'Christianity' a secularised meaning that is at variance with anything that it has ever meant since Christ himself appeared on earth. There are places where Robinson himself appears to want to do this, though he is neither intrepid nor consistent enough to carry the programme through to the end. It is, however, carried through quite remorselessly by Dr van Buren, in his work *The Secular Meaning of the Gospel*, which Robinson has spoken of with warm approval[3] and which I have discussed at what might seem inordinate length elsewhere in the present book.[4] It may seem paradoxical to suggest that Robinson shows insufficient sympathy with modern secularism, but I believe this is fundamentally the case. If we are to enter into a dialogue with the various systems of belief which compete with Christianity at the present day—and humanistic secularism is not the only one; there are Marxism, Islam and the various varieties of Buddhism and Hinduism—the first requisite, apart

[1] *Our Knowledge of God*, pp. 61 *et al.*
[2] *Honest to God*, p. 127.
[3] *The Honest to God Debate*, pp. 242, 249.
[4] Cf. ch. ii *supra, passim.*

from acquiring as accurate a grasp as we can of Christianity itself, is that we should take them really seriously as alternative outlooks upon the world and do our best to find out what are the points in which, *as systems of belief*, they agree and disagree with Christianity. It is here that I think we shall see that Robinson has failed so regrettably. There is nothing in his book which gets to grips with the really serious case for evolutionary humanism which is argued by Dr C. H. Waddington in his brilliant book *The Ethical Animal*.[1] There is nothing which shows that anxiety to *understand* a standpoint different from one's own which characterises Dom Bede Griffiths' remarkable article 'The Ecumenical Approach to Hinduism'.[2] Robinson concludes his Preface with the words: 'What I have tried to say, in a tentative and exploratory way, may seem to be radical, and doubtless to many heretical. The one thing of which I am fairly sure is that, in retrospect, it will be seen to have erred in not being nearly radical enough.' Whether the phrase 'in a tentative and exploratory way' can be justified except as a piece of defence-mechanism is doubtful; whether what he has tried to say can be legitimately described as 'heretical' may appear when we have found out what it is. But I think he is entirely correct in suggesting that it is not radical enough, for it does not get to the real roots of the matter. We must now pass from his Preface to the beginning of his main argument.

II

Robinson begins his first chapter, which is entitled 'Reluctant Revolution'[3] (though who is supposed to be reluctant we are not told) by remarking that the Bible speaks of a God 'up there'. While asserting that its picture of a three-decker universe was once taken quite literally, he admits that 'its more sophisticated writers, if pressed, would have been the first to regard this as symbolic language to represent and convey spiritual realities' and remarks that it 'had not become an embarrassment' to 'such an educated man of the world as St Luke' or 'the two most mature theologians of the New Testament, St John and the later

[1] Cf. pp. 205 *infra*.
[2] *Search*, III, p. 12 (May 1964).
[3] *Honest to God*, pp. 11–28.

Paul'. This fact itself calls for more consideration than Robinson gives it, for, as soon as the Church got out of a Semitic into a Greco-Roman setting, it was immediately confronted with a cosmology which did not postulate a three-decker universe, with a hemispherical firmament overarching a flat earth, but a system (or rather a large number of alternative systems) of celestial orbs and spheres and an earth which, whatever else it was, was approximately spherical.[1] And, to come down much later, throughout the Middle Ages there were two competing systems, the Aristotelian, which had a strong appeal on *a priori* grounds, and the Ptolemaic, which was much more successful in 'saving the phenomena'. The fact that the Church was so little bothered by this suggests that it was more successful in interpreting its scientific models than Robinson thinks; nobody who has studied Miss Sayers's brilliant discussions of Dante can suppose that the great Florentine poet thought of heaven in simply spatial terms. And Robinson himself admits that the notion of God as 'up there' has ceased to embarrass us, because 'we have long since made a remarkable transposition, of which we are hardly aware'. For, he writes (and the italics are his own), '*in place of a God who is literally or physically "up there" we have accepted, as part of our mental furniture, a God who is spiritually or metaphysically "out there"*'.

[1] Thus, to quote Dr R. M. Grant: 'It is often said that ancient people accepted a "three-storey universe"; they were wrong and we are right; therefore whatever they say about the universe is to be rejected. Examination of the evidence can indicate that (1) not all of them accepted such a cosmology, and (2) such a cosmology as such has little to do with the teaching of the New Testament.' (*Historical Introduction to the New Testament*, p. 85.) Again, Dr Alan Richardson has remarked:

> The Hebraic awareness of God as transcendent and immanent, as everywhere and nowhere, fitted ill into the Greek cosmic geography of the concentric crystal spheres, which must logically assign an appropriate place in the universe to every gradation of being, including the highest. But the medievals had inherited Greek science, and, since they found neither a rival cosmology nor a critique of the assumptions of the Aristotelian-Ptolemaic system in the Bible, they took it over without disquietude. One of the most curious misapprehensions of our time, common to famous scientists and men in the street, is that the medieval cosmology, which was shattered by the rise of modern science, derived its origin from the Bible. The extent of this misunderstanding serves to show how inseparably the medieval synthesis had riveted together biblical history and Greek science. It is still 'natural' to us, who have inherited Greek as well as Hebrew ways of thinking, to read the Bible with Greek eyes. (*History, Sacred and Profane*, pp. 68f.)

Now, this is a remark which I have found extremely illuminating, though not perhaps in the way that Robinson would intend; I shall return to this in a moment. He adds that 'there are, of course, those for whom [God] is almost literally "out there" ' and who, though they may have accepted the Copernican revolution in science, have still been able to think of God as in some way 'beyond' outer space. The argument now becomes extremely obscure. 'In fact,' we are told, 'the number of people who instinctively seem to feel that it is no longer possible to believe in God in the space age shows how crudely physical much of this thinking about a God "out there" has been. Until the last recesses of the cosmos had been explored or were capable of being explored (by radio-telescope if not by rocketry), it was still possible to locate God mentally in some *terra incognita*. But now it seems that there is no room for him, not merely in the inn, but in the entire universe: for there are no vacant places left.' The reference to 'the inn' is presumably light relief, for even the most extreme adherent of kenotic Christology can hardly have supposed that the Godhead in its totality was physically circumscribed within the spatial dimensions of the Babe of Bethlehem. What Robinson means appears to be that many people have thought that 'God' means a being who exists physically in a particular locality and that radio-astronomy has shown that there is no such being; the reference to 'rocketry', while contemporary, is admittedly irrelevant, as is shown by the words 'if not'. However, even if God did mean such a locally limited physical being, the conclusion would not follow. If the last recesses of the cosmos *had* been exhaustively explored by radio-telescope and no trace of God had been found, then (supposing that 'God' meant not just a spatially located physical being but also one who uniquely emitted radiation of certain specifiable wave-lengths or a specifiable pattern of such radiation), it might be claimed that God had been shown not to exist. But the fact that the universe is *capable* of being explored by radio-telescope proves nothing one way or the other; and, as for there being 'no vacant places left', modern research has shown that there is far more vacant space (or at any rate space in which the density of matter is minute beyond imagination) than was ever believed by ancient Hebrews or Greeks or medieval Europeans. Robinson himself immediately points out that the argument that he has stated is invalid, though for a different reason than that which I have given. He quite correctly states that modern astronomy holds that there is a limit set to observable space by the speed of light (it would be more accurate to say that it is set by the fact that at a certain distance physical objects will be receding at a speed equal to that of light), so that 'there is nothing to stop us, if we wish to, locating God "beyond" it. And there he would be quite invulnerable—in a "gap" science could never fill.' 'But', he adds—and this is where I find him puzzling—'in fact the coming of the space-age has destroyed this crude projection of God—and for that we should be grateful. For if God is "beyond", he is not *literally* beyond anything.'

Now this raises two questions, to which I do not find that Robinson gives an answer. First, who are these people who, accepting the Copernican revolution, did not think of God as literally or physically 'up there', but, until the advent of radio-astronomy and space travel, thought of him as physically and 'almost literally' (whatever 'almost' means in this context) 'out there'? I do not think I have ever met such a person, and I suspect he is an Aunt Sally of Robinson's. Secondly, supposing there was such a person, how has the space-age destroyed his 'crude projection'? Apparently, on Robinson's showing, by putting into his head an argument which has been shown to be quite invalid. Whether we ought to rejoice when hypothetical persons have false beliefs destroyed by invalid arguments I am doubtful. I have no doubt that the belief is false, but if I came upon someone who held it I should not talk to him about radio-astronomy; I should point out to him that the Church has always held that God is not limited to one particular physical locality, but is present *everywhere* 'by essence, presence and power' (to use the classical phrase of Christian theology) and I should try to explain to him what this means.

However, the consolation of this particular human oddity is only a preliminary to Robinson's main point, which is that the idea of a God *spiritually or metaphysically* 'out there' has got to die as well, and this, it is frankly recognised, is 'the God of our own upbringing and conversation, the God of our fathers and of our religion'. Robinson recognises that this is the God of whom the Bible speaks, and also that the question has been handled most effectively by such modern apologists as Dorothy Sayers, C. S.

Lewis and J. B. Phillips; 'their very achievement', he says, 'should make us hesitate to pull it down or call it in question'. 'I should like to think', he continues, 'that it were possible to use this mythological language of the God "out there" and make the same utterly natural and unselfconscious transposition as I have suggested we already do with the language of the God "up there". Indeed, unless we become used to doing this and are able to take this theological notation, as it were, in our stride, we shall cut ourselves off from the classics of the Christian faith, just as we should be unable to read the Bible were we to stumble at *its* way of describing God.' Now the 'transposition' referred to in the first of these two sentences was the transposition from the notion of a God 'up there' to that of a God 'out there'; we have been told this explicitly. But what is this new transposition to be; to what is the notion of a God 'out there' to yield? We must wait and see. In fairness to Robinson, we must be clear that the transformation for which he pleads is *not* the transformation from a literal or physical to a metaphorical or metaphysical interpretation of our phrases. The whole notion of God as 'out there' *in any sense* has to be abandoned, just as, according to Robinson, the notion of God as 'up there' *in any sense* was abandoned long ago. 'The signs are', he writes, 'that we are reaching the point at which the whole conception of a God "out there", which has served us so well since the collapse of the three-decker universe, is itself becoming more of a hindrance than a help.' There is, however, more to come, for we are told that there is not just a single, but a double crisis, and this bears upon the heart of Christian faith: 'The final psychological, if not logical, blow delivered by modern science and technology to the idea that there might *literally* be a God "out there" has *coincided* with an awareness that the *mental* picture of such a God may be more of a stumbling-block than an aid to belief in the Gospel.' Before seeing what Robinson proposes to put in the place of this obsolete notion, it will be well to raise a few questions about his argument up to this point.

In the first place, I am very doubtful whether there is any truth in the view that the Church coped with the crisis of Copernican astronomy by substituting the notion of God as 'out there' for the notion of God as 'up there'; I should at least like to see the evidence for this, and Robinson has certainly not produced it. What is, I think, true is that from the beginning the Church has interpreted its notion of God 'up there' as analogical, as is shown by the fact that it has supplemented it by the equally analogical notion of God as *everywhere*. But that it has ever made any very great use of the notion of God as 'out there' seems highly dubious. I should, however, like to add that, now that Robinson has suggested it, it seems to me to be a very useful notion indeed, especially in this space age, provided that we remember that, like all other spatial notions applied to God, it must be understood analogically and supplemented by others that are equally important. For if we are to think of God in images (and, being the sense-bound creatures that we are, we can hardly think of him in any other way), I do not see what better way there can be, in this gigantic universe, with its vast extent in both space and time which modern science has revealed to us, of expressing the universal creative activity of God in all its constituents and all its processes, than to say that he is 'out there'—meaning by this, not 'out' in one determinate direction at one determinate distance, but 'out' in all directions at all distances and at all times. At the very least, some such notion as this seems to be needed to supplement that which Robinson later introduces, if we are to avoid unbalanced anthropocentrism. When Robinson suggests that the *mental* picture of a God 'out there' may be a hindrance to the Gospel, I should wish to reply that *any* mental picture of God may be a hindrance if it is taken univocally in its unqualified everyday sense, even such biblical pictures as that of 'Father' and 'Shepherd', but that ordinary Christians find very little difficulty in making the necessary adjustments, while professional intellectuals might be expected to know something about the discussions of Christian theologians on the analogical nature of our language concerning God.

Robinson goes on to maintain that the abandonment of a God 'out there' represents a much more radical break than the transition to this concept from that of a God 'up there', since it will appear to be an outright denial of God. 'For', he says, 'to the ordinary way of thinking, to believe in God means to be convinced of the existence of such a supreme and separate Being. "Theists" are those who believe that such a Being exists, "atheists" those who deny that he does.' The word 'such' in this context is highly misleading, if it is taken to mean that 'out there' is commonly taken as both a literal and an exhaustive description of God. And he develops this assumption in a way that one can hardly avoid calling downright muddled:

> Suppose such a super-Being 'out there' is really only a sophisticated version of the Old Man in the sky? Suppose belief in God does not, indeed cannot, mean being persuaded of the 'existence' of some entity, even a supreme entity, which might or might not be there, like life on Mars? Suppose the atheists are right—but that this is no more the end or denial of Christianity than the discrediting of the God 'up there', which must in its time have seemed the contradiction of all that the Bible said? Suppose that all such atheism does is to destroy an idol, and that we can and must get on without a God 'out there' at all?

The following comments seem appropriate to this passage, which is very central to Robinson's argument:

(1) In any sense in which an intelligent Christian would be prepared to speak of God as a 'super-Being "out there"' he would not be adopting a version, however sophisticated, of 'the Old Man in the sky'.

(2) Christians have never thought of God as 'some entity, even a supreme entity, *which might or might not be there*', but as the one absolutely necessary Being.

(3) There may be people who call themselves 'atheists' who are so uninstructed as simply to reject the notion (however sophisticated) of the Old Man in the sky, while welcoming with acclamation Robinson's substitute, but to suppose that this is true of most intelligent people who call themselves 'atheists' is to insult their intelligence. Most of them know quite well what belief in God is and, for reasons which seem to them convincing, reject it. I think their arguments are false, but they are certainly to be taken seriously, and to suggest that 'atheists' are really unconscious crypto-theists is to do them a grave injustice. The transition in Robinson's passage from 'the atheists' to 'such atheists' conceals a serious logical flaw.

Robinson's subsequent question 'Have we seriously faced the possibility that to abandon such an idol may in the future be the only way of making Christianity meaningful, except to the few remaining equivalents of flat-earthers?' is presumably intended to suggest that we have not faced the possibility mentioned, but that if we did abandon the idol we should have little difficulty in making Christianity acceptable to the contemporary world. It may be relevant to observe that merely to abandon something, whether an idol or not, is hardly likely to make anything meaningful to anyone, unless we are clear what is to be put in its place. The question can therefore not be answered without seeing what Robinson has to say on this last point. We may, however, remark again that the idol which worries him so much seems to be an idol of his own fabrication, and I will anticipate the subsequent discussion to the extent of saying that I think something much more radical will be needed to commend the Christian faith to the modern secularised world than the substitution that Robinson proposes. In fact, he himself seems less than confident of its success. It will, he says, encounter the opposition not only of the fundamentalists but of 90 per cent of church people (we are not told how this figure is arrived at). 'Equally it will be resented by most unthinking non-churchgoers, who tend to be more jealous of the beliefs they have rejected and deeply shocked that they should be betrayed. Above all, there is a large percentage of oneself that finds this revolution unacceptable and wishes it were unnecessary.' It is not surprising that at this point Robinson himself asks whether it is 'really necessary to pass through this Copernican revolution'. 'Must we upset what most people happily believe—or happily choose not to believe? And have we anything to put in its place?' 'In some moods, indeed,' he replies, 'I wonder. But I know in my own mind that these are questions that must be explored. Or rather, they are questions that are already being explored on many sides.'

There follows in his book the moving autobiographical passage in which he describes his own development in the search for answers and his discovery of the three keys which he found in the writings of Tillich, Bonhoeffer and Bultmann. I shall refrain from detailed discussion of this section of Robinson's book in order to discuss the position which he has come to propound as his own. It is the less necessary, as a vast number of books have been written about all of these thinkers in recent years. None of them is easy to understand and their respective positions have seemed to those best qualified to judge as being incompatible. Their importance in the present context is through their function as providing the seminal principles for Robinson's own thought.

It is, however, interesting to remark that they all come from the background of German Protestantism, and that they all, in different ways, represent the reaction within German Protestantism from the extreme revelationism and supernaturalism of the school of Barth, Brunner and Heim. It has indeed been suggested that the emphatic secularist note which characterises Tillich, Bonhoeffer and Bultmann, to say nothing of Robinson himself, is the product of a violent swing from one extreme to the other, from a position which is all about God and grace to one which is all about man and nature. It is interesting to speculate what kind of book Robinson might have written if he had had behind him the Catholic tradition, with its doctrine of grace as perfecting nature and not destroying it. However, such speculations are trivial, and we must see what Robinson has to offer us himself. This takes us to his second chapter, entitled 'The End of Theism?'[1] It opens with the surprising statement that 'traditional Christian theology has been based upon the proofs for the existence of God'.

III

Surprising, I have said, because, although the 'proofs' have held a very important place in the Christian tradition, especially in the tradition of Catholicism, one has only to read the first question of the First Part of the *Summa Theologiae* to see that, for St Thomas Aquinas at least, Christian theology is based not upon any human arguments but upon divine revelation. And if this is true of a Catholic like Thomas Aquinas, it is true even more obviously of a Protestant like Luther. Be this as it may, Robinson's objection to the 'proofs' is the *a priori* one that 'the presupposition of these proofs, psychologically if not logically, is that God might or might not exist'. This statement is true, in the sense in which Robinson intends it, though I think most philosophical theologians would substitute 'metaphysically' for 'logically'. It must in any case be admitted that anyone who approaches the question of the existence of God must treat it as *psychologically* an open question, in the sense that, however firmly he is himself convinced that God exists, if he is to convince anyone else he must, for the purposes of his argument, begin by taking God's existence as problematical. Nevertheless, Robinson

[1] *Honest to God*, pp. 29–44.

objects that to take God's existence as problematical involves that 'such an entity, even if it could be proved beyond dispute, would not be God: it would merely be a further piece of existence, that might conceivably not have been there—or a demonstration would not have been required'. The objection, in fact, rests on the confusion between what is 'self-evident in itself and also to us' and what is 'self-evident in itself but not self-evident to us'; it is dealt with by St Thomas Aquinas in Book One, question ii, article I of the *Summa*. Now, the validity of arguing for the existence of God has notoriously been denied by extreme revelationists such as Karl Barth, on the grounds that man, in his finitude and his fallenness, is totally incapable of knowing anything about God, even that God exists, unless God directly reveals himself to him; but this is not Robinson's objection. What he insists is that 'God is, by definition, ultimate reality. And one cannot argue whether ultimate reality *exists*. One can only ask what ultimate reality is like.' It is hardly surprising that Mr David Jenkins has diagnosed this as 'a concealed and possibly inverted version of the traditional ontological argument',[1] the argument that God must exist, since the *idea* of God includes the idea of existing. This is, I think, a fair comment, but I would put my own objection to Robinson's assertion rather differently. We can, if we like, define God as ultimate reality, leaving the meaning of 'ultimate' vague enough to include something that in fact exists. But then, can we be sure that any existing being, however 'ultimate' in this vague sense, will be anything like what Christianity or any other respectable religion has meant by 'God'? As St Thomas has remarked, in the article to which I have referred above, some people have thought that God is a physical body. And, we might add, there are many people in mental homes who think that they themselves are God and ultimate reality. Robinson is making an important point in wanting to ask what ultimate reality or God is like; St Thomas, too, wanted to know and devoted nine questions of the *Summa* to the subject. But why, we may ask, is Robinson anxious to define 'God' so vaguely that it is impossible to dispute that he exists? We have, I think, already seen the answer. He is so determined to claim all men as implicit believers that he is going to use the word 'God' or whatever a man

[1] *The Honest to God Debate*, p. 198. Cf. p. 182 *infra*.

ultimately believes in, for whatever is, in Tillich's phrase, his 'ultimate concern'. But suppose a man's ultimate concern is with money, sex, cruelty or philately. We may, of course, say, in a highly metaphorical sense, that money, sex, cruelty or stamps are his 'god'. But, if we are trying to speak precisely, will it in fact be in the interest of clarity to say that we all believe in God, but he and Christians merely differ as to what God is like? Will it not be truer to say, with St Paul, that he has worshipped and served the creature more than the Creator? And suppose a man says quite sincerely that he does not believe that any reality is ultimate, in any proper sense of the word, and that none of his concerns is ultimate? It is difficult not to feel that Robinson is trying to pull the wool over the eyes of the unsuspecting unbeliever and is doing this at the cost of debasing the august name of God. In any case, the unbeliever may not be so unsuspecting; there was a passionate outburst, in a broadcast symposium shortly after *Honest to God* was published, by a lady who insisted that she had a great concern with ultimate reality and was an atheist, and was not going to be bullied into admitting that she was really a theist in disguise.

This 'ultimate reality' is identified by Robinson with what Paul Tillich calls 'the ground of our being' and in defence of this identification he quotes Tillich as attacking 'supranaturalism', that is to say the doctrine that God is 'a being beside others and as such part of the whole of reality. . . . He is seen as a self which has a world, as an ego which is related to a thou, as a cause which is separated from its effect, as having a definite space and an endless time. He is a being, not being-itself.' The quotation is from Tillich,[1] and Robinson admits that it applies to Deism rather than to theism in the traditional sense. But, characteristically, he alleges that although 'we know that [God] does not exist in space . . . we think of him nevertheless as defined and marked off from other beings *as if* he did. And this is what is decisive.' Such a statement as this is easy to make and difficult to contradict, as no indication is given as to who the 'we' are to whom it refers, though the subsequent assertion that this way of thinking is so interwoven into our way of thinking that it is difficult to criticise it without appearing to threaten the entire fabric of Christianity at least suggests that 'we' must be almost

[1] *Systematic Theology*, II, pp. 5, 11.

all the Christians who have ever lived. Furthermore, Robinson admits that it is assumed to be the Christian view by such non-Christians as Sir Julian Huxley. Nevertheless, in spite of the universal agreement of both Christians and non-Christians that this is the way in which Christians think about God, Robinson is determined to repudiate it, and the reason is clearly that, in spite of themselves, he is going to claim such people as Huxley as being really Christians without knowing it. 'The God [naturalism] is bowing out', he tells us, 'is the God of the "supranaturalist" way of thinking. The real question is how far Christianity is identical with, or ultimately committed to, this way of thinking.'

Before considering the answer which Robinson gives to this question I must make some comments on the passages I have just quoted. The phrase 'He [sc., God] is a being, not being-itself', which Robinson takes from Tillich as a statement of the supranaturalistic view, would certainly not be accepted by such an unashamed supranaturalist as St Thomas Aquinas. That God is 'being-itself' (*ipsum esse*) and that with creation there are more beings but not more being (*plura entia*, *non plus entis*) are Thomist commonplaces. So anxious is Robinson, however, to eliminate any kind of supranaturalism that he even condemns the picturing of God as a Person. What is quite amazing is his cool dismissal of all the traditional imagery about God as misleading, with the calm assumption that he himself has found a way of talking about God that is fully adequate. Generations of Christian thinkers have grappled with the problem as to how it is possible for a finite being to conceive God at all, and how we can distinguish images and concepts that are inadequate but informative from those that are definitely misleading; the classical discussions of analogical predication are only one example of this. Robinson, however, sweeps the whole lot into the waste-paper basket and substitutes the bare concept of ultimate reality or being. There is in any case something ironical for a theologian in the Catholic tradition, who, in spite of all his protests, has been accused for the last twenty years by his Protestant friends of depersonalising God by thinking of him in terms of being, to be told by Dr Robinson, on the strength of the writings of such unashamed Protestants as Tillich and Bonhoeffer, that the essential thing about God is that he is being-itself and that we must at all costs avoid thinking of him as a Person. Dr Macquarrie has seen a little farther than Robinson here, for he is not prepared to identify God with Being until he has convinced himself that Being is gracious. But then he proposes to drop reference to God altogether, and to substitute for the statement 'God exists' (which seems to him to treat God as merely one being among others) the statement 'Being is gracious'.[1] This seems to be carrying caution to excess, and one wonders what the simple believer will make of it. But then Macquarrie is a disciple of Heidegger, while Robinson is a disciple of Tillich.

However, to return to Robinson himself, having raised the question whether Christianity is committed to the supranaturalistic way of thinking, he admits that undoubtedly it has been identified with it and characteristically adds that somewhere deep down in ourselves it still is. ('Ourselves'—once again the elusive 'we'!) Furthermore, he tells us that the whole world-view of the Bible is unashamedly supranaturalistic, and remains so even when we have 'refined away the crudities and literalism of this construction'. 'How far', he asks, is 'Christianity . . . committed to a mythological, or supranaturalist, picture of the universe at all? Is it necessary for the biblical faith to be expressed in terms of this world-view, which in its way is as primitive philosophically as the Genesis stories are primitive scientifically?' The suggestion is made that Julian Huxley may have performed a valuable service in detaching Christianity from supranaturalism, and at this point Bultmann is introduced, with his programme of demythologising, and Bonhoeffer, with his programme for 'religionless Christianity'. Here we are not concerned with these in themselves, but only with the use that Robinson makes of them. Whether 'religion' meant for Bonhoeffer what it suggests to an English reader has itself been questioned,[2] but the statements which he makes without using the word are themselves sufficiently startling. 'God is teaching us that we must live as men who can get along very well without

[1] 'How is Theology possible?' in *The Honest to God Debate*, p. 188.

[2] Thus Dr Alan Richardson writes: 'The expression "religionless" means something quite different in English from what was intended by the German original, given currency by Dietrich Bonhoeffer. . . . By "religious" Bonhoeffer meant "metaphysical", "subjective", "individualistic", "pietistic"; "religion" for him means what in English might be called "religiosity".' (*History, Sacred and Profane*, p. 81, n. 1.)

him.' 'The God who makes us live in this world without using him as a working hypothesis is the God before whom we are ever standing. Before God and with him we live without God.' Such statements as these are clearly highly paradoxical, and remind us of some of the statements in which Christian mystics have tried to describe an experience which is strictly ineffable. Robinson, however, insists on taking them as strictly literal, and brings them into line with Tillich's assertion that theism as ordinarily understood 'has made God a heavenly, completely perfect person who resides above the world and mankind'. Robinson defends 'the Church's best theologians' from this charge, but strangely says that 'they would have been content with the essential orthodoxy of Professor Norman Pittenger's description of God as "the Reality undergirding and penetrating through the whole derived creation" '. This would seem to rule out both St Augustine and St Thomas from the ranks of the Church's best theologians, but in any case popular Christianity falls under the accusation of positing God as a 'supreme personality'. And Robinson rightly says that it is about the existence or non-existence of such a Being that contemporary linguistic philosophers do battle. His own solution is almost heroically naïve; it is that we should give up the battle for a personal God altogether. By doing this we shall placate not only the linguistic philosophers, but also Julian Huxley, who has registered the enormous sense of spiritual relief that has come to him from rejecting the idea of God as a supernatural being, and (posthumously) such avowed atheists or antitheists as Feuerbach and Nietzsche, who saw the supreme Person in heaven as the great enemy of man's coming of age. It is true, Robinson admits, that they acted in this way because they conceived God as a savage tyrant who impoverishes, enslaves and annihilates man, but their revolt would have been equally justified if they had believed that he was kindly old man who let his children do what they liked without interference. 'The nature of his *character* is here secondary', Robinson asserts, and in a rhetorical question he proposes to tear down the whole conception of a God 'up there', 'out there' or, in his own words, 'however you like to put it', and he backs up his case with a long passage from John Wren-Lewis. At this point his nerve seems to give way, and he tells us that 'to speak thus one is in danger, like the Psalmist, of condemning a whole generation—indeed many, many generations—of God's children'. 'There is nothing intrinsically wrong with [this language]', he tells us (somewhat surprisingly, in view of what he has previously said), 'any more than there was with the symbolism of a localised heaven.' Nevertheless, 'if Christianity is to survive, let alone to recapture "secular" man, there is no time to lose in detaching it from this scheme of thought, from this particular theology or *logos* about *theos*, and thinking hard about what we should put in its place'. Before turning to this task, Robinson has two more surprises in store for us. 'Our concern will not be simply to substitute an immanent for a transcendent deity. . . . On the contrary, the task is to validate the idea of transcendence for modern man.' In view of the derivation of the word 'transcendence' it is difficult to see how we can retain the idea while rejecting the whole conception of a God 'up there'; Robinson manages, however, to do this by reinterpreting it as burrowing into instead of as climbing over.[1] It is unfortunate that he was not able to refer to Canon G. F. Woods's essay on 'The Idea of the Transcendent' in *Soundings*. And, finally, he assures us that 'our concern is *in no way* [my italics] to change the Christian doctrine of God but precisely to see that it does not disappear with this outmoded view' of the world. Robinson's optimism is unbounded.

IV

Robinson embarks upon this task of 'validating the idea of transcendence for modern man', as he has called it, in the third

[1] In view of the way in which Robinson appeals to Tillich for support, the following passage from Tillich may not be irrelevant:

> The relation between the ground of being and its revelatory manifestations can be expressed only in terms of finite actions originating in a highest being and transforming the course of finite events. This is unavoidable. In the same way the relation of the ground of revelation to those who receive revelation can be conceived only in personal categories; for that which is the ultimate concern of a person cannot be less than a person, although it can be and must be more than personality. Under these circumstances the theologian must emphasise the symbolic character of all concepts which are used to describe the divine act of self-revelation, and he must try to use terms which indicate that their meaning is not categorical. 'Ground' is such a term. It oscillates between cause and substance and transcends both of them. (*Systematic Theology*, I, p. 173.)

chapter of his book, which bears the title 'The Ground of our Being'.[1] And, in spite of the reassuring words with which he ended his previous chapter, he now makes it plain that we are in for a very great transformation indeed. The translation from the God 'up there' to the God 'out there' represented, he tells us, no more than a change of direction in spatial symbolism: God was still thought of as 'a Being existing in his own right to whom the world is related in the sort of way the earth is to the sun. Whether the sun is "above" a flat earth or "beyond" a round one does not fundamentally affect the picture.' We must, I think, here interject that the comparison of the relation of God to the world with that of the sun to the earth is a complete travesty of the traditional position if it is taken as anything but the roughest and crudest metaphor; it makes no provision for the fundamental feature of the traditional position, namely the absolute self-existence of God and the total dependence of the world upon him. It is thus difficult to know what precise meaning to attach to the rhetorical question which Robinson now asks: 'But suppose there is no Being out there at all? Suppose, to use our analogy, the skies are empty?' Are we being invited to consider abandoning belief in God altogether? That would indeed be 'to change the Christian doctrine of God'. Or are we being asked simply to abandon a misleading metaphor in favour of some more adequate one?

Robinson at least makes it clear that something more is involved than would follow from the second alternative. He does indeed suggest that the metaphor of 'depth', which he proposes instead of that of 'height', would have considerable advantages simply as a spatial metaphor, since, as he says, 'we are familiar today with depth psychology, and with the idea that ultimate truth is deep or profound'. He also quotes from Tillich a somewhat questionable assertion to the effect that 'depth' has richer associations than 'height'. Nevertheless, he insists that 'we are not here dealing simply with a change of symbolism, important as that may be', not just substituting a God 'down under' for a God 'up there'. 'When Tillich speaks', writes Robinson—and he is clearly identifying his own view with that of Tillich as he understands it—'When Tillich speaks of God "in depth", he is not speaking of another Being *at all*. [The italics are Robinson's.]

[1] *Honest to God*, pp. 45–63.

He is speaking of "the infinite and inexhaustible depth and ground of all being", of our ultimate concern, of what we take seriously without reservation. . . . What Tillich is meaning by God is the exact opposite of any *deus ex machina*, a supernatural Being to whom one can turn away from the world and who can be relied upon to intervene from without. God is not "out there". He is, in Bonhoeffer's words, "the 'beyond' in the midst of our life", a depth of reality reached "not on the borders of life but at its centre", not by any flight of the alone to the alone, but, in Kierkegaard's fine phrase, "by a deeper immersion in existence".'

Now, we are not concerned with the question whether Robinson has correctly understood any of the three writers to whom he has here referred, though the correlation of Tillich and Kierkegaard is certainly somewhat strange; as Dr Kenneth Hamilton has shown,[1] there can hardly be two theologians whose attitudes are so directly opposed as are those of Tillich and Kierkegaard. We are concerned with what Robinson himself is trying to say, and we are badly hampered, in a passage such as that just quoted, by the fact that he takes in their crudest sense the metaphors which he rejects, while presumably intending those which he adopts to be interpreted benignly. It would be easier to be fair to him if it was clearer than it is that he is being fair to his opponents. He has warned us that his adopted category of 'depth' is not to be taken as spatial, even symbolically so; yet he insists on taking that of 'height' as so crudely spatial as hardly to be symbolical at all. What traditional theologian, unless he was an avowed deist, would describe God as a *deus ex machina*? And what are we to make of the assertion that 'He is "the 'beyond' in the midst of our life" '? The very use of the word "he" seems to beg a fundamental question, in view of what Robinson goes on to say (and has, as we have seen, already said) about the hazard involved in describing God as personal; and the use of the word 'beyond' suggests a reintroduction of the notion of God as 'out there'. Indeed, the phrase 'the "beyond" in the midst of our life' might well be taken as an unconventional assertion of the traditional doctrine that God is both transcendent and immanent. Robinson, in fact, goes straight on to say: 'For the word "God" denotes the ultimate

[1] *The System and the Gospel*, *passim*, especially ch. ii, 'Anti-Kierkegaard'.

depth of all our being, the creative ground and meaning of all our existence'; and this, if we take the word 'creative' in its normal theological sense, is a thoroughly traditional statement. We might compare with it the famous remark of St Thomas that God 'preserves things in no other way than by giving them existence; hence if he took away his action from them, all things would be reduced to nothing'.[1] There is, however, one significant difference, namely that Bonhoeffer and Robinson refer to '*our* life', '*our* being' and '*our* existence', while St Thomas refers to all things; and this, I believe, indicates both the strength and the weakness of Robinson's position. He is, it seems to me, so desperately anxious that God shall be inescapably involved in each one of us that he is indifferent, and indeed hostile, to the notion that God is the creator of the universe as a whole. Thus he tells us that the word 'God' is so conditioned by associations with *a* Being out there, that 'the line between those who believe in God and those who do not bears little relation to their profession of the existence or non-existence of such a being. It is a question rather of their openness to the holy, the sacred, in the unfathomable depths of even the most secular relationship.'

This assertion is reinforced by the following quotation from Martin Buber's famous, but obscure, work *I and Thou*:

> When he, too, who abhors the name, and believes himself to be godless, gives his whole being to addressing the *Thou* of his life, as a *Thou* that cannot be limited by another, he addresses God.[2]

'For', adds Robinson, 'in the conditioned he has seen and responded to the unconditional. He has touched the hem of the eternal.'

Now the apparently neuter connotation of the words 'the holy, the sacred', which Robinson himself uses, might well seem to indicate a belief that the ultimate reality was an impersonal substratum or stuff out of which the universe was made, while the quotation from Buber, whatever it may mean in its original context, seems, in Robinson's adoption of it, to be certainly personal, as the word 'Thou' suggests, but to be equally compatible with a worship of the self ('the *Thou* of his life, as a *Thou* that cannot be limited by another'). Any acquaintance with

[1] *S. Theol.*, I, ix, 2*c*.
[2] *I and Thou*, p. 76.

Indian religion will show how subtle, and at the same time how central, these distinctions are. In order to be quite fair to Robinson here, it will be necessary to quote the succeeding passage at length. It runs thus:

> The difference between the two ways of thought [i.e. traditional theism and Robinson's view] can perhaps best be expressed by asking what is meant by speaking of a *personal* God. Theism, as the term was understood in the previous chapter, understands by this a supreme Person, a self-existent subject of infinite goodness and power, who enters into a relationship with us comparable with that of one human personality with another. The theist is concerned to argue the existence of such a Being as the creator and most sufficient explanation of the world as we know it. Without such a Person 'out there', the skies would be empty, the heavens as brass, and the world without hope or compassion.

Down to the last sentence this may well be taken as a sufficiently accurate statement of the traditional point of view, though we might note in passing that Robinson's readiness to describe it simply as 'theism' while going on at once to reject it might seem to provide justification for MacIntyre's assertion that Robinson is clearly an atheist. The last sentence, with its reference to the 'Person "out there" ' instead of the God who is everywhere is, however, simply misleading. Against this, Robinson states his own position in what is really the central and pivotal passage of his book:

> But the way of thinking we are seeking to expound is not concerned to posit, nor, like the antitheists, to depose, such a Being at all. In fact it would not naturally use the phrase '*a* personal God'; for this in itself belongs to an understanding of theology and of what theological statements are about which is alien to it. For this way of thinking, to say that 'God is personal' is to say that 'reality at its very deepest level is personal', that personality is of *ultimate* significance in the constitution of the universe, that in personal relationships we touch the final meaning of existence as nowhere else. 'To predicate personality of God', says Feuerbach, 'is nothing else than to declare personality as the absolute essence.' To believe in God as love means to believe that in pure personal relationship we encounter not merely what ought to be, but what is, the

> deepest, veriest truth about the structure of reality. This, in face of all the evidence, is a tremendous act of faith. But it is not the feat of persuading oneself of the existence of a super-Being beyond this world endowed with personal qualities. Belief in God is the trust, the wellnigh incredible trust, that to give ourselves to the uttermost in love is not to be confounded but to be 'accepted', that Love is the ground of our being, to which ultimately we 'come home'.

Now, as we have already seen, Robinson is not an invariantly consistent writer and it would perhaps be possible to find passages elsewhere in his book which might seem to take some of the sting from this statement. However, if we are to do justice to him at all, we must in fairness assume that he is speaking deliberately and carefully in this central exposition of his position. And I wish to make the following comments on it:

(1) Robinson expresses complete indifference as to whether 'theism' is true or not.

(2) He does not naturally use the phrase '*a* personal God'; on the other hand he does want to say that 'God is personal'.

(3) This phrase—'God is personal'—means 'reality at its very deepest level is personal'. This phrase uses the spatial metaphor of 'depth' and so presumably needs interpretation if it is not to fall under Robinson's own condemnation of spatial images.

(4) What it means is that 'personality is of *ultimate* significance in the constitution of the universe, that in personal relationships we touch the final meaning of existence as nowhere else'. The notion of depth has now been replaced by that of ultimacy and finality, but these are not defined, either here or anywhere in the book. Their meaning is presumably taken as self-evident, but this seems to be at least open to doubt. Does Robinson mean that personal relationships are the most *valuable* constituents of the universe or that they will in the end be recognised as such? And if the latter, where, when and by whom? I am not asking these questions in order to be captious, but because they are just the questions to which a man who is agonising about life and trembling on the brink of hope and despair will want to have answered. The quotation from Feuerbach is, presumably, supposed to clarify Robinson's own assertion, but does little to this end. To know what Feuerbach means by 'absolute essence'

would involve a careful study of his peculiar philosophical system in which God is another name for the human species; how far Robinson goes with this particular form of nineteenth-century idealism he does not tell us.

(5) Personal relationships can be of many kinds, and some of them are very unpleasant indeed; hate, for example, no less than love. Do we touch the final meaning of existence in all of them, or only in some?

(6) It is perhaps the consciousness of this difficulty that leads to the introduction at this point of a new concept, that of 'God as love'; to believe in this, we are told, *means* (not just entails) that 'in pure personal relationships we encounter, not merely what ought to be, but what is, the deepest, veriest truth about the structure of reality'. What is meant by 'pure personal relationship' we are not told, but we shall see grounds for thinking that it refers simply to some kind of relationship between *human* persons. In any case, it seems odd to say that in a personal relationship we encounter a *truth*, however deep and very it might be. Perhaps what is meant is that relationships between human beings of the type described as 'pure' are the most valuable things that the universe offers us, but if so it seems unnatural to express this by saying that *God* is love. I shall return to this point in a moment.

(7) The word 'pure' is central to Robinson's exposition, but it is seriously ambiguous. Does it mean 'virtuous' or 'unmixed'? That is to say, is a pure personal relationship one which is perfectly good and loving or one which includes no impersonal element? A great deal turns on this.

(8) This belief in 'God as love' is described as 'a tremendous act of faith' made 'in face of all the evidence' and as a 'wellnigh incredible trust'. Its appeal to contemporary man will therefore seem to offer more difficulties than the earlier part of the book led us to hope.

(9) We are, in fact, given an alternative definition of belief in God; it is the trust that to give ourselves to the uttermost in love is not to be confounded but to be 'accepted', that Love (with a capital L) is the ground of our being, to which ultimately we 'come home'. Here there are introduced two new and unexplained metaphors, those of 'acceptance' and of 'coming home'. Now, acceptance would normally mean acceptance by

someone, and for a traditionalist it would mean acceptance by God. However, for Robinson there is no such person as God to do the accepting; the form of words 'God is personal' has been redefined to mean 'Personality is of ultimate significance' and 'God' as a name has been eliminated, in much the same way as 'infinity' as a name is eliminated when a mathematician redefines 'N tends to infinity' as meaning 'Whatever number M you like to specify, there will be a value of N that is greater than M'. Ultimate significance can do no accepting; perhaps it is the consciousness of this that leads Robinson to endow Love in this context with a capital L, as if it was the name of a person, but if so this is simply sharp practice and the wary unbeliever will see through it.

(10) Returning to (6) above, the following paragraph in Robinson's book confirms the suspicions there expressed. 'If this is true,' he writes, 'then theological statements are not a description of "the highest Being" but an analysis of the depths of personal relationships—or, rather, an analysis of the depths of *all* experience "interpreted by love".' There seems to be here a conglomeration of three different meanings that might be given to the term 'theological statement', namely (i) an analysis of the depths of personal relationships, (ii) an analysis of the depths of any or all experience, and (iii) an interpretation of either or both of these in terms of love. It is difficult not to feel that the undefined phrase 'interpreted by love' (it is, of course, taken from a hymn by J. G. Whittier) has been slipped in in order to suggest that an analysis of the depths of personal relationships will show that love is the key to their interpretation; if so, this is a begging of the question. And the following sentences give quite a different definition: 'Theology, as Tillich insists, is about "that which concerns us ultimately". A statement is "theological" not because it relates to a particular Being called "God", but because it asks *ultimate* questions about the meaning of existence: it asks what, at the level of *theos*, at the level of its deepest mystery, is the reality and significance of our life.' To speak of a *statement* as asking *questions* is linguistically queer, but we may let this pass. The point is that there is nothing about 'interpreted by love' here; in *this* sense a statement might be theological and affirm that, at the level of its deepest mystery, the reality and significance of our life was that we were the playthings of an

incompetent, capricious or malevolent spirit. In the next sentence, however, love gets smuggled in again: 'A view of the world which affirms this reality and significance in personal categories is *ipso facto* making an affirmation about the *ultimacy* of personal relationships: it is saying that *God*, the final truth and reality "deep down things", *is* love.' But, even with the peculiar Robinsonian definition of God embodied in this sentence, it is saying nothing of the sort, unless we assume that the personal relationships which are affirmed as being ultimate are relationships of love; and to assume this is to beg the question.

I am afraid that what I have been saying in the last few pages will seem to Robinson's supporters to be extremely hair-splitting and fault-finding, but it is, I am sure, very necessary. For Robinson is putting forward an interpretation of Christianity which he himself claims is far more than a restating of traditional orthodoxy in modern terms and is one in which the most fundamental categories of our theology—of God, of the supernatural, and of religion itself—must go into the melting. Now, anyone who proposes a revolution as radical as this must clearly expect his programme to be subjected to the most careful scrutiny, for to remodel the Christian religion so drastically on principles which turned out to be fallacious might clearly be nothing short of calamitous. And the conclusion to which my examination of Robinson's argument has so far led us is that it embodies a great deal of sheer ambiguity and confusion. It is for this reason—because he has not subjected his own arguments to a sufficiently minute scrutiny—that he seems to me to have erred, at the very heart of his exposition, not in being too radical but in not being radical enough. However, we must see how the sequel develops.

V

Having repeated his approval of Feuerbach's desire to transform 'theology' into 'anthropology', Robinson begins to lose courage. 'It is also clear', he says, 'that we are here on very dangerous ground. For, to Feuerbach, to say that "theology is nothing else than anthropology" means that "the knowledge of God is nothing else than a knowledge of man".' It is difficult to see how it could mean anything else to anyone who had an elementary knowledge of Greek vocabulary. It is thus hardly surprising that, as Robinson goes on to point out, 'his system runs out into the deification of man, taken to its logical conclusion in the Superman of Nietzsche and Auguste Comte's Religion of Humanity'. And he finds a similar defect in the humanism of John Macmurray. 'The question of God is the question of transcendence. It is precisely this that the location of God "up there" or "out there" was to express and safeguard and which its denial appears to imperil. But for Macmurray transcendence is a category that applies equally to humanity.' We find again in Robinson, as we did at the beginning of his argument, the desire to repudiate all spatial metaphors of height or distance as applied to God and yet to retain the metaphor of transcendence, which, by the very derivation of the word, would seem to be one of them. Macmurray, he goes on to affirm, is wrong in denying that transcendence is distinctively an attribute of God, but right in asserting it as a feature of all our experience:

> Contrary to what [Macmurray] says, our experience of God *is* distinctively and characteristically an awareness of the transcendent, the numinous, the unconditional. Yet that is a feature of *all* our experience—*in depth.* Statements about God are acknowledgments of the transcendent, unconditional element in all our relationships, and supremely in our relationships with other persons. Theological statements are indeed affirmations about human existence—but they are affirmations about the ultimate ground and depth of that existence.

This is one of the most revealing passages in Robinson's book and again I shall make a number of comments.

(1) We are told that an awareness of the transcendent, the numinous, the unconditional is a feature of *all* our experience—*in depth.* What is meant by the undefined, but spatially metaphorical, words 'in depth' I find it very difficult to understand; they plainly mean a lot to Robinson, for he has put them in italics. I cannot help suspecting that they are inserted because without them the assertion would be obviously false; it must be obvious on a moment's consideration that in *most* of our experience there is no awareness whatever of the transcendent, the numinous or the unconditional, in any ordinary sense of those words, and what is absent from *most* cannot be present in *all.* The maximum that could be alleged with any colour of plausibility

would be that this awareness is a feature of *some* of our experience; perhaps the words 'in depth' are intended to indicate this, though the syntactical relation of the phrase would be very odd. Does Robinson mean that this feature could be observed in any experience, as long as that experience is 'in depth', whatever that means? I am not at all sure about this, but I do not think the blame is altogether mine.

(2) 'Theological statements', we are told, 'are indeed affirmations about human existence—but they are affirmations about the ultimate ground and depth of that existence.' This is simply incoherent; if theological statements are *about* human existence, they cannot (in the same sense of 'about') be simultaneously *about* its ground and depth. It was the disowned Macmurray who said that they were about human existence; Robinson has indeed just told us that they are acknowledgments of the transcendent, unconditional element in all our relationships, for presumably 'theological statements' and 'statements about God' are synonymous terms.

(3) Here again, however, Robinson is extremely unconvincing, for he assumes without argument that 'to acknowledge the transcendent, unconditional element in all our relationships, and supremely in our relationships with other persons' necessarily involves making 'affirmations about the ultimate ground and depth of that existence'. 'It is not enough', he insists, 'to say that "religion is about human fellowship and community", any more than one can simply reverse the biblical statement and say that "love *is* God".' But this is, in fact, what Macmurray says and it is, as Robinson adds, what Feuerbach thought St John should have said, although St John was careful not to say it. But no reason has been given for supposing that Macmurray is wrong, except one based upon an equivocal use of the word 'about' on which I have already commented.

(4) Nevertheless, the position which Robinson has now come to state is very much more like the old-fashioned theism which he began by vigorously rejecting than anything which he has so far said. If an awareness of the transcendent, the numinous, and the unconditional is, or can be, a feature of even some of our experience and if it is recognised as the ultimate ground and depth of our human existence, we are certainly not far from affirming belief in the God of traditional Christian theology. But

Robinson is very far from having given any reasons for supposing that such a being exists.

(5) The suspicion that Robinson is after all really[1] an old-fashioned Christian theist is strengthened by his subsequent statements. He rightly quotes St John to the effect that apart from the relationship of love there is no knowledge of God, while also stressing that 'it is precisely [St John's] thesis that our convictions about love and its ultimacy are not projections from human love; rather our sense of the sacredness of love derives from the fact that in this relationship as nowhere else there is disclosed and laid bare the divine Ground of all our being'. And again: 'To assert that "*God* is love" is to believe that in love one comes into touch with the most fundamental reality in the universe, that Being itself ultimately has this character.' Robinson indeed maintains that 'the eternal *Thou* is met only *in, with and under* the finite *Thou*, whether in the encounter with other persons or in the response to the natural order', but he immediately adds, against 'naturalism, whether pantheistic or humanistic', that 'the eternal *Thou* is not to be equated with the finite *Thou*, nor God with man or nature'. The reference to 'response to the natural order' and to 'nature' is striking and welcome, for it is, I think, the first indication that Robinson has given in his book that we can find God anywhere except in the depths of our own selves. In fact, he seems to be saying, in an idiom derived from Martin Buber, very much what St Thomas Aquinas says in the earlier questions of the *Summa Theologiae*. Again, he writes:

> The necessity for the name 'God' lies in the fact that our being has depths which naturalism, whether evolutionary, mechanistic, dialectical or humanistic, cannot or will not recognise.

But what then becomes of the great programme of the radical recasting of the most fundamental categories of our theology, in which our ideas of God, the supernatural and religion itself were to go into the melting? Has it been abandoned? Only, I fear, for a moment, or at any rate only by that part of Dr Robinson which lies to the right of the line that runs through his middle.

(6) For, after the splendid recovery of St John's declaration that God is love, we find Robinson quietly slipping back into the

[1] Might we say 'in the bottom of his heart', or 'in depth'?

ambiguity by which he has claimed all good men as unconscious Christians. 'There are depths of revelation, intimations of eternity, judgments of the holy and the sacred, awarenesses of the unconditional, the numinous and the ecstatic', he writes, 'which cannot be explained in purely naturalistic categories without being reduced to something else.' 'Cannot' is perhaps a daring term, but this is at least a moving profession of faith. However he continues:

> The question of God is the question *whether this depth of being is a reality or an illusion*, not whether *a* Being exists beyond the bright blue sky, or anywhere else. Belief in God is a matter of 'what you take seriously without any reservation', of what for you is *ultimate* reality.

The gibe 'beyond the bright blue sky' may be ignored as a substitution of ridicule for argument; more attention is needed to the opening sentence. In saying that 'the question of God is the question whether this depth of being is a reality or an illusion' Robinson is slipping in the assumption that anyone who believes that the depth of being just described as 'depths of revelation' and so forth is a reality, is *ipso facto* a believer in the God of whom he has previously been speaking, the personal God of St John, the God who *is* love; and this is a begging of the question at issue. Again, it is quite true that 'belief in God is a matter of "what you take seriously without any reservation", of what for you is *ultimate* reality', if 'is a matter of' means 'depends upon'; but it is false if it is taken as meaning that anyone who takes *something* seriously without reservation, who takes *something* as ultimate reality, is a believer in God as St John describes him.

(7) Robinson continues: 'The man who acknowledges the transcendence of God is the man who *in* the conditioned relationships of life recognises the unconditional and responds to it in unconditional personal relationship.' This would certainly let in Macmurray as a theist, and almost certainly Feuerbach as well, in spite of Robinson's previous exclusion of them. But the fundamental point which is left in ambiguity is whether the necessary personal relationships are simply relationships with other human persons or whether, over and above these and indeed as their source and cause, there must be personal relationships with the personal ground of Being himself.

At this point Robinson finds it necessary to enquire whether the exposition which he has given is consistent with the teaching of the Bible about the 'otherness' and the omnipresence of God. The discussion is too short to be really adequate, but the conclusion manifests the same ambiguity which we have just noticed: 'God, the unconditional, is to be found only in, with *and under* the conditioned relationships of this life: for he *is* their depth and ultimate significance.' And this leads back, via a reference to Bonhoeffer, to a section headed 'The Way of the Irreligious'.

'Our contention', we are told, 'has been that God is to be met not by a "religious" turning away from the world but in unconditional concern for "the other" *seen through to its ultimate depths*' and, surprisingly, Macmurray is taken as the guide, with his assertion that God is 'the personal ground of all that we experience' and that encounter with God does not rest 'upon some special and extraordinary type of experience apart from which it could not arise'. This irrelevant type of experience is described by Robinson as 'mystical' or 'religious', though the terms are not generally taken as identical in meaning. If he is using the word 'mystical' in its technical sense, he is certainly right in saying that one can encounter God without it; every Catholic student of mystical theology would heartily agree with him, and so would every Catholic mystic. And I think he is also entirely right in saying that capacity for religious awareness is largely a question of natural endowment, and that 'to make the knowledge of God depend upon such experiences is like making it depend upon an ear for music'. But I find this rather difficult to reconcile with the importance which he has attributed a few pages back to 'depths of revelation, intimations of eternity, judgments of the holy and the sacred, awarenesses of the unconditional, the numinous and the ecstatic'. However, he goes on to quote the case of John Wren-Lewis, to whom 'belief in a personal God came . . . through the experience of discovering in a community "the creative and numinous power" inherent in *ordinary* personal relationships' and who found God as 'the "depth" of common non-religious experience'. That God can be found in common non-religious experience is again a commonplace of traditional theology, and has only been denied by extreme revelationists like Barth and by those who limit the manifestation of God to the activity of preaching like Bultmann. However, one need only read the article by Wren-Lewis entitled 'What are clergy for?' in *The Listener* of 12th March 1964 to see that for Wren-Lewis 'God' is merely a mythological personification of 'the vital energy of personal life' and that for him Robinson does not go nearly far enough. But whether Robinson is, in fact, a theist or, as MacIntyre maintains, an atheist, there is no doubt that he is a deeply committed Christian. It is therefore natural that he should go on to what he himself describes as 'the reassessment, in this whole context, of the person and work of Christ'.

VI

This task is undertaken in Robinson's fourth chapter, which is entitled 'The Man for Others'.[1] It begins as follows:

> The doctrine of the Incarnation and Divinity of Christ is on any account central to the entire Christian message and crucial therefore for any reinterpretation of it. It is also the point where resistance to reinterpretation is likely to be at its maximum and where orthodoxy has its heaviest investment in traditional categories. This is true both at the level of technical theology, where any restatement must run the gauntlet of the Chalcedonian Definition and the Athanasian Creed, and at the popular level, where one will quickly be accused of destroying the Christmas story.

This passage suggests a much less radical reconstruction of the Christian religion than the opening pages of the book would have led us to suspect. Here all that is mentioned is 'reinterpretation' and 'restatement', whereas we were told in the Preface that we were being called to 'far more than a restating of traditional theology in modern terms' and to a process in which 'the most fundamental categories of our theology must go into the melting'. However, we shall see exactly what is involved as we go on.

'Traditional Christology', we are not surprised to be told, 'has worked with a frankly supranaturalist scheme', which popular religion has expressed mythologically and professional theology metaphysically. 'For this way of thinking, the Incarnation means that God the Son came down to earth, and was born, lived and died within this world as a man.' We are not told that

[1] *Honest to God*, pp. 64–83.

this way of thinking is false or misleading, either as myth or as metaphysic, though Robinson's readiness to discard it would lead one to suppose that he thought it was one or the other; we shall, however, be surprised to discover that, as myth, he appears to wish to retain it, at least on Christmas Day. However, to resume, we are told quite accurately that for this traditional scheme 'as the God-man [Christ] united in his person the supernatural and the natural: and the problem of Christology so stated is how Jesus can be fully God and fully man, and yet genuinely one person'. 'The orthodox "answer" ', Robinson continues, 'to this problem, as formulated in the Definition of Chalcedon, is within its own terms unexceptionable—except that properly speaking it is not a solution but a statement of the problem. But as a correct statement, as "a signpost against all heresies", it had—and has—an irreplaceable value.' If it really has this irreplaceable value, it seems hazardous, to say the least, to propose to abandon it, though this presumably is what will be involved if we carry out Robinson's programme of casting into the melting 'the most fundamental categories of our theology—of God, of the supernatural, and of religion itself'. The untheological reader is not, however, allowed to judge the Chalcedonian Definition by reading it for himself, being merely referred in a footnote to the useful collection of *Documents of the Christian Church* edited by Dr H. Bettenson; instead he is presented with a travesty of it devised by Robinson. 'To use an analogy', he writes, 'if one had to present the doctrine of the person of Christ as a union of oil and water, then it made the best possible attempt to do so. Or rather it made the only possible attempt, which was to insist against all efforts to "confuse the substance" that there were two distinct natures and against all temptation to break the unity that there was but one indivisible person.' Now, to illustrate the careful and subtle language of Chalcedon by the crude illustration of oil and water is quite inappropriate, for while the illustration provides counterparts for the two natures it provides none for the one person, the 'one *prosopon* and *hypostasis*' into which, as Chalcedon says, they 'run together'. However, to continue with Robinson's analogy:

> It is not surprising . . . that in popular Christianity the oil and water separated, and that one or the other came to the top. In

> fact, popular supranaturalistic Christology has always been dominantly docetic. That is to say, Christ only appeared to be a man or looked like a man: 'underneath' he was God.

Something seems to have gone wildly wrong with the analogy here. The oil presumably corresponds to the manhood, if it is the Godhead that is 'underneath'; for, although the words 'one or the other' suggest that Robinson is not quite clear about this, the lighter substance will, in fact, always float on the heavier. But why the substance which is on top should be assumed to be only an appearance is very mysterious. What, in fact, the oil-and-water picture might be expected to suggest would be the Nestorian heresy, not the docetic; that is to say, both the natures would seem to be equally real, but no organic union would be evident between them. And, although it is fashionable in certain quarters to accuse traditional Christology, both popular and professional, of being docetic or monophysite, its tendency, when it has lost the delicate balance of orthodoxy, has been almost invariably towards Nestorianism. Thus in the Western Middle Ages popular devotion to Christ tended to parallel the adoration of a purely divine Jesus in the host with the tender devotion to a purely human Jesus in the crib and on the Cross, though neither of these, except in rare cases, reached the point of heresy. And so typical a traditional scholar as Père Galtier in his *Unité du Christ* goes just about as close to Nestorianism as is possible without actually falling over the brink.

However, after taking the view of Christ in which Mr Wren-Lewis describes himself as having been brought up as typical, Robinson writes as follows:

> Even if such a view would be indignantly repudiated by orthodox Churchmen, and however much they would insist that Jesus was 'perfect man' as well as 'perfect God', still the traditional supranaturalistic way of describing the Incarnation almost inevitably suggests that Jesus was really God almighty walking about on earth, dressed up as a man. Jesus was not a man born and bred—he was God for a limited period taking part in a charade. He looked like a man, he talked like a man, he felt like a man, but underneath he was God dressed up—like Father Christmas. However guardedly it may be stated, the traditional view leaves the impression that God took a space-trip and arrived on this planet in the form of a man.

Now, if orthodox churchmen would repudiate the view in question as indignantly as Robinson admits they would, the view would hardly seem to be as inevitable (or even as 'almost inevitable') as he asserts. And, having done his best to scandalise the orthodox by this piece of sensationalism, he cheerfully tells us that he is aware that this is a parody and probably an offensive one, while rapidly recovering himself with the assertion: 'But I think it is perilously near the truth of what most people—and I would include myself—have been brought up to believe at Christmas-time.' It may seem unkind to enquire what he was brought up to believe during the rest of the year, but the repeated hesitations and oscillations of language in which Robinson indulges are so endemic to his exposition that it would be unfair both to him and to his readers not to point them out. And, having confessed to an offensive parody, expressed in derisive references to Father Christmas and space-trips, he immediately backslides by a contemptuous reference to the Christmas collect and a well-known hymn of Wesley.

This somewhat pantomimic prelude, however, is only the preparation for Robinson's real attack on orthodox Christology. 'My point', he writes,

> is . . . to put the question whether the entire supranaturalistic frame of reference does not make anything but a Christological *tour de force* impossible. For as long as God and man are thought of as two 'beings', each with distinct natures, one from 'the other side' and one from 'this side', then it is impossible to create out of them more than a God-man, a divine visitant from 'out there' who chooses in every respect to live like the natives. The supranaturalist view of the Incarnation can never really rid itself of the idea of the prince who appears in the guise of a beggar. However genuinely destitute the beggar may be, he *is* a prince; and that in the end is what matters.

It is extremely difficult to see whether the 'supranaturalistic' view is here being accused of kenoticism or of docetism. 'Chooses in every respect to live like the natives' and 'genuinely destitute' suggest the former; 'divine visitant' and 'appears in the guise' suggest the latter. But at least it seems to be clear that, in spite of his earlier complimentary remarks about Chalcedon, Robinson is now repudiating it whole-heartedly, even if he is doing so only because he insists in drawing from it consequences that none of its traditional adherents would admit. That this is so is made plain by the set of rhetorical questions which follow:

> But suppose the whole notion of 'a God' who 'visits' the earth in the person of 'his Son' is as mythical as the prince in the fairy story? Suppose there is no realm 'out there' from which the 'Man from heaven' arrives? Suppose the Christmas myth (the invasion of 'this side' by 'the other side')—as opposed to the Christmas history (the birth of the man Jesus of Nazareth) has to go? Are we prepared for that? Or are we to cling here to this last vestige of the mythological or metaphysical world-view as the only garb in which to clothe the story with power to touch the imagination? Cannot the supranaturalistic scheme survive at least as part of the 'magic' of Christmas?

Clearly the answer to all these questions, taken in any literal sense, is intended to be 'No'. The whole of the previous discussion has been leading up to this. And presumably if the questions are taken in a symbolic or mythical sense, the answer should be 'No' again, as the whole of Robinson's argument has been based not upon the assumption that the traditional supranaturalistic way of thinking is false but that, for the present-day man, it is meaninglessness and impossible. What, then, is our surprise when to his last question—'Cannot perhaps the supranaturalistic scheme survive at least as part of the "magic" of Christmas?'—he gives the following reply:

> Yes, indeed, it can survive—as myth. For myth has its perfectly legitimate, and indeed profoundly important, place. The myth is there to indicate the significance of the events, the divine depth of the history. And we shall be grievously impoverished if our ears cannot tune to the angels' song or our eyes are blind to the wise men's star. But we must be able to read the nativity story without assuming that its truth depends on there being a literal interruption of the natural by the supernatural, that Jesus can only be Emmanuel—God with us—if, as it were, he came through from another world.

This I find completely baffling. We have been told that we must abandon the whole supranaturalistic way of thinking—and indeed that, if we are modern men, we cannot but abandon it—as being a factual account of the truth of the Incarnation. And we must abandon it, not merely as a crudely spatial concept but even as a metaphorical one; in the very first chapter of the book we were told that the God who is spiritually or metaphysically 'out there' is as repugnant to the modern mind as the God who is literally or physically 'up there'. But now we are told that, although we cannot assume that in the nativity there was a literal interruption of the natural by the supernatural, we shall be grievously impoverished if we do not accept the supranaturalistic scheme 'as myth'. I can only say that if I did not believe that there was a literal interruption of the natural by the supernatural, in the sense of traditional Christology, I should look upon indulgence in the Christmas narratives (except as a pretty fairy story) as a piece of dangerous self-deception and psychological escapism. If the myth is factually uninterpretable —if, in Robinson's words, 'as supranaturalism becomes less and less credible, to tie the action of God to such a way of thinking is to banish it for increasing numbers into the preserve of the pagan myths and thereby to sever it from any real connection with history'—I cannot see how the myth can 'indicate the significance of the events, the divine depth of the history'. It looks as if, in spite of everything, Robinson has lost courage at the last moment; at Christmas-time, if at no other, he must have his myths, and even if he cannot believe them he can none the less enjoy them. This does credit to the warmth of his human emotions, but on the plane of belief it would seem to involve him in sheer naturalism. Like Professor R. B. Braithwaite, he might be committed to an agapeistically policied way of life, while entertaining, without believing, the Christian stories. But if the whole notion—however spiritually or metaphysically understood—of God as visiting the earth in the person of his Son is incredible to the modern mind, then the obvious conclusion would seem to be the naturalistic view that Jesus is nothing more than a man. Perhaps he is, in Robinson's words, 'the most Godlike man that ever lived', and 'what he said and did was so beautiful and so true that he must have been a revelation, indeed, the supreme revelation of God', the divine being 'simply the human raised to the power of "*x*" '. Nevertheless—and this is another of Robinson's astounding inconsistencies—this is just what he refuses to admit, and not only because it disagrees with the New Testament but also because it disagrees with St Athanasius. 'To say that Jesus had a unique experience of God, that he displayed all the qualities of God, that he was like God or that God was like him—this can never add up to saying that he was "of one substance" with the Father.' It looks as if, after all, some of the most fundamental categories of our theology have been pulled out of the melting.

Before going on to see why it is that Robinson rejects not only the supranaturalistic but also the naturalistic view of Jesus and what he offers us in their place, it will be useful to enquire what he means by his assertion that the supranaturalistic scheme can survive 'as myth' and how he himself understands those elements in the Gospel which would normally be described as supernatural. He says very little about this in *Honest to God*, but he has made himself comparatively clear in two articles on the Virgin Birth and the Resurrection which he contributed to the *Sunday Mirror* of 22nd and 29th December 1963. In the former of these he remarks that 'the early Christians . . . were not convinced [that Jesus] was the Son of God because of anything that happened when he was born. They were convinced *by what they saw in him*. He showed them a new kind of living, a new kind of loving, quite out of this world. He seemed rooted in a security that couldn't be explained simply in terms of a human family background. In him they glimpsed something of the final mystery of life itself. *God* for them shone through him. And that has been true for Christians ever since.'

With a few qualifications this statement may be accepted as broadly correct. If we exclude from the description 'early Christians' the Blessed Virgin, St Joseph, Elisabeth and other close members of our Lord's family and use it to mean those persons who were drawn to him in his ministry as it is recorded in the Gospels, it is no doubt true that what convinced them of his uniqueness was the contact which they had with him and not information about his conception and birth. But three comments are needed. (1) Their contact with him did not consist simply of the impression which his character made upon them, great as that was and powerful as it was to lead some at least to abandon their trade and home and follow him. It consisted also in his teaching and his actions, and both of these were frequently supernatural and miraculous. (2) The fact that what convinced them that he was the Son of God was not anything that happened when he was born does not mean that what happened when he was born is unimportant or that those who knew about it thought it was. (3) The assertion 'that has been true for Christians ever since' can be true only in a very special and peculiar way. For while the first generation of Christians came to know Jesus by direct contact of the same kind as that by which they came to know one another, succeeding generations have come to know him only by reading about him in the Gospels, by hearing other people talk about him or (as they have believed) by meeting him in his body the Church. And all these ways involve serious theological problems about which no one is in a better position to know than Robinson.

However, what is more important is to see what the Virgin Birth means to Robinson himself. He is quite explicit:

> To say that new life was fathered and quickened in Mary by the Spirit of God is a profound way of expressing an inner truth about Jesus. It is to say that his birth and life cannot *simply* be thought of as a biological event; his significance is much deeper than that.
>
> This is what the Virgin Birth means for me, and this is a truth about him which I firmly believe. As regards the biological details, I am prepared to keep an open mind. *Nothing for me depends on them.*

This last sentence, which I have italicised, is most significant. I shall return to it later.[1] Now, to turn to the Resurrection.

After describing the shattering of the disciples' hopes by the crucifixion and death of Jesus, Robinson describes the sequel in these words:

> And then IT happened. It came to them—or rather, as they could only describe it, HE came to them. *The life they had known and shared was not buried with him, but alive in them.* Jesus was not a dead memory but a living presence, making new men of them.
>
> This overwhelming experience of the disciples is the great historical event which we call the Resurrection.

The last sentence should be noted. For Robinson, the Resurrection is not something that happened to Jesus; it is an experience of the disciples. It is therefore not surprising that, while Robin-

[1] I should like at this point to commend the extremely lucid and penetrating article on 'The Virgin Birth' by Dr Otto A. Piper in *Interpretation* for April 1964.

son admits that St Paul accepted the Empty Tomb, he adds that 'it was not central for him'. With an implicit but unacknowledged scepticism about the post-Resurrection narratives in the Gospels, he writes:

> Precisely what happened to the body we shall never know. The New Testament is silent [this is not strictly true; cf. Acts i. 1–11] —and we may be silent too. Believing in the Resurrection doesn't depend on any theory about it.
>
> Some will find it possible and natural to accept a literal vanishing or transformation of the elements which composed the flesh of Jesus. Others will think that what the disciples subsequently saw was a vision of Jesus alive: others again that it was what the psychic investigators would call his 'astral' body.
>
> *But all this is quite secondary* [my italics]. . . .
>
> No, the proof of the matter lay for them within. And it was clinched for them in what we call the Appearances. Exactly how physical or how psychological these were, I don't think it matters.

Robinson goes on to describe these 'appearances' as being of three types. The first was 'a sudden, startling conviction of Jesus's presence, as tangible as flesh and blood'. The second was 'a more gradual recognition of him behind other eyes and other lips'. The third—and this is emphasised by the words being printed in heavy type—was in the sacramental meal: 'Supremely for them, as for succeeding generations of Christians, it was in that act most familiarly associated with him that he made himself known—in the breaking and sharing of bread.' It is not altogether clear that this last experience is associated with the Eucharist—i.e. with the gathering of Christians to repeat what, at the last Supper, Christ commanded the disciples to do 'as his anamnesis'—or whether it is more widely referred to *any* meal that Christians may have together, but all the emphasis is in any case on the experience of Christians. What Robinson would have to say about Christians—and there are many of them, some of whom are among the most saintly—who never or almost never have anything that could properly be called an *experience* of this kind is not clear. 'The truth of the Resurrection', Robinson goes on to say, 'is a *present experience*. It cannot be proved by historical investigation, but only by a living faith.' The words 'living faith' are puzzling here, for, in any sense in which 'faith' has been used in the tradition of either Protestantism or Catholicism, it is almost the antithesis of 'experience'; it is 'the giving substance to things hoped for, the conviction of things *not* seen'.[1] As Dom Gregory Dix pointed out, it was the mystery religions that went in for 'experience'; Christians came together to *do* something because the Lord had commanded it.[2] It would, of course, be easy to play fast and loose with words like 'faith' and 'experience', which are used by different writers in a variety of ways. However, the important fact which stands out from this discussion is that for Robinson Christianity is essentially concerned with experiences which individual Christians have and which they identify as experiences 'of Christ', even if these experiences normally take place through their membership of the Christian community. It is not essentially concerned with things that happened to Jesus himself, not even with those events of the virginal conception and the rising from the tomb which Christians through the ages have looked on as of fundamental importance; and the accounts of these in the Gospels are simply myths with which Christians in a less critical age than ours embroidered their experience. I shall consider the implications of such a view for the Christian religion in another chapter;[3] here we are concerned only with the fact that Robinson expounds and supports it. It may, however, be added that it is difficult to see why, once we have agreed to interpret the supernatural stories in the Gospels as myths, we should not go on and interpret the natural stories as myths as well. In that case, however, there will be little ground left for Robinson's own Christology. But to this we must now return, after our excursion into Sunday journalism.[4]

Robinson's starting-point is unexceptionable; it is that nowhere in the New Testament is Jesus unambiguously described

[1] Heb. xi. 1.

[2] *The Shape of the Liturgy*, p. 153.

[3] Ch. v *infra*.

[4] In case it may be felt to be unfair to subject an article in a Sunday newspaper to detailed theological analysis, I will repeat a point made earlier in the text that, the wider an audience is for which an exposition is intended, the more important it is that it shall be scrupulously accurate and unambiguous. For, while a technical scholar may be expected to make his own criticisms, the inexpert reader is almost completely at the mercy of the writer.

as 'God' *tout court*. The same point has been made at great length by no less orthodox a scholar than Fr Karl Rahner, who has argued in a massive and exhaustive study that *ho theos* in the New Testament invariably signifies God the Father.[1] We have already seen that Robinson has admitted the adequacy, in its own setting, of the Chalcedonian definition. But now he bases himself on the first chapter of St John's Gospel, with its affirmation that 'the Word was *theos*'. Now *theos*, he says, is not the natural Greek expression for 'God'; that would be *ho theos*. But nor is it the simple equivalent for 'divine'; for that would be the adjective *theios*. The best translation we can achieve is 'What God was, the Word was'; and what this means is that Jesus was the complete expression, the 'Word', of God. The point is expanded at length, and I can quote only a few sentences here. 'Through him, as through no one else, God spoke and God acted; when one met him one was met—and saved and judged—by God.' 'Men's response to him *is* men's response to God: men's rejection of him *is* men's rejection of God.' 'Jesus never claims to be God personally: yet he always claims to bring God, completely.' There is nothing here that is very startling or novel, if we remember Rahner's point that, in the New Testament, *theos* does not mean what later theology means by the Trinity but what it means by God the Father. We have all the necessary basis for the later formulation that, while the Word is *true God*, he is *God from God*, God eternally begotten by God unbegotten. Our uneasiness will arise rather from the notion that Robinson has already expounded of what he means by 'God', in his chapter on The Ground of our Being. Unlike the run of liberal theologians Robinson does not tell us that for us God is identical with Jesus; rather he is anxious to tell us that Jesus totally subjects himself to God in obedience and love; and this God would seem to be very different from the mysterious ground of being whose very personality was seen to be ambiguous and questionable. Here are Robinson's own words:

> It is in Jesus, and Jesus alone, that there is nothing of self to be seen, but solely the ultimate, unconditional love of God. It is as he emptied himself utterly of himself that he became the carrier of 'the name which is above every name', the revealer

[1] *Theological Investigations*, I, ch. iv.

of the Father's glory, for the name of that glory is simply Love. The 'kenotic' theory of Christology, based on this conception of self-emptying, is, I am persuaded, the only one that offers much hope of relating at all satisfactorily the divine and the human in Christ. Yet the fatal weakness of this theory as it is stated in supranaturalist terms is that it represents Christ as stripping himself precisely of those attributes of transcendence which make him the revelation of God. The underlying assumption is that it is his omnipotence, his omniscience, and all that makes him 'superhuman', that must be shed in order for him to become truly man. On the contrary, it is as he empties himself not of his Godhead but of himself, of any desire to focus attention on himself, of any craving to be 'on an equality with God', that he reveals God. For it is in making himself nothing, in his utter self-surrender to others in love, that he discloses and lays bare the Ground of man's being as Love.

This is a finely written, and in many ways an impressive, passage, but it needs careful examination and comment.

(1) In the first sentence it is not entirely clear whether 'love of God' means 'love exercised by God' or 'love exercised towards God'. The latter meaning seems to be demanded by the context, but I suspect that the sentence which concludes the quotation has been arrived at by slipping from the latter to the former sense.

(2) The second sentence ('It is as he emptied himself . . .') seems to be intended as an echo of the famous passage in Philippians ii. 5–8, though there it is asserted that he was 'in the form of God' *before* he emptied himself (whatever 'emptied himself' means), while 'the name which is above every name' is not represented as being 'carried' with him *as* he emptied himself, but as bestowed on him by the Father (*ho theos*) as a reward for his humbling himself to the death of the cross.

(3) Although most commentators are agreed that in Phil. ii. 6 'emptied himself' does not refer to the act by which the Word became incarnate, but to his self-offering in his earthly life (probably in fulfilment of Isaiah liii),[1] what are commonly known as 'kenotic' theories do teach some self-stripping of the Godhead in the incarnation itself. Robinson's combined appre-

[1] See the references in my *Christ, the Christian and the Church*, pp. 25f, and E. R. Fairweather's Appended Note to F. W Beare's commentary on Philippians.

ciation and repudiation of them seems to amount to an acceptance of the commentators' view, namely that there is an emptying, but that it takes place *within* the incarnate life and not antecedently to it.

(4) Nevertheless, his criticism of 'the fatal weakness of this theory as it is stated in supranaturalist terms' is puzzling. For one would expect him, in view of his attacks on 'supranaturalism' in the earlier chapters, to denounce it as making (to use his own words) Christ into 'a divine visitant from "out there" who chooses in every respect to live like the natives', the 'prince' who has become a genuinely destitute beggar. In fact, Robinson criticises the theory because it represents the Word as stripping himself of those attributes of transcendence which make him the revelation of God. However, the following sentence seems to show that the real objection is that the theories associate his capacity to be a revelation of God with his possessing or having possessed attributes of transcendence at all.

(5) This may be what the next two sentences are intended to say, but their mutual connection is logically very odd. 'The underlying assumption is that it is his omnipotence, etc., that must be shed in order for him to *become truly man. On the contrary*, it is as he empties himself not of his Godhead but of himself, etc., that *he reveals God*.' The force of 'on the contrary' is not at all clear. Is what is meant that 'becoming truly man' and 'revealing God' are identical processes, but that this takes place in the way described in the second sentence and not in the way described in the first? Or is what is meant that he reveals God but does not *become* truly man at all? I suspect that the second alternative is correct, and that what is meant is that he reveals God by *being* truly man, and not, as the 'supranaturalists' would hold, by *becoming* man. In this case, the reference to the 'kenotic' theories seems to be quite irrelevant and the words 'being in the form of God'[1] in Phil. ii. 6 to be false.

(6) The second of these two sentences, as it stands, reads like pure traditional Christology. He does not empty himself of his Godhead, but (in the manhood which he has assumed) he does empty himself of himself and (being God as well as man) in

[1] It is noticeable that, while he manages to square with his view one of the possible meanings of *harpagmon* ('craving'), Robinson can do nothing at all with *en morphē theou huparchōn*.

doing this he reveals God. However, I do not think from the context that Robinson would accept the explanatory phrases that I have inserted in parentheses, for, in spite of his earlier use of John i, he is obviously very unwilling to say that the Word *became* man. However, unless, while he is 'emptying himself' he is himself God, it is very difficult to see how this emptying 'reveals God' or at any rate that it reveals him as a God of love.

(7) Finally, the last sentence in the passage quoted seems quite inconsequential if 'Ground of man's being' is taken as meaning (in accordance with earlier usage in the book) 'that from which man's being derives'. It would now have to be taken as meaning 'that which man's being essentially is'. With this assertion a traditionalist would agree: Christ, being perfect man, reveals in his utter self-giving what human nature in its fullest expression is. But this is to take 'Ground of being' in a new sense, and it leaves unsettled the question whether the Love with which the Ground of man's being is now identified is primarily love towards God or love towards men.

Once again I am conscious that the kind of analysis I have just been making will seem to many to be extremely finicky and fault-finding. I must, however, repeat that it is justified by the importance of the subject. For, when we are faced with a demand for a complete recasting of the Church's theology as it has been worked out over a period of nearly two thousand years, it is essential to find out what that demand implies and whether it is justified or not.

In developing his new Christology, Robinson takes up from Bonhoeffer a theme which he expresses in the following words:

> Jesus is 'the man for others', the one in whom Love has completely taken over, the one who is utterly open to, and united with, the Ground of his being. And this 'life for others, through participation in the Being of God', *is* transcendence. For at this point, of love 'to the uttermost', we encounter *God*, the ultimate 'depth' of our being, the unconditional in the conditioned.

No Christian, I imagine, would question the description of Jesus as 'the man for others', though I should expect him, on the evidence of the Gospels themselves, to describe him as *primarily* 'the man for God', the man who prays, 'Father, not my will but thine be done'. As, however, Love has been already identified with the Ground of man's being and with God, we are being told that, in Jesus, God has 'completely taken over' God. This seems to me to be very odd. Nor is it clear whether the next sentence, with its italicised '*is*', is meant as a synthetic statement or as a definition of transcendence. It appears to be the latter, in view of these sentences in the Bonhoeffer passage:

> This concern of Jesus for others the experience of transcendence. . . . Our relation to God not a religious relationship to a supreme Being, absolute in power and goodness, which is a spurious conception of transcendence, but a new life for others, through participation in the Being of God. The transcendence consists not in tasks beyond our scope and power, but in the nearest *Thou* at hand.

One cannot, however, be sure, and all that one can confidently say is that both Bonhoeffer and Robinson have a very peculiar use of the word 'transcendence'.

After the passage from Robinson just quoted there are a number of remarks with which hardly any Christian could disagree, concerning the complete self-giving of the incarnate Lord in his earthly life; we are told, for example, that in him 'the life of God, the ultimate Word of Love in which all things cohere, is bodied forth completely, unconditionally and without reserve in the life of a man—the man for others and the man for God' (this is one of the very few places in which the description 'the man for God' occurs, in comparison with the repeated occurrence of 'the man for others'). There are other statements, however, which are much more questionable. Thus we are told:

> The symbol of the Virgin Birth can only legitimately mean what the fourth Gospel takes it to mean (if, indeed, its description of Christians reflects that of Christ), namely, that the whole of his life is a life 'born not of the will of the flesh, nor of the will of man, but of God'.

Now, apart from the doubtfulness of the assertion that this is what the Fourth Gospel 'takes the Virgin Birth to *mean*',[1] the statement that the symbol of the Virgin Birth cannot legitimately

[1] Most biblical scholars would say that it is extremely doubtful whether the Fourth Gospel clearly asserts the Virgin Birth at all; whether it implicitly assumes it, is another question.

mean anything else seems extremely rash; it certainly meant something else to the authors of both the First and the Third Gospel. And it is surely doubtful whether anyone who was not already committed to accepting the Virgin Birth as part of the creed which he had inherited would think it appropriate to signify the complete self-dedication of Jesus to the service of others by the statement that he was conceived without the agency of a human father. We can indeed agree with Robinson that 'the source and spring of his whole being is God: his is a life conceived and sustained utterly by the Holy Ghost' and that 'he is for that reason only the more truly "the proper Man"'. But when we are told that 'he is perfect man and perfect God—not as a mixture of oil and water, of natural and supernatural—but as the embodiment through obedience of "the beyond in our midst", of the transcendence of love', two comments are necessary. (1) As has been previously said, the picture of 'oil and water' is not an accurate representation of orthodox 'supernaturalist' Christology, but rather of Nestorianism; (2) to describe his perfect Godhead as an 'embodiment through *obedience*' is to slip back into the 'liberal' Christology which Robinson claims to have transcended, according to which deity in Christ means nothing more than perfect humanity.

Again, Robinson tells us that what he believes St John 'is saying' in the words *sarx egeneto* ('became flesh') is 'not (as the later term "incarnation" suggests) that something from outside comes into and is encased in "flesh"' but that 'in the man Christ Jesus stands revealed, exposed at the surface level of "flesh", the depth and ground of all our being as Love'. Now, that something like this is *implied* by St John's words may well be admitted, but to affirm that this is what St John 'is saying' is to force upon the Evangelist a view which is unnatural to the phrase itself and inconsistent with its context. What on Robinson's interpretation is St John 'saying' when he writes 'All things were made by him, and without him was not anything made that was made'? The further assertion that 'unless it is read with supranaturalist spectacles, the Prologue requires as little "demythologising" as any part of the New Testament' might lead to the reflection that Robinson himself does not seem to have read the Prologue with an entirely naked eye; and the words 'as little' are surprising, in any case, as we were told in the opening pages of the book that the New Testament needed a great deal of demythologising indeed.

It is not altogether surprising that Robinson proceeds to declare that there is 'no final difference between the person of Christ and the work of Christ, the incarnation and the at-one-ment', though it certainly seems odd to say of anyone that there is no 'final difference' between his *person* and his *work*. 'The doctrine of the Atonement is not—as in the supranaturalist way of thinking—a highly mythological, and often rather dubious, transaction between two parties, "God" on the one hand and "man" on the other. . . . Even when it is Christian in content, the whole schema of a supernatural Being coming down from heaven to "save" mankind from sin, in the way that a man might put his finger into a glass of water to rescue a struggling insect, is frankly incredible to man "come of age", who no longer believes in such a *deus ex machina*.' Any educated supernaturalist may well feel moved to protest at the crudity with which his outlook is presented, and Robinson does, in fact, reconstruct it in more rational terms as follows:

> The relationship between God and man has been broken by original sin. Man could not pull himself up by his own shoe-strings, and thus the only hope of restoration was from God's side. Yet it was from our side that things had to be put right. It appeared hopeless. But God found the answer. For in Christ he himself became man, and as man reconciled us to himself.

And here is Robinson's comment:

> This construction no doubt gives expression or projection to genuine and deep-seated realities in the existential situation—and as myth should not be thrown out. But as an objective transaction supposed to have been accomplished outside us in time and space, it speaks today to remarkably few—to fewer indeed than the Christmas myth. The contrast is in fact instructive. Most people would genuinely *like* to believe the Christmas story, but wonder whether it *can* be true with the world as it is after nearly two thousand years. But in the case of the Atonement they ask with some impatience how anything done two thousand years ago on the Cross *could* affect me now. . . . At no point does the supranaturalist scheme appear less compelling. And yet at no point is the naturalistic view, even in its Liberal Christian form, shallower or more discredited than in

its estimate of what is wrong with the world and of what is required to put it right.

Before considering the 'third alternative' which Robinson recommends I will comment on Robinson's comment:

(1) The ambiguity with which he uses the word 'myth' is sharply prominent here. Even the most traditional theologian will be anxious to point out that the classical images which have been used, with more or less success, to depict different aspects of Redemption—the winning of a battle, the liberation of captives, the payment of a fine or a debt, the curing of a disease, and so on—are not to be interpreted literally, any more than, when we say that the eternal Word 'came down from heaven', we are describing a process of spatial translation. For here we are dealing with processes and events which, by the nature of the case, cannot be precisely described in everyday language. In this sense, these images may legitimately be described as 'myths', though the word is likely to mislead the ordinary reader by suggesting something that is simply false. The matter is quite different with such a statement as that Christ was born of the Virgin Mary; for, whatever aspects of the Incarnation outstrip the descriptive power of ordinary language, this at least is plainly statable in it. It means that Jesus was conceived in his mother's womb without previous sexual intercourse on her part with any male human being, and this is a straightforward statement which is either true or false. To say that the birth and death of Jesus Christ cannot *simply* be thought of as a biological event and to add that this is what the Virgin Birth *means* is a plain misuse of language, and no amount of talk about the appealing character of the 'Christmas myth' can validly gloss this over.

(2) As in earlier cases, Robinson shows here his puzzling indecision as to whether he wants to reject the 'mythological' statements altogether as meaningless to modern men and women or whether he wants to keep them while explaining that they are only to be understood as 'myth'. 'As myth', we are told, 'this construction . . . should not be thrown out.' It is only as an 'objective transaction supposed to have been accomplished outside us in time and space' that 'it speaks today to remarkably few'. Nevertheless Robinson proposes to discard it for a 'third alternative', and in this he is consistent with his original pro-

gramme that even the 'spiritual and metaphysical' interpretations of the 'myths' must go.

(3) We are told that most people would genuinely *like* to believe the Christmas story, but wonder whether it *can* be true with the world as it is after nearly two thousand years. 'The Christmas story' is a very ambiguous phrase. If it means that they would like to believe that nearly two thousand years ago a young married woman gave birth to a child in a stable and to indulge in sentimental feelings about it, it is difficult to see what there is in the state of the world today that produces difficulties for this belief. If, on the other hand, 'the Christmas story' is held to include the virginity of Mary, the appearance of the angels to the shepherds, the visit of the Magi and, behind all these, that the child of Mary was the incarnate Son of God 'by whom all things were made', it is an essential part of Robinson's thesis as originally stated that to modern man, 'come of age', this whole type of language and thought is just nonsense. One of Robinson's most puzzling characteristics is his nostalgic determination to enjoy as 'myth' the traditional images and stories which, even as myth, he has declared to be inacceptable to modern men. It looks as if the 'large percentage of [himself] that finds this revolution unacceptable and wishes it were unnecessary' has got the upper hand. But is this anything more than wishful thinking?

(4) At any rate, in the case of the Atonement it appears that what keeps modern man from belief is not the inacceptability of the traditional images and stories, 'frankly incredible' as they have been alleged to be. It is the notion that *anything* done two thousand years ago on the cross *could* affect me now. Whether the 'third alternative' to supranaturalism and naturalism which Robinson proposes avoids this difficulty we shall have to see.

The root-idea in this 'third alternative' is derived from Paul Tillich's assertion that 'the state of our whole life is estrangement from others and ourselves, because we are estranged from the Ground of our being, because we are estranged from the origin and aim of our life. . . . We are separated from the mystery, the depth, and the greatness of our existence. . . . We cannot escape, however. If that something is the Ground of our being, we are bound to it for all eternity, just as we are bound to ourselves and to all other life. We always remain in the power of that from which we are estranged.' This is indeed an admirable description of man's condition in original sin, as traditional Christianity understands it. What seems to me to be doubtful—and this is of central importance in view of the fact that Robinson makes this sense of union-in-estrangement the starting-point of his appeal to modern man—is whether the recognition of this condition is very widespread among the mass of our contemporaries in our technological civilisation and our paternalistic welfare-state. According to Tillich:

> The abyss of separation is not always visible. But it has become more visible to our generation than to the preceding generations, because of our feeling of meaninglessness, emptiness, doubt, and cynicism—all expressions of despair, of our separation from the roots and the meaning of our life. Sin in its most profound sense, sin as despair, abounds among us.

As a *Christian diagnosis* of the symptoms of our modern civilisation this may be perfectly correct; as a *description* of them it is surely doubtful, at any rate in the vast majority of cases. And, although Tillich is not to be blamed for this, it seems difficult to make this description agree with the statement of Bonhoeffer which Robinson has claimed to find so illuminating, that 'God is teaching us that we must live as men who can get along very well without him'. However, this is Robinson's application of Tillich's theme:

> It is this union-in-estrangement with the Ground of our being . . . that we mean by hell. But equally it is the union-in-love with the Ground of our being, such as we see in Jesus Christ, that is the meaning of heaven. And it is the offer of that life, in all its divine depth, to overcome the estrangement and alienation of existence as we know it that the New Testament speaks of as the 'new creation'. This new reality is transcendent, it is 'beyond' us, in the sense that it is not ours to command. Yet we experience it, like the Prodigal, as we 'come to ourselves'. For it is a coming home, or rather a being received home, to everything we are created to be. It is what the New Testament can only call *grace*.

This exposition is followed by a long extract from Tillich on the purely *gratuitous* character of grace.

The question that is immediately raised by Robinson's account is what precise part is played by Jesus Christ in this process of restoration. It would seem to be purely that of an example: what we are offered is the union-in-love with the Ground of our being, *such as we see it* in Jesus Christ. And if this is so, Robinson's position will not differ substantially from that of the disowned 'liberal' theologians. However, here is his comment on Tillich's description of grace:

> In all this we can recognise what St Paul is saying of the new creation or the new man 'in Christ Jesus'. It is nothing peculiarly religious—it is 'neither circumcision nor uncircumcision'. It is the life of 'the man for others', the love whereby we are brought completely into one with the Ground of our being, manifesting itself in the unreconciled relationships of our existence. It was manifested supremely on the Cross, but it is met wherever the Christ is shown forth and recognised in 'an entirely different mode of living-in-relationship from anything known in the world'. [This phrase is quoted from John Wren-Lewis.] For there, in however 'secular' a form, is the atonement and the resurrection. And the Christian community exists, not to promote a new religion, but simply to be the embodiment of this new being in love. And that means, to return to Bonhoeffer, 'participation in the powerlessness of God in the world'.

Here we have risen to the very heights of obscurity, but we must do our best. The new creation, or the new man in Christ Jesus (which is 'nothing peculiarly religious') is the life of 'the man for others', the love whereby we are brought completely into one with the Ground of our being (that is, in accordance with what we have been previously told, into one with God). Does this mean that we are brought into a real union with, that we are incorporated into, Jesus, who is living today no less truly than he was living in Palestine in the first century, and that we are in consequence brought into the very life of God? If so, then (apart from the characteristic reference to 'nothing peculiarly religious' and the ambiguities already remarked in the use of the phrase 'Ground of being' as a substitute for 'God') we would seem to have a statement, in Robinsonian language, of the traditional Catholic doctrine of incorporation into Christ and of grace as a participation in the divine life. This is, however, doubtful. Do this 'life' and 'love' which have just been mentioned signify the actual concrete human nature of Jesus or merely the *kind* of life which he lived and the *kind* of love which was expressed in it? Undoubtedly it was manifested supremely on the Cross, but what is meant by the subsequent statement that 'it is met *wherever* the Christ is shown forth and recognised, etc.'? Does 'shown forth' mean anything more than 'imitated', and does 'recognised' mean anything more than 'recognised as an example', or does it mean also 'recognised as the present source of this new mode of living'? Does 'living-in-relationship' mean 'living in relationship with other people' or also 'living in relationship with God'? Or is the identification of 'God' with 'the Ground of being' made in such a way that the two are simply identical? When we are told that the Christian community does not exist to promote a new religion, is 'religion' here intended in the abnormal Bonhoefferian sense or is it meant that the Church ought not to preach the Gospel but simply to rely on the power of its own life to attract outsiders?

These are, after all, questions of some importance, for on them depends the answer to the ultimate question whether the Christian's primary concern is with God or with other people. That is to say, admitted that there are two 'great commandments' for the Christian, is the commandment to love God the first, as Christ said it was, or is it really the second? Robinson's peculiar interpretation of God as the Ground of being, and the ambiguity which he imports into that interpretation, might almost lead one to suspect that in his view it is a serious error to distinguish between the two commandments at all. However, to return to the Atonement, it seems clear that, if Robinson is maintaining anything more than the liberal exemplarist theory which he professes to have repudiated, he would seem obliged to hold that, in some way or another, something done two thousand years ago on the Cross *does* affect us now and that it affects us because the incarnate Son of God who died there is now alive and incorporates us into his own self-offering.

It is, in fact, very difficult to see that Robinson's alleged 'third alternative' is really a third alternative at all. It seems to be a very obscurely worded version of one of the other two views, though which it is not easy to say. And I suspect that the fundamental reason for this obscurity is one on which I have already remarked, namely that Robinson is so anxious to persuade himself and others that all good men are 'really' Christians that he invests all his key-words and concepts with both a Christian and a non-Christian face and, having obtained recognition of the latter, adroitly substitutes the former for it.

VII

The conclusions to which I have been forced in examining the four explicitly doctrinal chapters of Robinson's book are reinforced by his fifth chapter, on 'Worldly Holiness'.[1] There is much in this which one can whole-heartedly applaud, in particular his denunciation of what most people would call 'pietism', but what, as we have seen, he strikingly but perversely insists on calling 'religion'. But once again we find ambiguity and incompleteness. There is a welcome and salutary denunciation of an individualistic attitude to the Sacrament of Holy Communion, but this goes with an almost entire indifference to its Godward aspect. With a neglect of the New Testament that is surprising in a biblical specialist, Robinson expounds his view of the Sacrament in entirely unbiblical language. 'The Holy Communion is *the* point at which the common, the communal, becomes the carrier of the unconditional, as the Christ makes himself known in the breaking and sharing of bread. *Holy* Communion is communion, community-life, *in sacris*, in depth, at the level at which we are not merely in human fellowship but "in Christ", not merely in love but in Love, united with the ground and restorer of our whole being.' Here there is at any rate the affirmation that Christ is alive and accessible today, a truth which was obscure in Robinson's discussion of the Atonement. 'At least', he adds, 'that is what Communion should be. But too often it is not the place at which the common and the communal point through to the beyond in their midst, to the transcendent in, with and under them, but precisely the opposite. It ceases to be the holy meal, and becomes a religious service in which we turn our backs on the common and the community and in individualistic devotion go to "make our communion" with "the God out there".' This sudden introduction of 'the God out there' in this context is very strange, for the common mark of individualistic devotion is that it tends to seek God within the soul, rather than 'out there'. But Robinson

[1] *Honest to God*, pp. 84–104.

seems determined to have all his *bêtes noires* in the same pen. 'This is the essence of religious perversion,' he writes, 'when worship becomes a realm into which to withdraw from the world to "be with God"—even if it is only in order to receive strength to go back into it. In this case the entire realm of the non-religious (in other words, "life") is relegated to the profane, in the strict sense of that which is outside the *fanum* or sanctuary. The holy place, where the Christ is met, lies not, as in the parable of the Sheep and the Goats, in the ordinary relationships of life: it lies within the circle of "the religious", from which the worshipper will go out to carry Christ's love into "the secular world".' Behind this passage there appears to lie an assumption that, if we make any distinction between the 'sacred' and the 'secular', we are denying any religious significance to the secular at all. Robinson has inserted at this point a somewhat obscure footnote saying that 'this is perhaps the point to recognise that so much of the discussion for and against "religion" is bound to be a matter of definition', but he pays no obvious attention to this reminder, which in any case might profitably have come very much earlier in the book. However, if there is *no* sense in which we have to withdraw from the world to 'be with God', even if only in order to receive strength to go back into it, there would seem to be no point in having churches or services at all, even the Holy Communion; it would be sufficient for us to live together, work together, eat together and play together as Christians, and so find the Ground of our being 'in depth' in the things of daily life. The whole complex of scriptural ideas that lies behind Christ's institution of the Eucharist is absent from Robinson's exposition. The Exodus from bondage, the New Covenant in the Blood of the sacrifice, the Lord's *anamnesis*, the Eucharistic banquet of the people of God in the kingdom of the Messiah, the showing forth of the Lord's death till he come—all these great themes receive not a mention. Any notion that *worship* is concerned with praising and acknowledging the 'worth' of God or that Holy Communion has any connection with thanksgiving ('Eucharist') is all but explicitly denied. 'The *purpose* of worship', we are told,

> is not to retire from the secular into the department of the religious, let alone to escape from 'this world' into 'the other

> world', but to open oneself to the meeting of the Christ in the common, to that which has the power to penetrate its superficiality and redeem it from its alienation.

And 'the *function* of worship'

> is to make us more sensitive to these depths; to focus, sharpen and deepen our response to the world and to other people beyond the point of proximate concern (of liking, self-interest, limited commitment, etc.) to that of ultimate concern; to purify and correct our loves in the light of Christ's love; and in him to find the grace and power to be the reconciled and reconciling community. *Anything* that achieves this or assists towards it is Christian worship. *Anything* that fails to do this is not Christian worship, be it ever so 'religious'.

The words which I have italicised in these passages are of central importance. Clearly no Christian could deny the relevance of the matters which are so strongly stressed as *criteria* for the discrimination between genuine and bogus worship. Robinson, however, sets them forward as the *purpose* and the *function* of worship, and neither of these is described by him as having any connection with praising, adoring or thanking God. He develops his exposition with reference to the position of the celebrant at the Eucharist in a way which would certainly alarm many of the most enthusiastic supporters of the Liturgical Movement. 'The so-called "eastward position", in which the priest stands with his back to the people, has', he says, 'the psychological effect of focusing attention upon a point somewhere in the middle distance beyond the sanctuary. It symbolises the whole way of thinking in which God is seen as a projection "out there" to whom we turn from the world. By contrast the "westward position", in which the president surrounded by his assistants faces the people across the table, focuses attention upon a point in the middle, as the Christ stands among his own as the breaker of bread.' This contrast is, I think, grossly exaggerated; the psychological associations of the two 'positions' are not nearly as various as is suggested. Many people complain that the westward position has the effect of focusing the attention of the people on the celebrant's face. However, in commending the westward position Robinson oddly slips back into the very images that he has so vigorously repudiated:

> There is equally here—or should be—the element of 'the beyond', the transcendent, as they lift their hearts to him as their ascended and triumphant Lord. But the beyond is seen not as that which takes one out and away from the earthly and the common, but as the vertical of the unconditioned cutting into and across the limitations of the merely human fellowship, claiming it for and transforming it into the Body of the living Christ.

This is finely said, but we ought to have been told it before. We must not place much stress on the appearance here of the word 'transcendent', for we have already seen that Robinson has his own use of this word to indicate not what is 'above' but what is 'within'. However, 'lift their hearts to him as their ascended and triumphant Lord' is surely a return not merely to the notion of 'out there' but to the even more despised notion of 'up there', and 'the vertical of the unconditioned' surely evokes the image of descent from above, rather than of explosion from within, unless—which is very unlikely—it is meant to suggest that of ascent from below. Again, the transformation of the merely human fellowship into the Body of the living Christ is splendid traditional theology—does not St Thomas Aquinas tell us that the *res* of the sacrament is 'the unity of the mystical Body'?—but this, too, should have been said before and not as an afterthought. What is, I believe, fundamentally lacking in Robinson's Eucharistic theology, as in his theology in general, is the Catholic conception of the *transformation* of the natural by the supernatural. Lacking this, he can ascribe to the natural the value which he rightly sees it to have only by finding divinity *within* it; one can perhaps at least say that this is an improvement on a common traditional Protestant view which denies all value to the natural at all. And I think the same judgment is to be made of his discussion of prayer as of his discussion of the Eucharist. Its strong and weak points are so similar that it really does not call for separate discussion.

Robinson's sixth chapter, entitled—in quotes—' "The New Morality" ',[1] has received a great deal of attention from those more competent to discuss it than I am, and I shall only remark that it seems to be quite coherent with the rest of his book. I shall therefore pass on to his final chapter—'Recasting the

[1] *Honest to God*, pp. 105–21.

Mould'[1]—in which he looks back on his argument as a whole and tries to see its general implications.

VIII

Starting from the familiar distinction which he draws from Bonhoeffer between the Gospel and 'Christianity' as a 'pattern of religion', Robinson somewhat unexpectedly observes that we shall not abolish our present pattern of religion 'even if we wanted to'. On the other hand, he asserts that unless we are prepared for the kind of revolution of which he has spoken the Christian faith and practice will come to be abandoned altogether. And this is because it is moulded, in the form in which we know it, by a cast of thought which belongs to a past age—a cast of thought which Bultmann calls 'mythological', Tillich 'supranaturalist' and Bonhoeffer 'religious'. He quotes Bonhoeffer for the view that the 'religious premise' is for modern man an obstacle to his acceptance of the Gospel comparable to that which the Law was for the first-century Jew. On the other hand, he insists that there is nothing wrong 'as such' with the religious premise, which has been, and still is, for millions 'the precondition of the Presence'. Nevertheless, he continues:

> What looks like being required of us, reluctant as we may be for the effort involved, is a radically new mould, or *meta-morphosis*, of Christian belief and practice. Such a recasting will, I am convinced, leave the fundamental truth of the Gospel unaffected. But it means that we have to be prepared for *everything* to go into the melting—even our most cherished religious categories and moral absolutes. And the first thing we must be ready to let go is our image of God himself.

This is, of course, almost exactly what Robinson said at the beginning of the book and one not unreasonably hoped that in the course of his discussion he was going to bring us some way at least towards the solution of this problem. However, if this last statement is to be accepted, we are apparently exactly where we were at the start, except that the issue seems to be rather more sharply defined. And what still remains obscure is how, if *every-*

[1] *Honest to God*, pp. 122–41. The title of this chapter is odd; the word 'mould' usually indicates the *matrix* in which the casting is done, not the object which is cast.

thing is to be cast into the melting, we can know whether the fundamental truth of the Gospel is being preserved or not. For literally everything is to go—'even our most cherished religious categories and moral absolutes'. Nevertheless a little later on Robinson brings in what he describes as 'the conviction about ultimate Reality that alone finally matters', a conviction which in fact matters so much that in order to help men to accept it we may have to 'discard every image of God—whether of the "one above", the "one out here", or any other', and this will presumably include the image of God as the 'Ground of being' as well. The conviction in question is the conviction that 'there is nothing in death or life . . . in the world as it is or the world as it shall be, in the forces of the universe, in heights or depths—nothing in all creation that can separate us from the love of God in Christ Jesus our Lord'. This, then, is presumably the 'fundamental truth of the Gospel', which will remain 'unaffected' when *everything* has gone into the melting, including *every* image of God. Now, I want in all seriousness to raise these questions:

(1) What reasons have we for supposing that this expression of 'the conviction about ultimate reality that alone finally matters' will survive the melting and recasting process? It is taken from the eighth chapter of the Epistle to the Romans, and, in spite of the fact that Robinson discreetly omits some significant words and gives the rest of the passage in the modernised language of the New English Bible, it is a highly 'mythological' statement, embodying the concepts of ancient cosmology and astrology. Nevertheless, Robinson is quite explicit about the matter: 'That', he says, 'I believe with all my being, and that is what at heart it means to be a Christian. As for the rest, as for the images of God, whether metal or mental, I am prepared to be an agnostic with the agnostics, even an atheist with the atheists.' How one is to be, in any sense that does not empty words of all meaning, 'an atheist with the atheists' while believing in the love of *God* is not clear. But presumably the image of God as one whose love is embodied in Christ Jesus our Lord is either not to go into the melting or will have a sufficiently high melting-point to emerge unscathed from it. I am not being facetious. 'The love of God in Christ Jesus our Lord' is not a concept that can be detached from its whole context in the New Testament and retained when everything else is abandoned; it is

part of the whole complex of thought and life and worship. The very words 'Christ' and 'Lord', in their New Testament meaning, are loaded with the religious context of first-century Judaism and Hellenism. This will lead to my second question.

(2) Has not Robinson been greatly misled by his favourite metaphor of 'melting' and 'recasting'? Granted, as we all must grant, that a tremendously difficult work of reformulation and explanation is needed in order to commend the Christian faith to every new generation and culture, this metaphor seems grossly inadequate to indicate the nature of the task, and this for two reasons. First, it suggests, especially in the extreme and unqualified way in which Robinson uses it, that nothing whatever will remain of the original shape, so that the whole inheritance of Christian thought and prayer and life will simply perish. And secondly, it suggests that the new form into which it is to be cast is to be entirely provided by contemporary culture, for everything that Christianity itself might have provided as a contribution to the new mould has been cast into the melting. In fact, as we have just seen, Robinson has, by the use which he makes of the verse from Romans, run away from the consequences of his own programme. And the confusion in which this has involved him is, I think, evident from the extraordinarily perverse use which he then makes of the story, related in the seventeenth chapter of Acts, of St Paul's encounter with the intelligentsia of his day on the Areopagus at Athens.

The point of the story is, of course, that St Paul made a valiant, but only partly successful attempt to express the Gospel in the thought-forms of his pagan hearers. It was not, *pace* Robinson, entirely unsuccessful: 'certain men clave unto him and believed'. Robinson is exaggerating when he writes: 'So far from the accepted mould of religious truth proving an insuperable barrier, there was apparently no point of contact at all. His gospel seemed utterly incomprehensible.' This is not, however, my main point of criticism, which is that Robinson interprets the whole episode in precisely the opposite sense to that which it is meant to bear.

'Paul', he writes, 'was dismissed as a setter forth of strange Gods, Socrates was condemned as an "atheist". Every new religious truth comes as the destroyer of some other god, as an attack upon that which men hold most sacred.' Now, it is, of course, true that St Paul's Christian Gospel seemed to many of his pagan hearers to be an attempt to destroy their gods, though if so it can hardly have been as 'utterly incomprehensible' as Robinson makes out. What St Paul was trying to do, however, was to find a point of contact between their existing thought-forms and the Gospel, which he was obstinately determined to proclaim, of 'Jesus and the Resurrection'. 'As I passed along and observed the objects of your worship, I found also an altar with this inscription: "To an unknown God". What therefore ye worship in ignorance, this set I forth unto you.'[1] As this verse and the sequel shows, St Paul was not pursuing the Robinsonian programme of casting his own images into the melting, but proposing them as the mould in which the amorphous intuitions of his pagan audience might be given concrete form. As Robinson himself says, St Paul's 'new religious truth [came] as the destroyer of some other god', though perhaps 'destroyer' is a less appropriate term in this context than 'fulfiller' or 'revealer of the true nature' would be. What is, however, astounding is Robinson's conclusion that, because Paul's 'new religious truth' came as an attack on the 'gods' of paganism, therefore the 'new religious truth' of twentieth-century secularism should be used to attack the traditional images of Christianity. It would be more in accord with St Paul's approach if the images of contemporary secularism were subjected to attack by the 'new religious truth' of Christianity, for, as Robinson has repeatedly insisted, traditional Christianity appears to the men of our day to be every bit as 'new' and indeed 'utterly incomprehensible' as Paul's Gospel did to the men of Athens. It is indeed true, as Robinson says, that 'the Christian gospel is in perpetual conflict with the images of God set up in the minds of men, even of Christian men, as they seek in each generation to encompass his meaning'. He is also right in saying that 'these images fulfil an essential purpose, to focus the unknowable, to enclose the inexhaustible, so that ordinary men and women can get their minds round God and have something on which to fix their imagination and prayers'. He is right, again, in adding, 'But as soon as they become a substitute for God, as soon as they *become* God, *so that what is not embodied in the image is excluded or denied*, then we have a new idolatry and once

[1] Acts xvii. 23.

more the word of judgment has to fall.' However, two distinct issues have here become confused. The first is that of the distinction between Christian and pagan images. The second is the distinction between using images as an aid to worshipping God and making them the object of worship, 'a substitute for God'. It simply does not follow that, because St Paul used the Christian images to correct and fulfil the pagan images of his time, therefore we should allow the Christian images to be destroyed by the secularist images of the present day. More positively, I would suggest that, if Robinson had paid more attention to the immensely detailed and conscientious discussions of traditional theology about the problem of knowing God at all, whether by concepts or by images, and about the way in which the biblical images have functioned in the thought and liturgy of the Church, he would have been neither so rash as to suppose that the Christian Gospel could survive the process of melting and recasting in a secular mould which he advocates nor so confident that Romans viii. 38 would emerge unscathed.

It is only fair to add, after the foregoing discussion, that Robinson goes on to argue that his position is neither that of non-Christian naturalism nor that of 'orthodox' supranaturalism. As an example of the former he takes the evolutionary humanism, the 'religion without revelation', of Sir Julian Huxley. 'I am convinced', he says

> that we should follow Huxley, who is here at one with Bonhoeffer, in discarding the supranaturalist framework. But whereas Huxley does it in the interest of religion without revelation, Bonhoeffer does it in the interest of Christianity without religion—not, of course, that Bonhoeffer desires to abolish religion in the way that Huxley wants to dispense with revelation: he simply wishes to free Christianity from any necessary dependence upon 'the religious premise'.

For Bonhoeffer, we may remember, being freed from the religious premise meant 'living as if God did not exist', knowing that God calls us to live as men who can get on very well without him. Robinson now makes the distinction between Huxley's position and Bonhoeffer's by identifying it with the distinction between the affirmations that 'love is God' and that 'God is love', and this again with the distinction between holding that love *ought to be* the last word about life and holding that, despite all appearances it *is*. It would be easy, but not very profitable, to question these identifications; it will be more fruitful to see what Robinson's positive affirmations are. And this, at least, seems to be plain:

> The Christian's faith is in Christ as the revelation, the laying bare, of the very heart and being of ultimate reality. And that is why, in the categories of traditional theology, it was so necessary to insist that he was *homousios*, of one substance, with the Father. For unless the *ousia*, the being, of things deep down, *is* Love, of the quality disclosed in the life, death and resurrection of Jesus Christ, then the Christian could have little confidence in affirming the ultimate personal character of reality. And this—not his religiosity, nor his belief in the existence of a Person in heaven—is what finally distinguishes him from the humanist and the atheist.

This is a moving confession of Robinson's devotion to our Blessed Lord, but it is questionable in its historical implications. When the Church declared at the Council of Nicaea that the Son was of the same *ousia* as the Father, it certainly did not mean that he was of the same *ousia* as *things*, however deep down, but that he was of the same *ousia* as their Creator. And to identify things with their Creator would be to fall into the pantheism which Robinson, no doubt quite sincerely, rejects. But, quite apart from this, if we give Robinson the benefit of the doubt and assume that by 'the being, of things deep down', he means God the Father, his statement would seem to assert that the Father is *homoousios* with the Son, rather than, as Nicaea asserted, that the Son is *homoousios* with the Father. This is not just a verbal point. For what was at issue at Nicaea was not the status of the Father, or of the 'Ground of being', but of the Son of God who was incarnate as Jesus. And what Nicaea declared was that the Son was not a creature, however exalted, but of the very same stuff, on the very same level of being, as the Father himself.[1] The word *homoousios*, as applied to the Son, was inserted into a Creed which began by proclaiming its belief in 'One God, the Father almighty, maker of heaven and earth and of all things visible

[1] Cf. G. L. Prestige, *God in Patristic Thought*, ch. x; J. D. N. Kelly, *Early Christian Creeds*, pp. 242ff; *Early Christian Doctrines*, pp. 231ff.

and invisible' and which went on to proclaim its belief in his Son Jesus Christ. It is, of course, true that the Christian's understanding of God has been immensely enriched by the conviction that he has been revealed in his only-begotten Son Jesus Christ our Lord, but to suggest that the *homoousios* was meant as a statement about the ground of being rather than about the Person of Jesus Christ is quite false as a matter of history. And I take it that the sentence 'For unless the *ousia*, the being, of things deep down *is* love, of the quality disclosed in the life, death and resurrection of Jesus Christ, then the Christian could have little confidence in affirming the ultimate personal character of reality' should begin 'For unless he was convinced that the *ousia* . . .', for it is presumably two beliefs that are, in Robinson's view, related as cause and effect or as antecedent and consequent. And even with this correction the statement seems odd, for unless he held the former of these beliefs, the natural consequence would seem to be, not that 'the Christian' would have little confidence in affirming the ultimate personal character of reality, but that the man in question would not be, in the normal sense of the word, a Christian at all. But, whether we make the correction I have suggested or not, the statement seems highly dubitable. For there *are* persons who confidently affirm the ultimate personal character of reality without attributing any special value to the life, death and resurrection of Christ, and indeed at the very beginning of his book Robinson has admitted this. I cannot but think that we have here yet another example of Robinson's questionable assumption that anyone who believes in the ultimate character of love must be 'really' a Christian, whether he thinks he is or not. This is confirmed by the final sentence of the passage, in which 'the Christian' is set over against 'the humanist and the atheist' as if no such people as non-Christian theists existed. And this is, as I see it, extremely unfair to non-Christian theists.

Turning now to defend himself against the 'supranaturalists', Robinson is conscious that they will suspect him of pantheism, 'for traditionally, the immanentist or pantheistic world-view has been countered in deism and theism with the assertion that the world owes its origin to *a* Creator, an almighty Artificer, who at a moment of time (or "with" time) made it "out of nothing" '. This statement can, of course, be taken as accurate only if the words 'Artificer' and 'at a moment of time' are referred to deism and the words ' "with" time' to theism, and even then a traditional theist will want to add a good deal of explanation. Why Robinson has italicised the word '*a*' before 'Creator' I cannot imagine. 'This', he says, 'is clearly a highly mythological and anthropomorphic picture. But it is entirely possible to demythologise it without lapsing into pantheism.' The subsequent sentences must be quoted at length:

> The essential difference between the Biblical and any immanentist world-view lies in the fact that it grounds all reality ultimately in personal freedom—in Love. For pantheism, the relation of every aspect of reality to its ground is in the last analysis a deterministic one, allowing no real room for freedom or for moral evil. It finds its natural expression in the mechanical or organic categories of emanation or evolution rather than in the personal categories of creation. But the Biblical affirmation is that built into the very structure of our relationship to the ground of our being is an indestructible element of personal freedom. We are not like rays to the sun or leaves to the tree: we are united to the source, sustainer and goal of our life in a relationship whose only analogy is that of *I* to *Thou*—except that the freedom in which we are held is one of utter dependence. We are rooted and grounded wholly in Love. And the doctrine of creation *ex nihilo* is that there is nothing in us or in 'all creation' which has ultimately to be attributed to some other ground or found some other explanation.

At this point the persevering reader may well feel astounded, for the view which Robinson is now commending appears to be in all essentials that of traditional theism. There are indeed a few phrases which need some precision. Thus, for example, the assertion that all reality is grounded in personal freedom does not immediately imply that this freedom is to be identified with Love, and indeed in the next sentence it seems to be implied that freedom may be exercised in a way that is morally evil. That the world is the immediate creation of a mischievous being is a view that has repeatedly opposed itself to orthodox Christianity in the course of the Church's history, and *prima facie* there might seem to be a good deal to be said for it. The contemporary man with whom Robinson is so much concerned cannot be relied on to make the identification of freedom with love on which so much of Robinson's position depends. And, in spite of his concern with Bonhoeffer and the Nazi prison-camp, he never really gets to grips with the problem of evil in the way in which, for example, Dr A. M. Farrer does in his books *Love Almighty and Ills Unlimited* and *Saving Belief*, and the late C. S. Lewis in *The Problem of Pain* and *Letters to Malcolm*. Again, the assertion that 'built into the very structure of our relationship to the ground of our being is an indestructible element of personal freedom' might leave it doubtful whether it is we ourselves or the ground of our being that is free, though the context makes it fairly clear that the reference is primarily to the ground. And we can only welcome the recognition that our relation to the ground is also one of 'utter dependence', for this rules out, as it has not been ruled out before, any suggestion of a God who is finite as we are. The next sentence is admirable: 'It is this freedom built into the structure of our being which gives us (within the relationship of dependence) the independence, the "distance", as it were, to be ourselves.' This is fine statement of the way in which the primary causal activity of God is compatible with a genuine but derived freedom of ourselves as secondary causes of our acts. But now the old complaint recurs: 'What traditional deism and theism have done is to "objectivise" this distance into the pictorial image of a God "out there".' And this 'projection of God *from* the world as a super-Individual is no more necessary an expression of transcendence than is mileage upwards from the earth's surface'. The odd thing here is that it has not occurred to Robinson that his metaphor of distance (even when subjected to his usual treatment of inclusion within inverted commas), just like his other metaphor of transcendence, carries with it precisely the suggestion of spatial separation that attaches to the metaphors of 'up there' and 'out there'. It is indeed remarkable that Robinson, unlike the despised 'supranaturalist' traditional theologians, never attempts to investigate the problems that are raised *whenever* we apply to God images and concepts derived from our everyday experience. The traditionalist will want to criticise him quite as much for the naïve and univocal way in which he applies the images and concepts which appeal to him as for the drastic way in which he dismisses those which do not, without any recognition of their essentially analogical character. Only once, I think, does he come near to recognising this problem, and this is on the page immediately following that passage I have just been discussing.

> To demythologise [he writes]—as Bultmann would readily concede—is not to suppose that we can dispense with all myth or symbol. It is to cut our dependence upon one particular mythology—of what Tillich calls the 'superworld of divine objects'—which is in peril of becoming a source of incredulity rather than an aid to faith. Any alternative language—e.g. of depth—is bound to be equally symbolic. But it may speak more 'profoundly' to the soul of modern man.

This invites the following comments:

(1) Traditionalist theology has, in fact, never rejected the metaphor of 'depth'. But, by combining it with the metaphor of 'height' and others as well, it has safeguarded itself against the danger of taking *any* of its metaphors too literally, a danger from which Robinson, with his monolithic image of depth, is very far from immune. But where traditional theology has developed an elaborate discipline (the 'doctrine of analogy') in order to determine in what senses our human concepts do and do not apply to the mysteries of our faith, Robinson is content to immunise his concepts by placing them in inverted commas. There can, in fact, be very few theologians who have made such extensive use of this simple protective device.

(2) It may be the case, though I am far from convinced of this, that the language of depth speaks more 'profoundly' to the soul of modern man. After all, 'modern man' is an abstraction no less than 'economic man' or 'average man', and what speaks profoundly to Mr Wren-Lewis may speak less profoundly to others. But, if it is true that, in some sense of the term 'modern man' (that is, the great majority of modern *men*) can be stirred by the notion of depth, while the notions of height and other traditional Christian notions leave him comparatively cold, may it not be that it is precisely in this respect that he needs to be converted? And if so, would not Robinson's energies have been better devoted to the task of working out a method of communicating these notions to modern man rather than to the denunciations which occupy such a large number of his pages?

In actual fact the section of the book with which we are now concerned seems to be very largely occupied with denials of the book's avowed thesis. Thus we read:

> It may be psychologically inevitable that the recognition of 'the infinite qualitative difference' between the Creator and the creature, between the holy God and sinful man, should find its symbolic expression in the cry, 'Depart from me'—that is in the setting of *space* in between. And it may be impossible to *imagine* the personal ground of all our being except as an almighty Individual, endowed with a centre of consciousness and will like ourselves and yet wholly 'other'. As symbols these images have their powerful and their proper place. They become idols only when the images are regarded as indispensable for the apprehending of the reality; they become dangerous only when they cease to mediate the reality and indeed become barriers to it.

Now, this statement is unsatisfactory in at least two respects. It falls into the snare of identifying man's creaturehood with his sinfulness, and, like the other passages we have just considered, it by-passes the problem as to how the 'reality'—the Holy God, the Creator—can be mediated to men by symbols at all. (Incidentally, we might enquire whether we are falling into idolatry if we regard as indispensable the images which Jesus himself used, such as that of 'Father'.) But what is quite amazing is the contrast between this recognition of the spatial images as having 'their powerful and their proper place' as 'symbols' and the wholesale rejection of them, even 'spiritually or metaphysically' understood, with which the book began. If, as we were there told, 'the most fundamental categories of our theology—of God, of the supernatural, and of religion itself—must go into the melting' and even 'the *mental* picture of such a God [i.e. God 'out there'] may be more of a stumbling-block than an aid to belief in the Gospel', how can we now be asked to admit that 'as symbols these images have their powerful and their proper place'? And if, as Robinson now suggests, it may be impossible to *imagine* 'the personal ground of all our being' except under these formerly repudiated images, what will have happened to us if we have accepted his earlier advice? We shall have committed ourselves and urged upon others, in the initial stages of Christian discipleship, an imageless Christianity which traditional spirituality has well known to be impossible to any who have not progressed very far along the path of mystical union. We can hardly be surprised that Robinson has had second thoughts; we can only regret that he has had them so late in the day. But, since he appears to be unconscious that he has shifted his position at all, it will be well to stress again the contrast between his original repudiation, in the most downright and rhetorical terms, of the traditional concepts and images of Christianity, as obstacles making belief impossible for modern man, and his later assertion that they have a powerful and proper place and may even be psychologically inevitable.

He goes on, in fact, to tell us that

> there are whole areas of response where the myth still occasions little difficulty. In prophecy and prayer, in liturgy and worship, the traditional imagery retains its numinous power. . . . Every generation can make such language its own, whatever the mould of its belief, whatever its projection of God. Liturgy, indeed, is the main medium of that transposition of which I spoke earlier, whereby we can readily accept and use a notation that on the face of it belongs to an entirely alien thought-world. In fact, as Canon Hugh Montefiore observes in another connection, our impasse is primarily an intellectual one.

The contrast is again unmistakable. If it is true that the traditional imagery retains its numinous power in prophecy and prayer, in liturgy and worship, the impasse being primarily an intellectual one, one would expect to find modern man in his hordes thronging our churches for the numinous experience induced by the preaching, prayer and liturgy, while demanding an intellectual interpretation of it altogether contrary to that experience. This is not, in fact, the case; nor should we expect it to be. Unless the symbols, 'spiritually or metaphysically' understood (to use Robinson's own term), are accepted as intellectually veridical, the exploitation of their 'numinous power' is at best the encouragement of escapism and at worst sheer dishonesty. The suggestion that a generation can make the supranaturalist language—the language of 'God up there' or 'God out there'—'its own' for purposes of prayer, liturgy and worship, while being unable to *think* of God except 'in depth' as the ground of being, is not only unconvincing in itself but is also clean contrary to the whole of Robinson's former argument. Liturgy, he tells us, is the main medium of the transposition of which he spoke earlier, but when we look back to the passage to which he refers we find that the transposition in question—the transposition of the notion of

'God out there' from literal to spiritual or metaphysical terms—was declared by him to be one that modern man will be unable to make without 'a century or more of reappraisal' and that in consequence the very notion itself was to be abandoned as 'more of a hindrance than a help'. 'Have we seriously faced the possibility', he demanded, 'that to abandon such an idol [the God 'out there'] may in the future be the only way of making Christianity meaningful, except to the few remaining equivalents of flat-earthers . . . ? Perhaps after all the Freudians are right, that such a God—the God of traditional popular theology—*is* a projection, and perhaps we are being called to live without that projection *in any form*' [italics mine].[1] It is indeed a far cry from this to the assertion that in liturgy we can 'readily accept and use a notation that on the face of it belongs to an entirely alien thought-world'. Robinson goes on to say that 'without the constant discipline of theological thought, asking what we really mean by the symbols, purging out the dead myths, and being utterly honest before God with ourselves and the world, the Church can quickly become obscurantist and its faith and conduct and worship increasingly formal and hollow'. But surely such a radical recasting of our theology as he began by demanding would make it impossible for us, while being utterly honest before God with ourselves and the world, to go on using the traditional imagery in prophecy and prayer, in liturgy and worship, whatever its numinous power. There will have to be either a much less radical melting and recasting of our thought than Robinson began by demanding or else a much more radical melting and recasting of liturgy than he has ended by conceding. With Robinson's desire 'to equip Christians, by the quality and power of [the Church's] community life, to enter with their "secret discipline" into all the exhilarating, and dangerous, secular strivings of our day, there to follow and to find the workings of God', I have every sympathy. My complaint against him, after making a detailed examination of his book, is that the programme which he sets forth, in so far as it is consistent at all (and I think I have shown that consistency is not its most marked characteristic), so far from transforming the secularised world in which we live by transfusing into it the redemptive power of Christ, would simply reduce Christianity

[1] op. cit., pp. 15, 17.

to a condition of impotence by conforming it to the pattern of the secularised world.

IX

I have written this chapter with very little reference to the many other discussions that Dr Robinson's book has provoked, because it seems to me that there may be some value in a thorough and systematic analysis of his argument which will supplement and not merely repeat what other writers have said. My conclusion is, however, not very different from that of Mr O. Fielding Clarke, in his invigorating little book *For Christ's Sake*. 'Where I disagree totally with Dr Robinson', he writes, 'is in the diagnosis of our condition and, therefore, in its cure. . . . What Christians need to do is not to think up new images but to deliver the goods! The Bishop complains that the Church is too turned in on itself, and his remedy is a century of juggling with images!'[1] And again: 'Our failure in proclaiming Christianity has not been a failure to have up-to-date images. On the contrary, it has been a failure to make the oldest images in our faith—the Cross and the Resurrection—real and sharply defined.'[2] With a wider outlook than Robinson, Fielding Clarke reminds his readers that the really serious alternative to Christianity with which the world is faced today is Marxism, with the immediate appeal which it makes to the hungry, the illiterate and the underprivileged. But for all his concern for the practical issues of poverty, malnutrition, illiteracy and sickness and his condemnation of affluent Christians for their only too common indifference to them, he reserves some of his severest strictures for the *trahison des clercs* of the theologians. 'Theology in general', he says, 'instead of acting as a beacon-light to guide the people of God, the laity, as they confront the problems of living for Christ in the world, has for generations been taking refuge in an ever more and more minute study of Christian origins. Theology is less and less about God and God's world, and more and more a department of ancient history, absorbed in minute details of historical and literary criticism. The whole business is wildly out of proportion.'[3] To do Robinson justice, I think it may well be the realisation of the inadequacy of theology as it has been under-

[1] op. cit., pp. 62f.
[2] ibid., p. 73.
[3] ibid., p. 85.

stood in British academic circles that accounts for the iconoclastic character of his book, though I think a contributory cause may be the lack of consideration of the peculiar situation and problems of contemporary man that has marked most of the Protestant biblical theology which has offered itself as the only alternative. Brought face to face with life as it is lived in all its variety in a great secular conurbation, Robinson has recognised the almost complete irrelevance of academic theology to the lives of ordinary people. The tragedy of the situation is that he has found nothing to turn to for inspiration but fragments of Bultmann, Bonhoeffer and Tillich.

Of other criticisms than Clarke's, the most penetrating that I have seen are those of Mr David Jenkins and Mr Alasdair MacIntyre, printed in the symposium *The Honest to God Debate.* (MacIntyre's paper originally appeared in a longer version in the journal *Encounter.*)

I think MacIntyre is going too far when he opens his discussion by saying that 'what is striking about Dr Robinson's book is first and foremost that he is an atheist',[1] though there are, as we have seen, trends in his thought which if he followed them out consistently would certainly issue either in atheism or in sheer indifference as to whether God existed or not. And I thoroughly agree with MacIntyre's protests against Robinson's 'translation' of statements about God into statements about human concern, for to describe as 'translation' what is really 'substitution' enables one to run with the theistic hare and hunt with the atheist hounds. (Actually, the metaphor which Robinson favours is that of 'recasting' rather than that of 'translation', but the essential point is the same.) A similar protest against 'reductionism' in theological discourse has been made more recently by Mr Hugo Meynell in his penetrating book *Sense, Nonsense and Christianity.* But perhaps the most useful feature of MacIntyre's essay lies in his assertion that Bonhoeffer's Christianity is really intelligible only in the context of 'helplessness' of his Nazi prison-camp and that outside that context it loses its specifically Christian character and merely 'clothes ordinary liberal forms of life with the romantic unreality of a catacombic vocabulary'.[2] His further assertion, that theologians who wish to

[1] op. cit., p. 215.
[2] ibid., p. 222.

translate what they have to say to an atheistic world are doomed to one of two failures, since if they succeed in their translation what they say has been transformed into the atheism of their hearers, while if they fail in their translation no one hears what they have to say but themselves, is not, I think, true, unless we take a very unnatural and restrictive view of what constitutes 'translation'. For it is tantamount to saying that we can never use another person's language in order to convince him of something of which he was not convinced before; and this is patently false. I think, however, that MacIntyre's assertion is true of the kind of translation which Robinson advocates and practises, for this, if carried out consistently (which it is not), would be directed to changing not a man's beliefs but simply his attitudes.

Mr Jenkins's essay, while it is written with great restraint and courtesy, is, in fact, very destructive indeed. Thus, for example, after referring to the 'scandalous poverty' of much current 'theism', with its neglect of the great theological treasure that is to be found in the Fathers of East and West and in the great mystics and masters of the spiritual life, he remarks that 'the true extent of the scandal is peculiarly well shown by the fact that not only does the theism against which the Bishop protests seem to many people to be recognisably the theism of the Christian Church (and the only possible theism—hence the need and justification for atheism) but also the Bishop actually seems to be trapped in this belief himself.'[1] Again, commenting on Robinson's assertion 'I have never really doubted the fundamental truth of the Christian faith—though I have constantly found myself questioning its expression', Jenkins comments, 'I am unable to be at all clear what it is that the Bishop has never really doubted. I do not think one could be altogether blamed for being inclined to deduce that what the Bishop has never doubted is that somehow or other his own "attitude" or "feeling" or "commitment" is "right".'[2] He very relevantly remarks that Robinson talks about his 'faith' and 'commitment' without saying what his faith is *in* or what his commitment is *to*. He gets right to the heart of the matter in his comment on the way in which Robinson tries to *define* God into existence with the formula 'God is, by definition, ultimate reality. And one cannot

[1] ibid., p. 195.
[2] ibid., pp. 196f.

argue whether ultimate reality exists.' 'We have,' Jenkins pointedly observes, 'I think, detected some very determinedly anti-traditional-metaphysic thinkers trying to get away with a concealed and possibly inverted version of the traditional ontological argument'[1] (the argument that the *idea* of God includes the idea of existing, and therefore God must exist). He also points out the way in which Robinson oscillates between asserting that the 'Ground of being' is something other than the stuff of our ordinary life and existence and equating the two. Jenkins's essay is so brief and yet so pungent (unlike the discussion with which I myself have been wearying my reader) that it should be sufficient merely to direct the reader's attention to it. I will only mention one further point which Jenkins makes and in which he turns Robinson's argument back on itself. 'It is by no means self-evident', he writes, 'that images of depth are richer or more satisfactory than images of height—and that especially in the area of personal relationships and personal development. Here is a matter for urgent discussion between psychologists and theologians. How far does "depth" imagery correlate with desires to escape from reality as it is manifested in persons, to "return to the womb" and to get away from the stretching demands of integration in relation with and with reference to others? And how far does "height" stand for the demand always to go further than every outgoing experience wherein the self is expressed on behalf of other selves? . . . It might perhaps be true that the problem of transcendence is the problem of the fulfilment of human personality in a fullness of personality that embraces all personal possibilities in a Transcendent which (who) is fully personal.'[2]

I shall conclude this already overlong discussion with some comments on the concluding essay in *The Honest to God Debate*, in which Robinson himself, under the title 'The Debate Continues', offers some further remarks about what he describes as 'the first round of the debate'. After some introductory remarks of an autobiographical kind he characterises the present situation as 'a currency crisis', one that 'affects all the traditionally accepted means of exchange among Christians and between Christians and the world in which they live: doctrinal formulations, moral

[1] ibid., pp. 198f.
[2] ibid., pp. 202f.

codes, liturgical forms, and the rest'.[1] The task with which we are confronted is, he says, a double one. 'First, we must be prepared to ask with rigorous honesty what is the real cash value of the statements we make and the forms we use. . . . But the second task is that of finding a new currency, that will be convertible in the modern world. And the most distinctive fact about this world is that it is a *secular* world.'[2]

How far the metaphor of currency is really helpful in this context might, I think, be questioned, but that the present-day world is a secular world can hardly be doubted. And I think he is quite right in saying that secularisation, as we know it, is a modern phenomenon, although quite wrong in supposing that Mr Harry Blamires, to whose book *The Christian Mind* he makes a passing reference, would deny this. He continues:

> I do not believe that this age is wicked (and certainly not wicked above all others) because it is secular. I believe that the process of secularisation represents the same kind of shift in man's whole way of looking at the world as that which marked the transition from the Middle Ages to the Renaissance. That is to say, it is of its nature something towards which the Christian faith as such is neutral.

Then he adds, somewhat inconsistently, 'Or, rather, the Christian must welcome and respond to it as a God-given fact, as the world-view within which Christ has to be made flesh for modern man.'[3] I am reminded of the story of the Irishman during the war who, when he was reminded that he was a neutral, replied, 'Yes, but who am I supposed to be neutral against?'

Since secularism is by definition the belief that there is no God, it is difficult to see why the Christian should welcome it as a God-given fact, except in the sense that all evils provide opportunities for the grace of God and for the exercise of Christian virtues; this does not, however, appear to be what Robinson means. The phrase 'the world-view within which Christ has to be made flesh for modern man' is highly questionable, with its suggestion that the incarnation is a psychological process which has to be repeated within successive world-views. But what seems to me to be most open to dispute—or at least in need of

[1] ibid., p. 243.
[2] ibid., pp. 247f.
[3] ibid., p. 249.

clarification—is the comparison of the modern process of secularisation with the transition from the Middle Ages to the Renaissance. The term 'Renaissance' is itself very ambiguous. If it is intended to signify the upsurge of an attitude to life in which God is believed not to exist and man to be the primary object of his own concern, then the transition from the Middle Ages to the Renaissance would seem to be not something comparable with modern secularisation but the first phase in it. If, on the other hand, the Renaissance is taken to include merely the scientific, technological and artistic aspects of the situation, there would seem to be no comparison to be made between the transition from the Middle Ages to the Renaissance, in *this* sense, and secularisation, which involves the total rejection of any transcendent reality beyond the phenomena of the senses. But in any case, what would seem to be called for is neither 'neutrality' on the part of Christians nor 'welcome and response', but a sympathetic and critical assessment of the situation from the standpoint of the Christian faith. However, we can, I think, agree with Robinson's diagnosis of secularisation as 'a revolt against three ways of viewing the world, and probably four, which have been intimately bound up in the past with the presentation of the Christian gospel'. He continues:

> The fourth (to take it first) is the whole possibility of *metaphysics* as a meaningful enterprise. Whether, or in what sense, the Gospel can be given expression without recourse to metaphysical statements I do not know. That is why I have left the issue open. So much depends on what one means by metaphysics, and I am not a linguistic philosopher.[1]

It is difficult to know what to do with a passage like this. But it seems to break down somewhat as follows: (1) We must first decide what we mean by metaphysics. (2) Then we must decide whether metaphysics so defined is meaningful. (3) Then we must decide whether the Gospel can be expressed without metaphysics. (4) Then, in the light of our answers to (2) and (3) we must decide whether the Gospel can be expressed at all. (5) Linguistic philosophers come into this somewhere. (6) Robinson is not a linguistic philosopher. (7) Therefore Robinson has left 'the Issue' (i.e. presumably, No. (3)) open.

[1] ibid., p. 249.

The whole passage reads very much like a confession of incompetence. One thing, however, is, I think, clear, and that is that from the beginning of his exposition Robinson has not left the issue open. He has opted for one particular metaphysical doctrine ('ground-of-being' metaphysics) and tried to give expression to the Gospel in that. For reasons which I have stated at length, I do not think he has succeeded. It is, however, interesting to notice that at this point he speaks in terms of great appreciation of Dr Paul van Buren's book *The Secular Meaning of the Gospel*. As I have discussed that book in detail in another chapter, I need not say much about it here. But it is worth noting that it embodies a very consistent and unambiguous attempt to secularise the presentation of the Gospel. And, although Robinson seems not to have observed this, its conclusion is that there is no God (not even in the 'ground-of-being' sense) and that neither Jesus nor anyone else survives bodily death.

Robinson has little to say in amplification of his previous explanation of what he means by saying that God is personal; it is 'that at its deepest level the reality in which [the Christian's] life is rooted cannot be described exhaustively in terms of impersonal, mathematical regularities but only in the last resort in terms of an utterly gracious and unconditional love, which he can trust as implicitly as at another level he can trust the regularities which science describes'.[1] (Can this really mean that Robinson's trust in God is no firmer than his trust in scientific theory, or has he for once been guilty of careless writing?) But he goes much farther than he has gone before in 'translating' statements about God into statements about our experience. 'The doctrine of the Trinity', he says, 'is not, as it has often been represented, a model of the divine life as it is in itself. It is a formula or definition describing the distinctively Christian encounter with God.'[2] Nevertheless he says quite categorically that 'the doctrine of the Trinity is about God'. And again, 'the doctrine is to the experienced reality what the map is to the earth or a model for the scientist',[3] so that what the doctrine describes is the reality experienced and not the experience itself; not, in spite of the earlier statement, the encounter. Robinson's

[1] ibid., p. 253.
[2] ibid., p. 254.
[3] ibid., p. 256.

language may be imprecise, but here at least his meaning seems to be fairly orthodox.

The next feature of secularism, he tells us, is its rejection of the *supranaturalistic* world-view, and here he has nothing very fresh to say. But what is very noticeable is the defensive attitude which he now adopts. There is nothing about the most fundamental categories of our theology going into the melting, and he explicitly denies that the language about depth or the ground of being was 'anything radically new'. And, while expressing his personal gratitude to Tillich, he says that 'if dogmatic theologians or philosophers cleverer than [him]self find [Tillich's ontology] unsatisfactory [he] will not argue with them'. Furthermore, he withdraws any impression he may have given that he was trying to *define* God into existence, 'the impression that anyone who takes seriously the depth and mysteries of life must believe in God'. He rephrases his question thus: 'The question of God is whether these experiences of depth (and everything else in life) are to be interpreted in terms of "Being as gracious" [the term is borrowed from Dr John Macquarrie]—that is, for the Christian, in terms of the grace of our Lord Jesus Christ and the love of God and the fellowship of the Holy Spirit.'[1] Again he writes: 'Tillich's phrase "the ground of being" is simply a possible (and quite traditional) way of indicating another "projection" (apart from supranaturalism and naturalism) in which all the great biblical language about God may be cast. It is not in any sense intended to be a substitute for the images of Father and the rest, or to do business for them.'[2] This is indeed a welcome clarification, but one is left wondering whether Robinson has seen its implication. This is that the attempt to persuade the atheist that, because he had an ultimate concern 'in depth', he 'really' believed in God must be abandoned as dishonest. All that the great programme of 'radical recasting' and throwing everything into the melting has resulted in is the simple fact that modern man can now be told that, if and when he has brought himself to believe that the ground of all being is the personal loving Father who is revealed in Christ, he need not think of the Father as 'up there' or 'out there'. This is something that might surely have been done with less fuss.

[1] ibid., pp. 260f.
[2] ibid., p. 263.

In discussing the third characteristic of secularism—its rejection of the *mythological*—Robinson adds little to what he has said before. One thing seems plain: that, while he does not deny the possibility of the miraculous events which the Gospels describe, he considers the question of their factuality quite secondary; what matters is their 'theological *significance*'. What is not considered is whether, at least in some cases, the theological significance will be the same if the factuality is denied. This is a very large question, and I have discussed it elsewhere in this book.

In his comment on the last characteristic of secularism—its rejection of the *religious*—Robinson does little but repeat the paradoxes of Bonhoeffer. ' "God is teaching us that we must live as men who can get along very well without him", that is, without having to bring him in.' Nevertheless, we are told that we can find him after all. 'Our God is the God who forsakes us—only to meet with us on the Emmaus road, if we are really prepared to abandon him as a long-stop and find him not at the boundaries of life where human powers fail, but at the centre, in the secular, as "the 'beyond' in our midst".'[1] I do not know whether other people find this as obscure as I do. Do we *not* find him 'at the boundaries of life where human powers fail'? Was that not, in fact, where Bonhoeffer found him in the prison-camp? Is he not, in fact, to be found *everywhere*? Robinson seems to suggest that we can find him everywhere *except* in the sphere of religion, but his use of the term 'religion' is so idiosyncratic that we are left wondering about his exact meaning. The following paragraph, however, seems to make one point clear.

Bonhoeffer's insistence that Christ must be met 'at the centre of life', we are told, 'echoes that of Christian spirituality all down the ages'. Bonhoeffer has, however, introduced a 'new factor' which is so important that its description is printed in italics—'*at the centre of a life where a religious sector can no longer be presupposed as a special point of entry or contact*'. And this means that 'men and women are coming to commitment to Christ as the clue to life not because they are specially drawn by "religion" nor because he meets them as the answer to their "religious" needs. . . . They look for a Christ who could be Lord of a genuinely secular world, who does not require of them that they

[1] ibid., p. 271.

become religious first before they can become Christian.'[1] And this contribution, we have been told above, could not have been made before the middle of the twentieth century.

In discussing this we are inevitably hampered by the ambiguity of the term 'religious' in Robinson's usage, but I take it that what is meant is that large numbers of men and women today develop an intense devotion to Christ and an intense desire to find him in the occupations of their daily life which they share with their non-Christian friends, but have no desire to become members of the Christian Church, take part in religious services, receive the sacraments, say their prayers or confess their sins. This does not seem to me to be anything very new; what is new is the assumption by a Christian bishop that this is a good thing. Robinson quotes from the Dutch Professor Hans Hoekendijk a passage containing the following sentences:

> We will not be able really to get alongside man in our modern world unless we begin to 'dereligionise' Christianity. Christianity is a secular movement, and this is basic for an understanding of it. We have no business to make it a religion again. That would mean a correction of what Christ has done. And we have no business to make a Christian into a *homo religiosus* again, a religious man, a normal human being plus something. The Christian is simply a man who is in the process of being restored to normal manhood.[2]

This is extremely revealing, for it manifests an assumption that the 'religious' and the 'secular' or, to use the traditional terms, the 'supernatural' and the 'natural', are radically opposed. This opposition is, of course, characteristic of a type of Protestantism which has been extremely influential, for which the fallen 'natural' man is incurable and whose 'religion', while it may rescue him, by faith in Christ, from eternal damnation, can do nothing to transform his natural condition. It is hardly surprising that modern men who have been brought up to think of religion in these terms should react into a violent secularism which is compatible with devotion to Jesus Christ but for which the whole paraphernalia of religion is anathema. The Catholic doctrine, that grace both presupposes nature and supernaturalises it, making it not less but more natural in the process,

[1] ibid., pp. 271f.
[2] ibid., pp. 272f.

justifies no such antithesis.[1] It will agree with Hoekendijk that 'the Christian is simply a man who is in the process of being restored to normal manhood', but it will add that the means by which he is being restored is supernatural grace. So far from this making 'religion', in the proper and normal sense of that word, unnecessary, it will demand it. But equally religion demands the secular as the medium for its redemptive activity. And it is only in this way that the secular can achieve a true understanding of itself. What we are called to in this twentieth century is not the abandonment of the accumulated treasures of our Christian heritage, but their putting at the service of the contemporary world. This will involve us in tasks of interpretation which will tax us to the uttermost as we try to interpret Christian truth not only to Western industrialised, secularised man, but also to the people of the East and of Africa, with their own great heritages of philosophic thought and religious practice. After this long and, I fear, extremely tedious examination of Dr Robinson's programme, I can only repeat, though in a sense presumably different from that which he intended, that, in its exclusive concern with one small section of our own community, it is not too radical but not nearly radical enough. It does not get down to the roots.

[1] Cf. ch. iv *infra*.

CHAPTER FOUR

SCIENCE, THE SECULAR AND THE SUPERNATURAL

L'extraordinaire univers, si naturellement naturel, à la fois et si surnaturellement chrétien! Solide, stable, créé dans le temps mais pour l'éternité, ce monde où chaque nature est douée de son être et de son efficace propre n'en opère moins qu'en vertu de l'efficace divine, dont son être est d'être l'effet, et en vue de Dieu qui, comme il en est la cause, en est la fin.

—Étienne Gilson.

ONE VERY NOTABLE feature characterises the restatements, reinterpretations and recastings of the Christian religion which we have been considering in this book, and in particular those of Dr van Buren and Dr Robinson. This is the assumption that anything that can be described as 'supranatural' or 'supernatural' is old-fashioned and indefensible and that anything that can be described as 'secular' is up to date and commendable.

It is related of a well-known English philosopher that when he was asked 'Do you think life is worth while?' he replied 'It all depends on what you mean by "while".' It is, in fact, always well to pay careful attention to the definition of one's terms, especially when they have acquired emotional or evaluative overtones, and, as in the context of the present discussion, this is particularly true of these two words 'supernatural' and 'secular', I shall specify as clearly as I can the senses in which I propose to use them. In doing this I shall, I think, simply be clarifying their normal use in educated English.

By 'the secular' I shall mean that whole body of thought and activity which is concerned with man's life in what is sometimes called 'this world', a life which begins with the fertilisation of an ovum by a spermatozoon and ends with bodily death. Thus there is excluded from the sphere of 'the secular' any concern which a man may have with a possible future life after death and any concern which he may have, even during 'this life', with an order of reality (if such there be) which transcends the experience of the senses. Thus, as I shall use it, the word 'secular' will correspond to one of the traditional meanings of that much overworked word 'natural'. 'Secular', it must be noted, is not simply synonymous with 'material', if this last word is taken to refer to physical matter, as it normally is today. A man who believed in neither God nor immortality but ascribed supreme value to the acquisition of mathematical knowledge or the appreciation of music could be validly described as a secularist, but hardly as a materialist. And, of course, a man may believe in the reality and importance of the secular without being a 'secularist'; that is to say, he may believe that 'this world' is real and valuable without believing that it is the only reality or that its reality and value are supreme and ultimate. It may be useful to quote the following words from Dr Demant in this connection:

> The essential characteristic of secularism is independent of the nature which secularism gives to what it regards as ultimately real; it is still secularist even when that reality is mental or spiritual, and not only when it is material or biological.[1]

And again:

> The ancient paganisms, the Bible and the Christian Church all have this in common, that they hold the source of all things to be a divine reality which transcends the world as well as operating in it. The secularisms of today have this in common, that they hold the meaning of the world to lie within itself.[2]

By 'the supernatural', in contrast, I shall mean the whole body of thought and activity which is concerned with man's life as a member of 'another world', which sees his life in 'this world' as deriving ultimately from that 'other world', and which sees his final destiny as lying in that 'other world' and beyond bodily death. If a man is a Christian theist, he will associate that 'other world' with a beneficent Creator, upon whose will 'this world' is dependent for its existence and its preservation and in union with whom his own beatitude will consist. In this sense, which is

[1] *Religion and the Decline of Capitalism*, p. 113.
[2] ibid., p. 111.

that commonly given it by theologians, the term 'supernatural' has, of course, nothing to do with spooks and hauntings—'Tales of Terror and the Supernatural'; nor is the contrast between the supernatural and the natural the same as the contrast between the miraculous and the non-miraculous, if 'miraculous' is taken, as it usually is, to refer to some *ad hoc* intervention of divine power into the natural order of things, obeying no rules and conforming to no principles of prediction. As Christian theology sees it, the grace which human beings receive through prayer and the sacramental life of the Church is strictly supernatural, for it is directed towards the attainment of the vision of God in heaven; it is, however, not strictly miraculous, for, no less than the workings of the natural order, it has its own pattern of operation to which it conforms. On the other hand, a miracle, while it can hardly avoid being supernatural in its source, may be purely natural in its end and purpose, as if, for example, by divine intervention a sick man is restored to bodily health. To consider the relation between the supernatural on the one hand and the secular or natural on the other is one of the purposes of this chapter.

As writers such as Ogden, van Buren and Robinson have rightly emphasised, the world in which we live today is dominated by the achievements and outlook of science, and no argument will be needed to establish the fact that science, as such, is entirely concerned with the secular. Its successes in this realm are too obvious to need comment. It is no disparagement whatever of science if one adds that this very success in the secular realm has produced in the great mass of civilised people today an attitude which may be fairly described not merely as secular but as secularist, an attitude for which 'this world' is the only reality of which they need seriously to take account. While this attitude has, of course, affected scientists themselves, it has, I think, affected them rather less than most other people, for they are in a better position to recognise the limitations of their own expertise. The really hard-boiled secularists are to be found today far more among philosophers and historians than among scientists; but they are to be found most of all among the people who make no claim to be intellectuals of any kind, among the great mass of our population, who have been conditioned, by the gigantic achievements of scientific technology, to accept the world as simply so much raw material for human enjoyment and exploitation, without any consideration of its ultimate basis and source. As regards scientists themselves, Dr W. H. Thorpe has recorded his judgment that 'a far higher proportion than formerly of practising biologists are, at least in this country, active and concerned members of various Christian communities and communions',[1] and this is, I think, true no less of physical than of biological scientists. Certainly a large number of books have appeared in recent years in which scientists of very varied types have given reasoned expression to their conviction of the truth of Christianity and have argued not merely that Christianity and science are compatible but also that it is only in the light of Christian doctrine that the scientific exploit and achievement can be seen to make sense. The Jesuit palaeontologist Pierre Teilhard de Chardin, in his much discussed work *The Phenomenon of Man*, has provided perhaps the most famous example of this, but there are works by other writers, such as the late Sir Edmund Whittaker,[2] Dr William G. Pollard[3] and Dr J. D. Lambert,[4] beside that of Dr Thorpe from which I have just quoted, which are not less impressive for being less lyrical and visionary and whose writers cannot be suspected of having any professional axe to grind.[5]

Now, the first point which needs to be stressed is that Christian theology, while it holds that man's existence has a supernatural ground and that his final destiny is in the supernatural realm, holds not less emphatically that the secular realm, just because it is God's creation, has a God-given status of its own and that science, whose concern is, as we have seen, with the secular realm has a genuine, though dependent autonomy. To see the matter in its true proportions we must indulge in a brief historical retrospect.

It has been remarked by a number of writers, in particular the late Alfred North Whitehead, that the rise of empirical science is closely connected with belief in the Christian doctrine of God. 'Faith in the possibility of science', Whitehead wrote, 'generated

[1] *Biology and the Nature of Man*, p. xi.
[2] *Space and Spirit.*
[3] *Chance and Providence; Physicist and Christian.*
[4] *Science and Sanctity.*
[5] Not, indeed, that Teilhard received very much encouragement from the authorities of his Church and his order.

antecedently to the development of modern scientific theory, is an unconscious derivative from medieval theology.'[1] For the scientific method makes two assumptions: first, that there are *regularities* in the world, since otherwise there would be nothing for science to discover; secondly, that these realities are *contingent* and so need to be looked for, since otherwise they could simply be predicted *a priori*. This combination of assumptions is completely incompatible with the fundamental position of ancient Greek thought, which was that, in so far as the world is intelligible, it is so because it embodies pure forms which can be known, and can only be known, by philosophic contemplation, and that in so far as the world does not embody the pure forms it cannot be known at all. The combination of assumptions is, however, fully compatible with the Christian doctrine of creation, for which the world owes both its origin and its continuing existence to the activity of a God who is both intelligence and will, both rationality and power, consistent and yet free. Because he is rational, the world which he makes will embody patterns and regularities; but because he is free, the particular patterns and regularities which it embodies can be discovered (in default of direct information from God himself) only by examining it for ourselves, that is by applying the scientific method; and the astounding success which has followed the application of the scientific method provides very strong confirmation of the assumptions on which it is founded. The point was thoroughly understood by the great pioneers of English

[1] *Science and the Modern World*, ch. i. Cf. my *Christian Theology and Natural Science*, ch. iii.

M. Rémy Chauvin, after discussing the tradition of Brahmanism and Buddhism and its resemblances with and differences from the motivational system of Western Christianity, concludes that, for all their admirable heroism, the rejection of the world and the doctrine of *karma* which characterise these great Asian religions thwart the evolutionary march of the religious motivation of man and are in addition basically antagonistic to the scientific spirit. He writes:

> Christianity supported with its immense authority two essential concepts: (*a*) The world has a meaning, since it is the work of a sovereignly intelligent God. (*b*) This meaning is adapted to man and renders the universe worthy of interest, since it is the work of a sovereignly good God. . . . It is not by chance that science, while born in Greece, has developed only in Christendom. And if in the Middle Ages we almost did take the 'oriental' turn of which De Rougemont speaks, we caught ourselves very quickly. (*God of the Scientists, God of the Experiment*, p. 104.)

science. Dr Richard S. Westfall has pointed out, in his enthralling book *Science and Religion in Seventeenth-century England*, that the scientific 'virtuosi' of the seventeenth century—men such as Boyle, Hooke and, above all, the great Newton—made a devoted attempt to reconcile the newly born mathematical physics with the Christian religion. The tragedy was that, because the Newtonian physics was basically deterministic, the only places where there appeared to be room for divine activity were in the initial bringing of the universe into being and in the filling up of the gaps which were believed to exist in the deterministic structure. Newton himself believed that there were two very notable gaps within which God's intervention was needed to keep the fabric in existence. He had to prevent the fixed stars from collapsing together and he had to prevent the irregularities in the motions of the planets and their satellites from bringing the solar system to destruction.[1] When, however, Laplace showed that in fact the solar system was stable under these irregularities, there was very little left for God to do. (The other problem—why the stars did not collapse together—was tactfully mentioned only in undertones until the advent of relativity-theory.) Dr Westfall has traced in detail the way in which, almost unconsciously and certainly unintentionally, as time went on, the virtuosi brought about their reconciliation of Christianity with science by modifying Christianity to the point of destruction. (There may be a lesson for some of our contemporaries here!) 'While they were protesting vigorously that natural philosophy was in harmony with Christianity, they were quietly and perhaps unconsciously altering Christianity to meet their own definition.' Thus Providence was interpreted simply as 'the general benevolence of the original creation and the continual sustenance of the natural order'. 'In theory natural religion was meant to supplement Christianity, to provide it with a rational foundation; in practice it tended to displace it.' 'In defending Christianity in this manner, they prepared the ground for the deists of the enlightenment—the mechanical universe run by immutable natural laws, the transcendent God removed and separated from his creation, the moral law which took the place of spiritual worship, the rational man able to

[1] Cf. E. A. Burtt, *Metaphysical Foundations of Modern Physical Science*, pp. 280ff.

discover the true religion without the aid of special revelation.'[1] Thus, in Whitehead's words, we get the Newtonian forces as nothing less than the imposed conditions provided by a God who 'made his appearance in religion under the frigid title of the First Cause and was appropriately worshipped in white-washed churches'.[2] What physics failed to do in the eighteenth century in the matter of eliminating God was triumphantly completed by evolutionary biology in the nineteenth, when natural selection successfully ousted divine design. No longer could it be maintained that God had thoughtfully provided the horse with backward-turning ears so that it could more efficiently hear its master's voice. But that is another story.

It must be emphasised at this point that the progressive elimination of God in the course of this rearguard action was due to the fact that the basic laws of Newtonian physics were completely deterministic in their form; the only room left for God was in the gaps, if any such there were, in which they failed to apply. Furthermore, their success in the fields of physics and astronomy was so outstanding that phenomena, such as those of electricity and magnetism, which were discovered later, were forced into line with them, and it was even assumed, though direct proof was lacking, that biological phenomena could be reduced to them as well, so that human freedom tended to vanish no less than divine control. It is therefore important to stress the fact that the basic laws of physics which have now replaced those of Newton are not deterministic. (At the very least we may say that the supporters of determinism, such as Bohm and De Broglie, are now a struggling minority, who justify themselves by their faith rather than by their works.)[3] The exact way in which this basic indeterminacy may be related both to divine control and human freedom cannot be discussed here, but I would in passing refer to the very interesting way in which Sir John Eccles, in *The Neurophysiological Basis of Mind*, has constructed a possible model for the interrelation of human volition and the laws of quantum mechanics.[4] The essential point is that the postulate on which the flight from traditional

[1] op. cit., pp. 71, 102, 106, 219.

[2] *Adventures of Ideas*, ch. viii.

[3] Cf. D. Bohm, *Causality and Chance in Modern Physics*, *passim*; Louis De Broglie, *The Revolution in Physics*, pp. 220ff.

[4] Cf. my *Christian Theology and Natural Science*, pp. 225ff.

theism was based has been abandoned by modern physicists. Whether the flight was necessary, given the initial postulate, may itself be doubted, but the question is now purely academic, as it presupposes an abandoned hypothesis. And in saying this I am, of course, implying no disparagement of the colossal intellectual stature of Newton and his successors.

The way is now open for a clear reaffirmation, from the side of Christian theology, of the God-given autonomy of the positive sciences. That God is free to intervene in the natural order, when he sees fit, is admittedly involved in any belief in his sovereignty and his power. That he will not do so incessantly or capriciously is no less involved in his rationality and wisdom. Just what such intervention will involve when it does occur is, I think, very difficult to say, though I agree with C. S. Lewis that the metaphor of God feeding into nature new food for her to digest is more helpful than that of God forcibly overruling nature's laws.[1] There is nothing unscientific in holding that the introduction of a new factor into a situation will produce new effects, and such a new factor is what, from the scientist's point of view, such an intervention will be. But it must be stressed that, if God does so intervene, he intervenes into a situation which itself exists only because he has established it and maintains it. It is worth remarking that traditional theology, while it has looked upon miracles as being striking and sometimes startling manifestations of God's activity, has been equally anxious to see his activity as involved in the day-by-day existence and functioning of the natural order of the world, and has, in fact, based its classical arguments for God's existence and attributes on the latter rather than the former. It is well known that the Church's official attitude to alleged miracles is one of considerable scepticism and reserve; this is not due to cynicism or timidity. It is due, first, to the conviction that, though miracles undoubtedly occur, they will not occur very frequently, since God has given the world a metaphysical structure and a nature which, while basically open to new influxes of divine activity, is in general sufficient for the purposes for which the world was made;[2] secondly, because it is in general very difficult to distinguish a genuine miracle from a spurious one; thirdly, because it is not

[1] *Miracles*, ch. viii.

[2] Cf. the quotation from C. S. Lewis on p. 236 *infra*.

usually important to distinguish them in any case, since miracles will usually have done whatever they were meant to do simply by occurring; and fourthly, because people ought not to be encouraged to base their religion on stunts or thrills. It may, nevertheless, be added that, while in a credulous age many events will no doubt be taken as being miraculous when they are not, in an incredulous age many events will be taken as not being miraculous when they are.[1] In any case, neither credulity nor incredulity is the preserve of any particular age; there are credulous readers of our Sunday papers, and there are incredulous characters in the Gospels. However, the point that I am concerned to make here is that, while on the Christian view miracles will sometimes occur, this does not alter the fact that the Christian belief in a God who is both free and rational provides the soundest justification for that empirical investigation of the universe which is specially characteristic of modern science. In contrast, the tough-minded secularist philosophy of Hume, for all its claims to be scientific and empirical, is unable to provide any grounds for supposing that the world will manifest any future regularity at all. There are, of course, deplorable examples of stupid interference by well-meaning but ill-informed theologians and religious officials in purely scientific matters (Galileo and the Inquisition, Huxley and Wilberforce spring to all our minds), but such interference is not peculiar to religious dogmatists. The case of the Soviet biologist Lysenko will strike a note in our memories, and we may also recall the protest made by Sir Bernard Lovell in his Reith Lectures of 1958 against the domination of cosmological research in Russia by Marxist presuppositions.[2] Even scientists themselves can be intolerant to one another; there are, for example, the cases of the shocking persecution of Cantor by his fellow mathematician Kronecker

[1] As Dr R. M. Grant has written: 'It is held that ancient people accepted miracles while modern ones rightly reject them. Such a generalisation is false. In antiquity, as in modern times, some believed in miracles while others did not. Such conclusions, negative in the face of contemporary scholarly clichés, can be reached not by reading modern summaries but by looking at the heterogeneous testimonies given by first-century men.' (*Historical Introduction to the New Testament*, p. 85.) And again, with regard to the New Testament miracles: 'We cannot get rid of these stories by ascribing them to an "ancient world view". The ancients were well aware that bodies heavier than water sink in it.' (ibid., p. 328.)

[2] *The Individual and the Universe*, ch. ii.

and the attacks of Kolbe on his fellow chemist Van 't Hoff.[1]

There is, however, one quite serious point which has been raised recently with great frankness by a Catholic scientist, Dr Peter Anderson, in a paper entitled 'Does Science foster materialism?'[2] It is concerned with intercessory prayer, and the author points out that, as a result of scientific research, more and more of the events which Christians used to look upon as under the direct and unmediated direction of God, and which they were accustomed to make the object of intercessory prayer—the weather, recovery from sickness and so on—are now seen to be included in the normal operation of natural laws, so that to expect God to intervene to change their course would be tantamount to demanding a succession of miracles in the strict sense. Thus Dr Anderson writes:

> There was time when a patient's recovery from pneumonia was thought to be in the hands of God and now it is in the hands of drugs. In fact, of course, God acts no more nor no less directly in this crisis than he did before the discovery of sulphonamides, but sloppy theological ideas allow us to think that he does. It has often seemed to me that the frequency with which we offer prayers for fine weather reflects the rather undeveloped state of the science of meteorology.

There is clearly a very large question here and I wonder whether sufficient attention has been given to the element of indeterminacy which, in the view of the dominant 'Copenhagen school' of theoretical physicists, is inherent in the elementary processes of nature. But I entirely agree with Dr Anderson's insistence that science has done a great service to religion, as well as providing a specious ground for unbelief, in making it difficult for us to look upon the filing of requests for particular benefits as the central concern of prayer. He continues as follows:

> Now, I am not advocating that we should no longer pray for the sick or for clement weather; all I am trying to suggest is that there is something seriously wrong with the theological basis of our prayer if its tone is radically altered—or it ceases altogether

[1] Cf. M. Polanyi, *Personal Knowledge*, pp. 190, 156.

[2] Bulletin of the Philosophy of Science Group of the Newman Society, May 1964, pp. 6ff.

—when some new discovery of science dispels ignorance of natural events. Surely what is needed is a reorientation of these prayers in a way which emphasises man's *total* dependence on God, rather than as subscribing to a view of God acting by a spasmodic granting of favours, and warding off dangers here and there. I am suggesting that sloppy religious teaching does not lead to a concept of God acting *totally* through all the phenomena we observe, nor to a concept of grace whereby man lives totally with something of the life of the God in him, but on the contrary to a view of God acting piecemeal, here and there listening to a prayer and *intervening* in the illness or the thunderstorm, acting in those spheres of life where we do not understand the phenomena—where we cannot with any confidence predict the result. If this is the basis of our prayer, of how man sees his relationship with God, then we must expect that every discovery of science which dispels ignorance and every application of technology which gives a feeling of security and well-being, leaves one less aspect of life into which God enters. And consequently we must expect science to foster materialism; and we must attribute this, not to any fault of science and the pursuit of knowledge, nor to any fault of those who develop techniques which give man greater security, more leisure and so on, but to sloppy religious teaching.

This is, I think, a thoroughly accurate diagnosis of the situation and it is fully in line with our previous discussion. There are, in fact, two theological maxims that are very relevant to our present concern. Grace, we are told, presupposes Nature; and Grace does not destroy Nature but perfects it. That is to say, in our present vocabulary, the supernatural neither ignores the secular nor rejects it, but needs it as the foundation and the material for its own task, while at the same time stimulating the secular to perform *its* own task according to its own proper methods. This is, of course, the statement of an ideal situation, which can only be approximated to in actual practice. In a fallen world, there are only too likely to be misunderstandings, infringements of territory, attempts to dominate and the like, arising from human perversity and stupidity. The fact nevertheless remains that, as Christianity envisages him, man is a being who is organically part of the secular order, while at the same time having a supernatural origin and a supernatural destiny; and these two aspects of his existence, while they are interwoven in a way whose complexity baffles description, are nevertheless distinct and discernible. In an ultimate sense, the secular exists for the sake of the supernatural, for man's earthly life ends with his bodily death, while his supernatural life does not. Nevertheless, the secular has a real autonomy, although a secondary one; so that, for example, a scientist will best make his scientific work subserve man's supernatural destiny, not by applying to the custodians of supernatural revelation for directives about his experimenting and his theorising, but by doing his scientific work to the best of his ability in accordance with its own traditions and canons. There may, of course, be occasions in the course of his work when he is faced with difficult ethical problems, and the decisions which he then makes will, it is to be hoped, be related to the beliefs which he holds as a Christian about the nature, dignity, predicament and destiny of the world and of man. It is, however, not only the scientist who is a Christian who is faced with ethical problems; they arise for everyone, whether Christian or non-Christian, whether scientist or non-scientist, in the mere process of living a human life and doing a human job. And, while it is true, in a sense, that being a Christian raises ethical problems that would not otherwise arise (though it would be truer to say that it directs attention to ethical problems that might otherwise be ignored), it is also true that it frequently helps in the decision of ethical problems that might otherwise be practically insoluble. Thus, for example, the Christian belief in the *theological* unity of the human race (which does not, of course, prejudge the question of its *biological* unity) would indicate a very definite answer to the ethical problem whether it is legitimate to use members of particular human groups as mere raw material for experiments, the results of which may be hoped to be of benefit to others. The moral issues which face both scientists and other workers in the secular field are, however, often extremely complicated, and they have become more so in recent years, especially in those realms, such as psychology, neurophysiology, chemotherapy and genetics, where scientific research has rendered possible new and potentially alarming interferences with human personality and indeed with the future of the human race. The solution of these problems needs, as I see it, the closest co-operation between theologians and workers in the various secular fields in an atmosphere not of conflict but of mutual respect and confidence; much fruitful work of this kind is, in fact, being done, but much more is needed.

The dual character of the secular order as having its own genuine autonomy and as at the same time being instrumental to man's supernatural destiny provides the key to the inspiring and controversial figure whom I have already mentioned, Père Teilhard de Chardin. Both from the theological and from the scientific point of view, it is easy to convict him of rash and undisciplined speculation, though some of the difficulty of assessing his achievement arises from the antecedent difficulty of knowing to what literary *genre* his works belong. They are neither straight theology nor straight philosophy nor straight science, nor yet a combination of the three; they might perhaps best be described as theologico-scientific rhapsody. It is not surprising that some detached observers have found them exciting and inspiring, and others exciting and infuriating; we can set Sir Julian Huxley on the one side[1] against Dr Medawar on the other,[2] while we have also the critical but sympathetic studies of Père Rabut[3] and M. Nicolas Corte.[4] With all his limitations, both as a scientist and as a theologian, the conviction that underlay his scientific research was that, simply by doing his job as a palaeontologist, he was helping to bring the world that God had created and redeemed towards the end for which God had created and redeemed it. For him, therefore, the discovery and study of human origins, the tracing of human evolution and the forecasting of man's future were simply an extension into the secular realm of the activity in which he was engaged when he said Mass at the altar each morning, a perfecting and a utilisation of nature by grace. Whether he was entirely successful is a matter of doubt; it is arguable that, in his anxiety to maintain the organic relation between the secular and the supernatural, he failed to respect the proper autonomy of either and that both his theology and his science suffered in consequence. Be that as it may, his writings are unique of their kind, and we can learn a great deal both from his success and

[1] Foreword to the English edition of *The Phenomenon of Man.*

[2] Review of *The Phenomenon of Man* in *Mind*, LXX (1961), pp. 99ff.

[3] O. Rabut, *Dialogue with Teilhard de Chardin.*

[4] *Pierre Teilhard de Chardin: his life and spirit.*

from his failure. What as a theologian I heartily acclaim is his burning conviction that the work of the scientist who is a Christian (and in his case a Christian priest) is itself an extension of the priestly activity by which the Church as Christ's body offers God's creation to him, and is an organic part of that transformation of the world and of the human race by the redemptive grace of God which will culminate in the consummation which Christian theology sums up as 'the Resurrection of the Body' and 'the Life Everlasting'. Many biologists, in particular Sir Julian Huxley[1] and Dr C. H. Waddington,[2] have stressed the fact that, with the appearance in the evolutionary process of man as a conscious, rational and reflective being, evolution itself reaches a new stage, for man can understand the nature of the process and can therefore deliberately influence its future course. The question thus arises what that course should be, and it is a very live question in view of the possibilities of changing the natures of living beings, including man, which research in genetics is now beginning to provide. Without indulging in the wilder type of science-fiction we must frankly face the question 'What do we want man to be?' May I answer this question by quoting some words which I have written elsewhere:

> The Christian, remembering that God himself has become man, can only reply that he wants man to be man. This may sound a somewhat unadventurous and uninspiring answer, but it is in fact nothing of the sort. Christianity does not believe that God became man simply in order to bring human history to a full stop and to reduce man to the status of a divinely certificated fossil. The Incarnation did not only set upon man the seal by which God guarantees man's imperishable importance and inalienable dignity; it brought into the world a new thing and inaugurated a new era of human history. The human organism which the Son of God took from his Virgin Mother and in which he died and rose from the dead was not destroyed by his resurrection and ascension; it was transfigured and glorified and made accessible to men. . . . By the new birth of baptism [a man or woman] becomes a member of the restored human race, whose first member and head is Jesus Christ, as by his natural birth he became a member of the fallen human race, the race of the sons of Adam. His further

[1] Cf. 'The Evolutionary Process', in *Evolution as a Process*
[2] *The Ethical Animal*, *passim*.

> progress is then not progress within the natural order, but within the supernatural order of grace and redemption, though within the supernatural order the natural order will itself be fulfilled and transfigured. And what is God's will for individual human beings is his will for the human race. Sir Julian Huxley was speaking more truly than perhaps he realised when he wrote that with man a new method of evolutionary transformation has come into being, though 'evolutionary' is too weak a word to use. It is the method of incorporation into Christ's body and of being transformed into his likeness. What secularised man may do with his newly acquired power over himself it would be hazardous to predict. . . . The Christian has a different ideal, the building of human beings as living members into the organism of the Body of Christ. This is a task in which science, like every other human activity, can play its part, but only if it is determined that men are to be men. . . . For Christian faith, the ultimate term of human evolution is the Total Christ, consisting of Head and members in intimate union sharing a common supernatural life, as 'one mystical person',[1] in that final transfiguration of the whole created order which theology knows as the Resurrection of the Body for the Life Everlasting.[2]

I have tried, in the course of this discussion, by an initial clarification of the meanings of the terms 'secular' and 'supernatural', to show that it is possible to recognise the legitimate claims of the secular without becoming a secularist and without abandoning the traditional Christian belief in the primacy of the supernatural. I think it is through his omission to make this very necessary clarification that Dr Robinson's discussion is both ambiguous and confused; Dr van Buren, on the other hand, seems to me to be perfectly clear and to be quite simply a secularist. I hope I have also shown that it is possible for a Christian to be, in an accurate sense of the term, a *humanist*. It is a good many years ago now since M. Jacques Maritain drew the distinction between anthropocentric and theocentric humanism, and argued that the latter, in which man's life is orientated not towards himself but towards God, is the only humanism that does justice to man's nature as it actually is, that offers satisfaction to his deepest needs and aspirations and that justifies the

[1] St Thomas Aquinas, *Summa Theologiae*, III, xix, 4*c*.
[2] *Christian Theology and Natural Science*, pp. 314ff.

dignity which he believes himself to possess.[1] Anthropocentric, or as I would call it secularistic, humanism is, however, extremely vocal today and it usually claims to find its justification in the outlook and discoveries of modern scientific method. It is often called simply 'scientific humanism', though I would myself dispute this name on the ground that it begs the issue by the implied assumption that secularism and science go hand in hand. It has certainly considerable appeal in our modern technocratic civilisation, and theologians such as Ogden, van Buren and Robinson have been very much influenced by it. None of them, however, has subjected it to a rigorous examination. The most impressive attempt which I know to erect a secularist humanism on the basis of modern science is that which Dr C. H. Waddington adumbrated in 1942 in his book *Science and Ethics* and to which he has given more developed expression in his later work *The Ethical Animal*, which was published in 1960. I shall therefore give it detailed consideration.

The earlier attempts, such as those of the eighteenth-century rationalists, to construct a system of human ethics on a secularist foundation had at least the advantage of being able to start from a stable concept of man, even if it was the ancient Greek concept of man as a rational or a political animal and not the Christian concept of man as created in the image of God. With the advent of evolutionary theory the matter has become far more difficult, for man now appears as merely a product of the evolutionary process and, as Lord Russell argued in his famous essay 'A Free Man's Worship', it is difficult to see why he should be of any importance to the universe as a whole. However, Dr Waddington argues extremely ably and consistently and his discussion merits the most careful attention.

Like Sir Julian Huxley, Dr Waddington is anxious to maintain that, although man is a product of evolution, he is a product of a quite unique kind, at any rate as far as this planet is concerned. He sees man as the outcome of a succession of evolutionary improvements each of which is of a comparatively rare type ('open', as contrasted with 'closed', anagenesis) which does not, as is generally the case, render further improvements impossible. Further, with the arrival of man an entirely new mechanism of evolution has become possible—'socio-genetic'

[1] *True Humanism*, 1938 (French original, *Humanisme intégral*, 1936).

evolution—in which information is handed on from one generation to another, by a process of social teaching and learning which is vastly more speedy in its overall results than the process of mere biological heredity. 'In man', Dr Waddington writes, 'we have, in addition to the biological evolutionary system, a second one in which the mechanism of social transmission fills the role which in the biological realm falls to genetics, that of passing information from one generation to the next.'[1] And, he claims, what makes socio-genetic evolution possible is man's power to form ethical beliefs.

Dr Waddington's central theme is that evolution provides a criterion by which ethical judgments may be made. He admits that this assertion may look like a form of the naturalistic fallacy, which tries to define good in terms of some non-moral concept, but he claims to have eluded this snare. 'What I am trying to do', he says, 'is not to formulate another description by which goodness can be recognised, but a criterion by which beliefs concerning the nature of goodness can be judged', and he points out that a criterion for judgment is of a different logical status from the notion which is being judged;[2] what I do not find convincing, however, is the way in which he gets from one to the other. I fully agree with his assertion that an 'ought' can depend on an 'is',[3] but it seems to me that this transition can be validly made only if the ethical agent has a teleological character (i.e. if it embodies a purpose) deriving from a transcendent cause. You can run with the hare and hunt with the hounds only if the leading hound is the hound of heaven. It seems to me to make sense to assert that the good for man is that which promotes his attainment of the end for which God has made him, but I do not see how, without falling into a circular argument, one can hold with Dr Waddington that the evolutionary process itself provides a criterion for assessing the validity of ethical judgments,[4] even if one agrees with him that evolution itself manifests a 'direction' and that this is 'not merely a direction in which

[1] *The Ethical Animal*, p. 103. Canon G. B. Bentley has, however, remarked that this process of social transmission is sometimes, as at the present day, partly counteracted by a reluctance of the young to imitate or learn from their elders.

[2] op. cit., p. 176.

[3] ibid., p. 54.

[4] ibid., pp. 176, 204 *et al.*

progress happens to have occurred, but, in some of its aspects at least, it has the character of an inevitable consequence of the nature of the evolutionary process and the organisms involved in it.'[1] For, although it might be false, it would not be meaningless to say that the direction of the evolutionary process was bad and that we ought to do all we can to change it. Dr Waddington has an attractive belief in the general rightness of the evolutionary process and the worthwhileness of man, but this needs for its justification a theistic metaphysic or something very like one. The evolutionary process cannot be a judge in its own cause; only a criterion which transcends it can judge it. And in any case what Dr Waddington says elsewhere about man's power over socio-genetic evolution suggests that the evolutionary process itself may not be so inevitable as the passage I have quoted implies.

For, we must observe, Dr Waddington asserts that ethical beliefs furnish an evolutionary dynamic as well as an ethical criterion, when we come to the human level. 'Ethical beliefs', he says, 'play an essential role in enabling the human race to continue evolving in a direction which in general terms continues that of animal anagenesis, but by a mechanism which is peculiarly characteristic of *homo sapiens*.'[2] And again, 'the specifically human mode of evolution, based on socio-genetic transmission of information, essentially requires the existence, as a functional part of the mechanism, of something which must have many of the characteristics of ethical belief.'[3] That Dr Waddington is himself uneasy about his criterion is suggested by the fear which he shows of the consequences of consistently following out *any* ethical belief or system of ethical beliefs. 'So soon as it becomes employed as a guide for action', he tells us, 'a metaphysical system must attract to itself some degree of belief; and if, being a comprehensive system, it is taken as the sole guide, it becomes the vehicle for a monotone belief of the kind which, I have argued, is in danger of leading to a destructive schismogenesis. Thus the search for a unified metaphysics remains either an intellectual pastime having no important effects on human action, or it leads belief into the dangerous

[1] ibid., p. 65.
[2] ibid., p. 201.
[3] ibid., p. 202.

confinement of a single dimension.'[1] If, however, Dr Waddington is right in asserting that 'a complete system of thought . . . if it could be found, would bring to end the process of evolution which is the essence of the whole world of living things of which man is a part',[2] what are we to think of Dr Waddington's own system? In any case, is evolution to go on for ever? And what will happen to man if it does?

I think the basic weaknesses of Dr Waddington's thesis are apparent. You cannot use the evolutionary process as an ultimate criterion of ethical beliefs and at the same time use your ethical beliefs as the criterion by which you try to influence the evolutionary process. Furthermore, to identify the inevitable direction of the evolutionary process with the fulfilment of human welfare is to make a very large assumption indeed. Lord Russell exposed that fallacy in the essay to which I have referred; it is by no means obvious on empirical grounds that the evolutionary urge is specially interested in the happiness of man. Dr Waddington makes heroic efforts to escape from his vicious circle, but he never succeeds; only the appeal to some transcendent principle, such as the God of Christian theism, could enable him to do that.

I must also comment on another fallacy into which Dr Waddington falls, in common with most secularist humanists, and which helps him to gloss over the weaknesses which I have just mentioned; this is his habit of writing in terms of a hypostatised abstraction called 'man'. There is, of course, no harm in using the word 'man' in a sentence as long as we remember that it is really a collective term for 'men'; but Dr Waddington uses it as if 'man' was some kind of enduring entity, whose misery at one time could be compensated by its prosperity some centuries later. It cannot be too strongly emphasised that, apart from the theological sense (which Dr Waddington would not accept) in which we are all one man in Adam and in Christ, there is no such being as *man*, there are only *men*; and no glorification of the evolutionary process and its inevitable direction can contradict the equally inevitable and far more obvious fact that it is the individual men who are born, toil, suffer, rejoice, love, hate and, in the end, die. It is only in his last chapter that Dr Waddington

[1] ibid., p. 193.
[2] ibid., p. 195.

makes any real attempt to get to grips with the fact of death, and it is revealing that when he does he talks of death as if it was a quality of human nature rather than an event which each man has to undergo. 'We have', he says, 'to accept the fact that, in spite of the advances which man has made in some respects over his biological predecessors, it [*sc.*, death] still remains an essential part of his nature',[1] as if mortality was something like binocular vision or bipedal locomotion. The only suggestion that he can make about the problems raised by the ethics of death is that the answer is to be looked for in a consideration of the 'richness of experience' of those people who actually come into existence—a vague and easily abused criterion if ever there was one. And, while he finds it impossible to avoid some notion of original sin and of the Fall, he can only interpret them in terms of psychology and does not take seriously their radically moral character. Again and again, as one reads Dr Waddington's brilliant book, one is conscious that what it needs to hold it together is a rational theism of the type held by traditional Christianity. For, as is clear from his remorseless attacks on Taoism and Zen Buddhism,[2] what he is really concerned to defend is the general ethical outlook which he has inherited from a Christian cultural past, though he neither recognises its source nor perceives the only ground on which it can be rationally vindicated. No doubt it is chiefly the shortsightedness of Christians themselves that is to blame for his failure. I hope at least that my criticisms of his argument will have provided a concrete illustration of the thesis that I have tried to maintain in this discussion, that the supernatural, as traditional Christian theology conceives it, is no enemy to the scientific and the secular, but on the contrary provides their justification.

There is one further matter which needs attention in view of its importance in the sequel. I have emphasised that, on the Christian view, miracles, in the strict sense of an *ad hoc* intervention by divine power over and above God's normal concurrence with the natural processes, will not be expected to happen very frequently and that in any alleged case of a miracle it is wise to

[1] ibid., p. 213.

[2] It is perhaps noteworthy that the secularist Waddington is far less sympathetic towards Zen Buddhism than the Catholic Dom Aelred Graham; cf. the latter's *Zen Catholicism*.

adopt a provisionally negative attitude. Nevertheless, the middle way between scepticism and credulity is not easy to achieve in practice and, as in other matters, the attitude of the individual will be not unaffected by his personal temperament. But, when all allowance has been made for the psychological factors involved, the fact will remain that, as a mere matter of logic, miracles may be expected to occur more frequently in a religious context, especially that of the Church which is the continuing body on earth of the Incarnate Son of God, than in a purely secular one. The setting of the laboratory is one in which, so far as is humanly possible, the scientist isolates his experiment from all influences other than that which he is interested in investigating. Divine intervention would be such an extraneous influence, and, although it is perhaps the only disturbing influence against which the scientist cannot in principle erect an absolute barrier, we may expect that God will respect the nature of the task on which he is engaged and will not make it unnecessarily difficult by *ad hoc* manifestations of his power. Scientific research is difficult enough in any case, without the scientist having to take account of miracles. The matter is quite different when the setting is not that of the laboratory but of the Church, for here the context is not that of the secular but of the supernatural; and it is, of course, a perfectly sound logical and methodological principle that when fresh causes are at work fresh effects are to be expected. There are, furthermore, situations of a mixed nature in which the two settings overlap and intermingle; the increasing co-operation between the clergy and medical and psychological practitioners in dealing with the sick provides just such an instance. In such a case the task of discrimination will be extremely difficult, but the principle is nevertheless clear. The matter is well illustrated by a friendly controversy between two French Catholic scientists, who both share the same theoretical outlook. M. Lhermitte, in his book *Le Miracle*, takes up an extremely sceptical attitude to the greater number of the allegedly well-authenticated miracles of modern times; he has been criticised by M. Rémy Chauvin, in his *God of the Scientists, God of the Experiment*,[1] for demanding in the case of miracles a

[1] op. cit., pp. 80ff. Chauvin well observes: 'If God worked miracles every five minutes, all science would be in fact impossible. But at the rate God maintains, science and religion can painlessly coexist' (p. 86).

standard of evidence that no scientist would dream of requiring in any normal scientific question.

The principle at issue—namely that where fresh causes are at work fresh effects are to be expected—applies with special force in the case of the miracles which are recorded in the New Testament in connection with the person of our Lord. There is a tendency among many present-day theologians, which seems to me almost morbid, to minimise, and indeed often to eliminate completely, the miraculous element in the Gospels. The ground on which this is usually defended is that the writers of the Gospels, like other people in the ancient world, were credulous folk who expected miracles to happen and therefore thought they had happened even when they had not. It is, of course, easy to meet this contention with the retort that many present-day theologians, like many other people at the present day, are incredulous folk who do not expect miracles to happen and will therefore think that they have not happened even when they have. This retort is indeed not without relevance, but the further point is often made that the 'reality of the Incarnation' involves that Jesus had no powers at his disposal other than those that are available to ordinary human beings like ourselves. This position, which emphasises the human element in the Incarnation to the virtual exclusion of the divine, is itself open to the objection that it is very unwise for us to lay down *a priori* the detailed nature of a case that is *ex hypothesi* unique. The potentialities of human nature which is unfallen and is united to the Second Person of the Holy Trinity are not necessarily identical with those to which it is limited in the case of fallen creatures like ourselves. The reliability of the Evangelists is, of course, a legitimate matter for discussion; but, if the events which they describe were in themselves probable, we cannot simply rule out their testimony and convict them of unreliability on the grounds that they believed the events to have occurred, however predisposed they may have been to expect them. If our belief in the probability of the events itself rests upon our belief in the deity of Christ, we cannot, of course, use the occurrence of those events as the ground of our belief in his deity, though we can use them in order to acquire increased understanding of his character both as human and as divine. But if we are prepared to admit, even as a possibility, that Jesus was divine, or even that without being divine he was unique, then we must, as a matter of logic, discard any attempt to discredit the Gospel accounts on the ground that they record abnormal occurrences. What other ways lie open to us, by which we may assess their authenticity, we shall enquire later on.

CHAPTER FIVE

FACT AND THE GOSPELS

A certain group of scholars, mostly German or influenced by German Protestant theology, has rushed to abandon positions before they were attacked, and to demythologise the Gospel message when there was no clear evidence that intelligent minds outside the Church were any more frightened by her mystery than by her morals.

—G. I. Bonner.

I

I SUGGESTED IN the opening chapter of this book that there were three chief reasons for the markedly anti-supernaturalist attitude which is characteristic of the presentations of the Christian religion by a great many theologians today. The first is the positivist emphasis which is dominant (though less self-assured than it once was) in contemporary Anglo-Saxon philosophy. I made no attempt to discuss it exhaustively, as it has received detailed and very adequate consideration from many writers, some of whose works I mentioned, and there seemed to be little point in saying over again what had been said very clearly elsewhere. In any case, it can have had very little direct effect upon continental, as contrasted with Anglo-Saxon, theologians, for on the Continent philosophy has in recent years meant existentialism rather than linguistic analysis. The second reason, which has been much more pervasive and has operated quite as much on the subconscious as on the conscious level, is the assumed incompatibility of a supernaturalist outlook with the methods and achievements of modern science; this was the subject of the last chapter. The third reason, to which I now turn, arises from the recent course of biblical scholarship, based upon form-criticism and culminating in the demythologising programme of Bultmann and his disciples; according to this, the supernatural element in the Gospels and in primitive Christianity generally can be convincingly shown to be due to the mythopoeic activity of the early Church in its reflection upon its own religious experience. It is with reluctance and trepidation that I venture to make some remarks about this matter, for I can make no pretensions to be a biblical scholar and I am very conscious that I am laying myself open to the retort 'Ah, but if you knew as much about the subject as we do, you would see how impressive and inevitable our insights are!' Nevertheless, there are a number of reasons why some consideration of the work of the biblical theologians by a theologian whose professional interest lies in a different field may not be entirely impertinent and worthless. In the first place, while expert biblical study requires long application to a variety of ancillary techniques and a profound study of the biblical texts themselves, the arguments which biblical theologians use are not for the most part unintelligible to the educated outsider and are, in fact, offered for his consumption in a swarm of books, articles and broadcast talks. Secondly, while biblical scholars are for the most part extremely confident in the way in which they express their conclusions, close attention often reveals that they are very much at odds with one another; the educated outsider may therefore well feel disposed to look into the general assumptions and the method of inference which have led to a particular scholar's judgment upon a particular point. Thirdly, the fact can hardly be concealed that, tactless as it may be to refer to the matter, the whole technique of interpretation which has characterised the work of biblical theologians in general since the volumes of Dr G. Kittel's massive *Theologisches Wörterbuch zum Neuen Testament* began to appear, has been subjected to the most devastating criticism, from the angle of technical philology, by Professor James Barr. Respect for the large number of distinguished scholars who have been the targets of his concentrated fire restrains me from listing their names here. It is, however, not irrelevant to observe that no serious attempt appears to have been made to reply to his arguments in detail; they have been met with an embarrassed and, at least in public, a practically unbroken silence. Again, it may be noted that the extreme scepticism about the reliability of their material which is manifested by many New Testament scholars does not seem to be supported by the small number of ancient historians who, having done their initial work in the non-biblical field, have later turned their attention to the origins of Christianity. The earlier work of William Ramsay and Cuthbert Turner in this respect is paralleled by Mr A. N. Sherwin-White's recent book *Roman Society and Roman Law in the New Testament*, which, like Professor Barr's works, has been largely ignored by those who have most reason to take account of it. There seems, in fact, to be a deeply rooted tendency in the minds of many biblical theologians to approach their subject in a mood of quite exaggerated scepticism. This may be due to a laudable desire to attract the outsider to the Church by persuading him that it is possible to be a Christian on the basis of a much smaller body of reliable factual material than has generally been supposed to be necessary; I suspect that his usual reaction is a decision that if the factual basis of Christianity is so limited and precarious he might just as well stay where he is, and a suspicion—no doubt quite unjustified—that the biblical theologians would themselves abandon the formal profession of Christianity if they had not a vested interest in its propagation.

It is perhaps worth while to notice that the assertion that the supernatural element in historic Christianity is an accretion upon the originally unsupernatural life and teaching of Jesus is no new thing. Without telling again in detail the story which is related in Albert Schweitzer's famous book *Von Reimarus zu Wrede* (*The Quest of the Historical Jesus*), we may recall that F. C. Baur and the Tübingen School in the middle of the last century maintained that the bulk of the New Testament writings were of second-century origin, and that even the great Adolf Harnack considered that the specifically supernatural and 'Catholic' character of historical Christianity was due to the introduction into an originally ethical Jewish religion of an alien Hellenistic metaphysic. What is really impressive, however, is the fact that, on purely scholarly grounds, the intrusion of this corrupting force into the original Gospel has been pushed back to an earlier and earlier date, so that now it has to be located within the New Testament itself or even into the sources out of which the New Testament books were compiled. It is interesting to compare the reactions of different Protestant scholars to this phenomenon. When Heinrich Schlier became convinced in 1948 that *Ur-Catholicismus* was endemic to the New Testament he took the logical step of becoming a Catholic.[1] On the other hand, Dr Anders Nygren, having concluded, in his *Agape and Eros*, that the basic Christian doctrine of the love of God had begun to go astray even in St John and that St Augustine, instead of being, as had been commonly maintained, the one really sound Christian teacher between St Paul and Luther, was in fact the founder of medieval Catholicism, was remarkably untroubled by this; what else, he seems to imply, could we expect in a fallen world in which even redeemed man is incurably corrupt? The same attitude is even more striking in the book entitled *The Problem of Catholicism* by the Waldensian scholar Dr Vittorio Subilia; for him, apparently, even the teaching of Jesus himself was infected by his gnostic environment, but once again, so far from being disconcerting, this seems to Subilia to be just what one ought to expect. The majority of the Bultmannites and post-Bultmannites, however, would not, I think, hold that gnosticism was primarily the enemy or even that the supernaturalising agency, whatever it was, was evil at all. The mythologising of the earthly life of Jesus as a result of the spiritual experience of the primitive Church was an inevitable and indeed a desirable process, given the thought-forms of the age, and it got to work on the traditional material, whether oral or written, long before this was assembled into the form of the canonical Gospels; but we men of the twentieth century cannot think in this way and so we must reverse the process, with Heidegger's existentialist philosophy to do for us what the myths did for the primitive Church. Before turning to the specifically Bultmannian approach it will I think be interesting and instructive to see how the problem of *Ur-Catholicismus* was handled by the distinguished German scholar Dr Martin Werner, whose chief work, *The Formation of Christian Dogma*, appeared in an extensively revised English edition in 1957.

Werner's thesis is briefly as follows. The primitive Church had two basic beliefs: the expectation of an immediate return of Jesus, and a doctrine of Jesus as the Son of Man which was, in fact, an angel-Christology. When the expected return did not take place, the Church, with great adroitness, preserved its own existence by substituting a new religion for the old. Henceforth

[1] Cf. Hans Küng, *Structures of the Church*, ch. vi, §3, for the contrast with Käsemann.

Jesus was considered to be divine, and with this there went a thorough de-eschatologising of Christology. Thus Catholicism came into being. What, then, must be the programme of the modern Protestant? First, obviously, to discard the new doctrine and recover the old. But then the real problem arises, for the old doctrine was, in fact, false, as the early Church had discovered. In Werner's own words:

> In duly reckoning with the fact of the necessary de-eschatologisation of doctrine, Protestantism cannot regard this doctrine of the eschatological Christ, in its original historical sense, as a dogma. In the same way it also abandons the Catholic doctrine of the Trinity and the Two Natures, which emerged in the Early Church, as the erroneous product of an illogical and arbitrary de-eschatologising of the primitive doctrine of Christ. Protestantism, however, understands the Primitive Christian doctrine of the eschatological Christ as an expression of the notion of a special revelation of God in history concerning the principle of human existence.[1]

Catholicism thus gets buffeted on both cheeks, first for departing from the primitive faith and then for departing from it in the wrong way. The ultimate problem for the Protestant is therefore how to live by a religion which has been proved to be false; the final answer seems to be a kind of Bultmannite existentialism, though Bultmann is hardly referred to throughout the book. The primitive faith, we are told, identified the historical person Jesus of Nazareth 'in some way' with the eschatological Christ, but, 'since due consideration must be given to the necessary process of de-eschatologising, Protestantism cannot deal with the issue here as though this identification had the status of dogma'.[2] What the ordinary Christian is to do about his religion while this necessary process is going on is not entirely clear, but we are assured that it 'does not mean the end of Christianity, as the protagonists of Protestant and Catholic reaction suspect in their confusion and anxiety. Rather can one reckon with the hope that the end of error and mis-development in the history of Christianity may be hastened and the world be shown what ultimately is the nature of Christian faith.'[3]

If learning is identical with knowledge, this is an almost

[1] op. cit., p. 329.
[2] ibid.
[3] ibid., p. 330.

incredibly learned book; Werner's acquaintance with biblical, classical and patristic literature is colossal. Moreover, he is remarkably skilful in fitting his facts into the framework of his theory. It is, however, often difficult to see how the theory follows from the facts, and I think the theory itself and the programme which is proposed as a consequence of it will strike most readers as ingenious, but perverse and unlikely. It will, I think, be worth while to enquire how Werner makes his theory plausible, if not to his readers, at least to himself, for the method of argument which he relies on is one of which we can hear echoes in a good many other quarters. He appears, in fact, to combine three ways of thinking.

First, he has a striking capacity for seeing two notions as contradictory which other persons will see as either complementary or identical. Thus, he sees the doctrine of deification as denying and supplanting the Pauline *mystique* of 'being in Christ'.[1] Again, he sees the Pauline doctrine that baptism is a dying and rising again with Christ as denied and supplanted by the view that in baptism the whole man is raised to immortal life by the Spirit.[2] Similar substitutions are alleged to have occurred in the doctrine of the Eucharist, of Redemption and of the Person of Christ. Secondly, Werner has no conception of any kind of development in the verbal expression or the intellectual understanding of a truth; if the words are not the same, then a new doctrine has taken the place of the old one. Thus we find repeated references to the 'new dogma' of the divinity of Christ;[3] the question is never even raised whether the unconditional allegiance which Jesus evoked from his followers in the Gospels was not an implicit admission of deity. Thirdly, there is a recurrent tendency to assume that any material which is compatible with a particular position is positive evidence for it, even if it is equally compatible with the opposite view; thus, for example, Werner writes, with reference to Phil. ii. 6: 'The pre-existent Christ did indeed exist in "divine form"; but Paul himself had *expressly denied* that, despite this, "equality with God", in the strict sense, could be asserted.'[4]

[1] ibid., p. 170.
[2] ibid., pp. 177f.
[3] e.g. pp. 236, 255.
[4] ibid., p. 122 (italics not in original).

Dr H. E. W. Turner has criticised Werner's thesis in the following words: 'Its root difficulty lies in the fact that it involves a radical recasting not only of the theology and experience of the early Church, but also of the New Testament itself. In both, Werner has abstracted only those elements which support the exposition of his theory. Despite his superficially impressive documentation his picture of New Testament Christology is little better than a caricature. There are more points of contact between the New Testament and the later Church than he seems prepared to allow.'[1] Dr S. G. F. Brandon, in his Introduction to Werner's book, writes off Turner's criticism as vitiated by the professedly apologetic character of Bampton Lectures, as if Werner himself had no axe to grind. We may, however, recall Dr J. N. D. Kelly's warning, in his Presidential Address in 1956 to the Oxford Society of Historical Theology, against reading the statements of the earlier fathers in the light of the preoccupations and ideas of the fourth century and in consequence of detecting changes of belief where no such changes exist. *Mutatis mutandis* this warning would seem to apply, when set a stage farther back, to Werner's manner of argument. If he had only managed to feel the Church as the living Body of Christ, instead of as a repository of documents, he might have seen in its doctrinal evolution not the substitution of one religion for another, but the ever-deepening understanding of the mystery of the Word incarnate under the guidance of the Spirit. On his two main contentions, I would offer the following comments, which may have some relevance in other contexts as well. (1) The primitive Church undoubtedly felt itself to be living under the shadow of the eschatological judgment of God; this was a common feature of late Judaism, and Christian Jews would, of course, identify it with the return of Jesus the Son of Man on the clouds of heaven. The judgment was not simply a future event at the end of history, but the basic concept in terms of which all events in history were to be interpreted. No doubt, in their longing to see again the Master whom they had loved so dearly, many Christians, whether Jewish or Gentile, would hope and persuade themselves that the actual return of Jesus, as the consummation of history as well as its interpretative principle,

[1] *The Pattern of Christian Truth*, p. 22.

might occur in their own earthly lifetime. But it appears to have been in a Gentile rather than a Jewish setting that this chronological aspect of Christ's return became so dominant that the death of certain Christians before it had happened produced a serious religious crisis. And it is noticeable that, when St Paul has to deal with it at Thessalonica, he does not treat it as a deep theological problem, but brushes it off almost casually: when Christ returns, those of us who have died will be brought out from the grave and those who have not will be raised up from the earth to meet the Lord; it will happen without warning and nobody knows when, so the important thing is to be perpetually ready for it.[1] St Paul shows no such concern with the immediacy of the second coming as he does, for example, with the resurrection of Christ from the dead; the latter is of such centrality to his faith and his preaching that without it both would be a hollow sham.[2] There seems no reason to suppose a crisis of the magnitude and universality that Werner postulates, but rather a gentle movement of adjustment, in which no doubt there was regrettable loss of the sense of urgency (though it is doubtful anyhow whether it is altogether healthy to live under a perpetual sense of crisis)[3] but in which this was compensated by a deepening of the sense, which had never been absent, of the indwelling of Christ in his Body the Church and in its members.

(2) The primitive Jewish-Christian theology, of course, thought of Jesus as an angel before his human birth; believing in his pre-existence (and Werner does not seem to have seen the significance of the fact that it did believe in his pre-existence), how else, in its own terms, could it conceive him? But, as Père Daniélou has pointed out in his *Theology of Jewish Christianity*,[4] it looked upon him as the one angel who was *uncreated*, and as the *archē*, the *bereshith*, in whom God had created the world. What difference is there, other than a verbal one, between saying, with primitive Jewish Christianity, that the Son is the one angel who is *not* created and, with the Epistle to the Hebrews, that he is *not* an angel (i.e. a created being) but 'has by inheritance

[1] I Thess. iv. 13–v. 10.

[2] I Cor. xv. 12–18.

[3] Cf. St Paul's strong words in II Thess. to those who had given up working in expectation of the second coming.

[4] op. cit., ch. v.

obtained a more excellent name than they'?[1] Werner's theory that the divinity of Christ was a new invention on the part of the Church seems quite baseless.

I have given this attention to Werner's book, not because it is a typical example of contemporary New Testament study—it belongs, in fact, as the date of the original German edition (1941) indicates, to a rather earlier phase of scholarship—but because it manifests particularly clearly certain assumptions and attitudes which, usually in a much subtler form, have become endemic among students of Christian origins. Their common feature is an uneasiness with the notion of the supernatural, which is found even among those who do not in principle deny its existence. It shows itself in a tendency to eliminate the supernatural where this is possible, to minimise it where it cannot be eliminated, and to treat it as in any case of very secondary importance.[2]

[1] Heb. i. Daniélou makes it plain, of course, that there were heretical types of Jewish Christianity, just as there were of Gentile.

[2] A good example of this can be found in two passages from that very able New Testament scholar John Lowe, whose preoccupation with the government of a great college and cathedral and comparatively early death precluded the full contribution which he might have made to biblical studies. He had certainly no theoretical prejudice against the supernatural, and his monograph *Saint Peter* is written with great independence and lack of bias. But on pp. 46f. we read: 'We have seen that John xxi. 15ff., though good evidence for the mind of the Church at the turn of the first century, has little claim to be regarded as an authentic dominical utterance. Luke xxii. 31–32 has greater claim to be considered as a genuine saying of Jesus. It does not fall under the suspicion which attaches to post-resurrection utterances, and it is found in a source which contains much good early tradition.' The implications of this last sentence are obvious, and are confirmed by the fact that the earlier passage relating to John xxi begins: 'Whoever wrote this, and whatever claim it has (probably very little) to be based on a saying of the Lord . . .' (p. 23). So, 'we have seen' means in fact 'I have said', for no reasons are given for the disclaimer just quoted. Clearly, the inauthenticity of any alleged post-resurrection utterance is taken for granted as too obvious to need argument; yet nobody who knew Dr Lowe would suppose that he doubted the Resurrection.

Another instructive instance can be quoted from Dr R. H. Fuller, though he safeguards himself as far as possible. He writes as follows:

> Form-criticism itself, though its results are often thought to be largely negative, does in fact provide valuable criteria to enable us to distinguish between the authentic sayings of Jesus and creations of the post-Easter church. Thus we can, for historical purposes, eliminate from the sayings of Jesus anything which clearly pre-supposes the post-Easter situation, and which reflects the faith of the post-Easter church. For

II

To return to the main theme of this chapter, the application of the method of form-criticism to the New Testament is usually considered to have been initiated by Martin Dibelius in 1919, with his book *Die Formgeschichte des Evangeliums*. It was concerned with the bridging of the gap between the actual events of the life of Jesus and the accounts of them which we have in the Gospels. It is usually held that St Mark is the earliest of the four Gospels to be written, at least in the form in which we have it, and that it dates between A.D. 65 and 70. St John is commonly held to be the latest and, while the extremely late date proposed by some scholars in the last century is now abandoned, it can hardly have

---

> here the presumption is that their *Sitz im Leben*, their creative milieu, is in the life of the Church, and not in the life of Jesus. Secondly, we can eliminate any material which can be paralleled in contemporary Judaism, for here too the presumption is that the sayings in question have (historically speaking) been erroneously attributed to Jesus. This material would include sayings which are paralleled in Jewish apocalyptic and in Rabbinic tradition. Of course, these methods are not foolproof, and one cannot help feeling that German scholars often proceed as if they were. They yield no complete certainty, for on some points Jesus *could* have agreed with the post-Easter church: but usually, in a saying of this class the post-Easter situation is clearly reflected. Jesus might also have quoted or used with approval Rabbinic teaching. The most we can claim for this method of elimination is that it provides a safer course than Stauffer's principle of *in dubio pro tradito*. (*The New Testament in Current Study*, pp. 40f.)

This is extremely revealing, for even the qualifications which Fuller makes show the odd assumption that, although Jesus might occasionally have agreed with the post-Easter church or have adopted an apocalyptic or rabbinic idiom, he could not have done it very often, and certainly not on most of the occasions when the Gospels say he did. We may reasonably enquire (but without success) for the ground of this assumption. Again we might reasonably expect that anything that Jesus said in the post-Easter situation would reflect the faith of the post-Easter church, since (1) people usually speak in the context in which they find themselves, (2) Christians will presumably hold that the faith of the post-Easter church was true and (3) what Fuller describes as the reflection of the faith of the post-Easter church in the alleged sayings of Jesus might be the other side of something much more important, namely the reflection of the authentic sayings of Jesus in the faith of the post-Easter church. Fuller's criterion would render it *a priori* impossible for the evangelists to have recorded accurately the post-Resurrection sayings and acts of Jesus. It is well to have presuppositions so clearly brought out into the open; usually they are latent and can only be surmised.

been written before A.D. 90 or 100.[1] Matthew and Luke are situated in between. There is thus a gap of something like thirty or thirty-five years at the least between even the latest events of the life of Jesus and the earliest of our written Gospels, and, even when the 'synoptic' Gospels (Matthew, Mark and Luke) have been dissected into hypothetical earlier written sources, the time-interval between events and written records remains considerable. How did the accounts of the events reach the writers and what had happened to those accounts in the interval?

The answer of the form-critical school is as follows (I quote from an extremely lucid account by Professor R. P. C. Hanson):

> The Form Critics . . . confidently draw the conclusion that for the most part the ingredients of this material circulated during the oral period as isolated units, without reliable indication of the context or time in which they first originated. Even if the Church had from an early stage exercised particular care in preserving accounts of the works and words of Jesus as a sacred *paradosis*, they believe that we must accept the evidence of the form in which these accounts have reached us that they cannot for the most part be regarded as direct statements taken down from the lips of people who had been eyewitnesses of the events recorded shortly after they had taken place. They must have passed through a period of oral transmission between their first utterance, or their first being described by eyewitnesses, and their reaching written form in the gospels, or earlier in the gospels' sources.[2]

As a somewhat extreme example of this position, Hanson quotes from an article by Professor D. E. Nineham, who sees the Gospels as almost devoid of any eyewitness character at all, but who takes them as giving expression to an authoritative interpretation and insight into the words and works of Jesus on the part of the Church.

[1] However, the posteriority of John to the synoptics ought not to be too confidently assumed. The very independent scholar Dr R. M. Grant writes: 'All the evidence is ambiguous. . . . On specific literary and historical grounds, then, it cannot be proved that John is either earlier or later than the synoptic gospels. The only grounds on which this point can definitely be "proved" lie in a general theory of the development of early Christian thought, and the chief support of this theory is provided by the Gospel itself. Since the argument is circular we shall do well to neglect it.' (*Historical Introduction to the New Testament*, pp. 154f.)

[2] *Tradition in the Early Church*, pp. 13f.

> What we have [writes Nineham], incorporated in the gospels, is the insight into the meaning of the events described which had been given and tested in forty or fifty years of the Church's experience of Jesus as the living Lord. . . . The gospels were not meant to give us an uninterpreted picture of Jesus' ministry so full and detailed that we could interpret its significance for ourselves. They were meant to admit us to that understanding of, and relationship with, Jesus which was vouchsafed to the apostolic Church. At the same time they make possible sufficient historical knowledge of the person and ministry of Jesus for us to assure ourselves that the early Christians were not making bricks without straw; and also for us to see the sense in which their interpretations were intended and were legitimate and to set about the task of reformulating them in terms of our own needs and experience.[1]

Now, it must in fairness be recognised that Nineham's position, though extreme, is not, at any rate in intention, destructive. As conservative a scholar as Dr Alan Richardson would stress the way in which, in any historical account, fact is inevitably intermingled with interpretation, even if the latter mainly takes the form of selection of material believed to be important.[2] What is characteristic of Nineham is the immense stress which he places upon the interpretative activity of the Church, which he takes to be virtually infallible, in contrast with its power to preserve an accurate record of fact, which he clearly takes to be virtually non-existent. (Not entirely non-existent, for there is what Hanson aptly describes as 'that vivid but vague phrase', 'not making bricks without straw'.) And this assumption raises a colossal and basic theological issue to which Nineham gives no attention. ('How much straw, in any case', we might enquire, 'to so many bricks?') As Hanson remarks, 'How are we to know that this is the right insight, as, on this assumption, it is not the insight of the apostles? Others can regard this insight as a disastrous misinterpretation of the original message.'[3] And, in view of the widespread assumption that the form-critics' case is virtually unshakeable, it is relevant to draw attention to a number of scholars of distinction who either reject it or else

[1] 'Eyewitness Testimony and the Gospel Tradition. III', in *J.T.S.* XI (1960), pp. 263f. The two earlier parts of the article appeared in vol. IX (1958).
[2] Cf. *History, Sacred and Profane, passim.*
[3] op. cit., p. 15.

accept it only in a very diluted form. Both O. Cullmann and H. Riesenfeld are quoted by Hanson for the view that the apostles as eyewitnesses and not merely inheritors of information were responsible for the *paradosis*, with Vincent Taylor in support. Riesenfeld, in a paper on *The Gospel Tradition and its Beginnings* which acquired some notoriety when it was read at Oxford in 1957, emphasised the fact that, whatever else he was, our Lord was a Jewish rabbi, and not unreasonably deduced that his teaching would have been very largely given in stock rabbinic fashion to be learnt by heart and handed down by word of mouth. In this view, one of the chief functions of the apostles was to watch over this tradition, which was regularly taught and passed on in the Church's gatherings for worship. It was this context of ordered instruction and not one of imaginative *mythopoeia* that was the *Sitz im Leben* of the transmission of the Gospel in the oral period.[1] A much more developed statement of this thesis has been given by the Swedish scholar Dr B. Gerhardsson in his book *Memory and Manuscript*, in which comparison is made with the actual teaching practice of the rabbinic schools in the first century A.D. In Hanson's words:

> He puts forward a theory that the tradition about Jesus was in the earliest days of the Church transmitted as authoritative oral tradition, memorised as accurately as the oral Torah or *Mishnah* was memorised and transmitted in contemporary Rabbinic Judaism, and was preserved, taught and commented upon in a halakic manner by the apostles themselves and not least by Paul, in whose letters we can clearly detect a process of this sort taking place. He argues that this 'holy tradition' was passed on in the early Church by careful memorisation orally until it gradually came to be written down, at first only in notebooks (codices, not scrolls), in order to aid the memory: by the middle of the second century these 'notebooks' had percolated throughout the Church in the form of gospels and epistles; then began the process of this written *mishnah*, so to speak, becoming recognised as the holy Scriptures, the new sacred Torah, of the Christian Church. He expressly denies some of the most dearly held assumptions of the Form Critics. . . . He emphasises strongly that the apostles were from the

[1] As R. M. Grant says, 'the evangelists regarded their function as that of bearing witness to Jesus Christ, not that of composing edifying fiction' (*Historical Introduction to the New Testament*, p. 302).

> beginning thought of as eyewitnesses, and insists that there must have been from the first a demand for some such testimony as the apostles gave.[1]

Furthermore, Dr C. H. Dodd, who may be regarded as the *doyen* of English New Testament scholars, has argued for the substantial historicity of the Gospel accounts in a number of books, including his recent voluminous treatise *Tradition in the Fourth Gospel*. So authority is by no means all on one side.

Now it is clearly not within the competence of an outsider to settle a dispute between New Testament experts, but it is certainly within his competence to recognise the fact that such dispute exists. And this is extremely relevant at a time when the ear of the public has been largely monopolised by the more sceptical type of form-critics and their followers and a widespread demand has been made for the reinterpretation of Christianity on the basis of a complete lack of reliable information about the actions and teaching of Jesus. With Hanson we may stress the importance of such work as Gerhardsson's without taking it as the last, or the only relevant, word on the subject. But it may legitimately lead us to question some of the more confident assertions to which we have become accustomed from the other side, and if we sometimes feel a little nettled that our simple trust has been imposed upon, are we very much to blame?

It will at this point, I think, be interesting to examine the comments which have been made upon the form-critical movement by a scholar to whom I have already referred as having received his training and practised his craft in the field of secular ancient history, namely Mr A. N. Sherwin-White, in his Sarum Lectures on *Roman Society and Roman Law in the New Testament*. Having remarked upon the success of ancient historians in developing critical techniques which, as he says, have led them to 'believe that a hard core or basic layer of historical truth can be recovered even from the most deplorable of our tertiary sources', he continues:

> So, it is astonishing that while Graeco-Roman historians have been growing in confidence, the twentieth-century study of the Gospel narratives, starting from no less promising material, has

[1] op. cit., pp. 15f.

> taken so gloomy a turn in the development of form-criticism that the more advanced exponents of it apparently maintain—so far as an amateur can understand the matter—that the historical Christ is unknowable and the history of his mission cannot be written. This seems very curious when one compares the case for the best-known contemporary of Christ, who like Christ is a well-documented figure—Tiberius Caesar. The story of his reign is known from four sources. . . . These disagree amongst themselves in the wildest possible fashion, both in major matters of political action or motive and in specific detail of minor events. Everyone would admit that Tacitus is the best of all the sources, and yet no serious modern historian would accept at face value the majority of the statements of Tacitus about the motives of Tiberius. But this does not prevent the belief that the material of Tacitus can be used to write a history of Tiberius. The divergences between the synoptic gospels, or between them and the fourth gospel, are no worse than the contradictions in the Tiberius material.

Having given a comparable example from the tribunate of Gaius Gracchus, Mr Sherwin-White takes account of a foreseeable objection:

> The objection will be raised to this line of argument that the Roman historical writers and the Gospels belong to different kinds of literature. Whatever the defects of our sources, their authors were trying to write history, but the authors of the Gospels had a different aim. Yet however one accepts form-criticism, its principles do not inevitably contradict the notion of the basic historicity of the particular stories of which the Gospel narratives are composed, even if these were not shored up and confirmed by the external guarantee of their fabric and setting.

The following point is very important:

> That the degree of confirmation in Graeco-Roman terms is less for the Gospels than for Acts is due, as these lectures have tried to show, to the differences in their regional setting. As soon as Christ enters the Roman orbit at Jerusalem, the confirmation begins. For Acts the confirmation of historicity is overwhelming. Yet Acts is, in simple terms and judged externally, no less of a propaganda narrative than the Gospels, and liable to similar distortions. But any attempt to reject its basic historicity

> even in matters of detail must now appear absurd. Roman historians have long taken it for granted.[1]

The mention of Christ entering the Roman orbit at Jerusalem has reference to an earlier chapter in which Sherwin-White discussed the trial of Christ. By making use of his encyclopaedic knowledge of the different types of legal process that existed in the Roman Empire and the circumstances under which they were severally applicable, he has most impressively shown that the objections to the historical accuracy of the synoptic accounts that have been brought by such scholars as Juster, Lietzmann and Winter are really devoid of substance and that even the Johannine variations from the synoptic account have no historical improbability. But, to resume:

> What to an ancient historian is most surprising in the basic assumptions of form-criticism of the extremer sort, is the presumed tempo of the development of the didactic myths—if one may use that term to sum up the matter. We are not unacquainted with this type of writing in ancient historiography, as will shortly appear. The agnostic type of form-criticism would be much more credible if the compilation of the Gospels were much later in time, much more remote from the events themselves, than can be the case. Certainly a deal of distortion can affect a story that is given literary form a generation or two after the event, whether for national glorification or political spite, or for the didactic or symbolic exposition of ideas. But in the material of ancient history the historical content is not hopelessly lost.

An interesting example is now adduced from Herodotus. 'The parallel with the authors of the Gospels', we are told, 'is by no means so far fetched as it might seem. Both regard their material with enthusiasm rather than detached criticism.' The case taken is that of the murder of Hipparchus in 514 B.C., and it is shown that, although when Herodotus wrote in the mid-fifth century there was a popular mythical version of the event which, in fact, was congenial to Herodotus's own sympathies, the story which he gives is different from the popular version and was verified a generation later by the research of Thucydides. The lesson drawn from this is as follows:

[1] op. cit., pp. 187ff.

> All this suggests that, however strong the myth-forming tendency, the falsification does not automatically and absolutely prevail even with a writer like Herodotus, who was naturally predisposed in favour of certain political myths, and whose ethical and literary interests were stronger than his critical faculty. . . . Not that one imagines that the writers of the Gospels set to work precisely like either Herodotus or Thucydides. But it can be maintained that those who had a passionate interest in the story of Christ, even if their interest in events was parabolical and didactic rather than historical, would not be led by that very fact to pervert and utterly destroy the historical kernel of their material. It can also be suggested that it would be no harder for the Disciples and their immediate successors to uncover detailed narratives of the actions and sayings of Christ within their closed community, than it was for Herodotus and Thucydides to establish the story of the great events of 520–480 B.C. For this purpose it matters little whether you accept the attribution of the Gospels to eyewitnesses or not.

Reverting to his stock instance, Sherwin-White adds;

> The impression of a historical tradition is nowhere more strongly felt than in the various accounts of the trial of Christ, analysed in Roman terms in the second lecture. Consider the close interdependence of Mark and Matthew, supplementing each other even in particular phrases, yet each with his particular contribution, then Luke with his more coherent and explicit account of the charges and less clear version of the activity of the Sanhedrin, finally John, who despite many improbabilities and obscurities yet gives a convincingly contemporary version of the political pressure on Pilate in the age of Tiberius.[1]

And the author concludes with an intriguing remark on the parallel between the technique of the synoptic writers and the 'father of history' Herodotus. 'It is', he says, 'as though this was the natural manner in which a primary innovator, with no models to follow, instinctively wrote history, especially when the narrative of events was controlled by an idea rather than the mere desire to explain what happened.'[2] Sherwin-White modestly admits, in his Preface, the lack of focus to which he is liable through

[1] op. cit., pp. 189ff.
[2] ibid., p. 192.

his lack of expert knowledge of Judaic and Christian material; but he has amply vindicated his suggestion that 'it may be useful if someone from the Roman side looks again at the old evidence, even where there is no new material, and appraises the New Testament setting in terms of modern Romanist developments'.[1]

Before leaving the subject of the ancient historians it may be interesting to quote the following piquant and characteristic passage from Dr R. M. Grant in connection with the speeches recorded in the Acts of the Apostles:

> The tendency towards uniformity in these speeches has been explained as due to the common practice of ancient historians who invented speeches suitable to the occasions they were describing. In this regard, recourse is often had to a statement by Thucydides, to the effect that when he did not have records of what was actually said he tried to compose something appropriate. Those who thus appeal to Thucydides usually neglect the rest of what he said: he stated that when he did have reliable reports he used them. Since we do not know that Luke did not have reliable reports, we cannot say that he did more than rewrite his sources, or perhaps write them for the first time from oral tradition. It should be added that Thucydides did not provide the only model known to ancient historians, in any event; Polybius, in the second century B.C., severely criticised some of his predecessors for inventing speeches and said that the historian's business was to record what was actually said. And while we know that Luke's contemporary, Josephus, liked to make up appropriate speeches—one of them was supposedly delivered in a cave just before all the witnesses committed suicide—we do not know that Luke followed his example.[2]

III

We may rightly be grateful to the form-critics for reminding us that the Gospels are primarily evidence for what their authors believed about the events which they recorded and are only secondary evidence for the events themselves. This is equally true of secular history and biography, and it does not warrant us in assuming that we cannot get behind the beliefs of the writers

[1] ibid., p. v. 'Romanist', of course, refers to Roman history, not to Roman Catholicism.

[2] *Historical Introduction to the New Testament*, p. 141.

and of the community of which they were members to the events which they profess to record. Even contradictions or demonstrable errors on specific points need not destroy the credibility of a narrative as a whole. A student of Boswell's *Life of Johnson*, to take an example, can never have *logical* certainty of the truth of any of the stories and utterances that he finds in it. Nevertheless, he can have *moral* certainty of the truth of some of them, and even if he feels doubtful about the reliability of Boswell's work in details he may still hold it to be accurate in its general bearing. Again, there is a very real sense in which Macaulay's *History of England* is primarily evidence for Macaulay's belief about what took place in seventeenth-century England and for his own political creed, and is only secondary evidence for the seventeenth century itself. Nevertheless, one can even learn something about James II by reading Macaulay; and a Christian may presumably hold that the primitive Church was guided by the Holy Spirit in a way that Boswell and Macaulay were not. A judgment in this matter will, of course, depend on what one believes about the Church, and I should not expect to carry with me a scholar such as Dr Subilia, for whom the Church has been infected with gnosticism since its foundation. However, even when treated by the ordinary canons of historical criticism which one would apply to any other ancient document, the Gospels seem, as Mr Sherwin-White's investigations confirm, to be very much more factual than the Bultmannite school would admit, and I strongly suspect that the present phase of scepticism will prove to be a passing one. When we are faced with an apparent contradiction between two accounts of the same incident the question, of course, arises how they are to be reconciled; there is nothing new in this. But unless we have a preconceived bias against the supernatural we have no ground for assuming that the correct solution is to be found by rejecting or minimising the supernatural element in either or both of them. We must furthermore remind ourselves—and this is perhaps the aspect of the situation which New-Testament scholars seem to find it most difficult to admit—that the key to the problem may lie in some event of history, some point of law or custom, or some linguistic idiom of which we are as yet, and perhaps always will be, altogether ignorant. It is, I think, a salutary exercise for any theologian to work through the pictures in a dozen consecutive numbers of *Punch* and ask himself how many of the jokes would be entirely unintelligible to someone who studied them in a hundred years' time without any knowledge of their local and temporal setting; the English reader may perhaps grasp the point even more clearly if he substitutes the *New Yorker* for *Punch*.[1] How many scholars, again, are always conscious of Grant's point that, while when we have two accounts we can choose between them, when we have only one we cannot invent an alternative? Or of his equally pointed remark that those who, when faced with an apparent contradiction, accept the evidence which contradicts the main line of Christian witness are assuming that the forgers included a few authentic elements for the benefit of modern critics.[2]

In any case, the notion of interpretation needs more careful consideration than it sometimes receives. It is, of course, true that the Church would naturally tend to record those acts and words of Jesus which threw light upon the problems with which it was actually faced, though we have only to read the Gospels and the Epistles to see that it believed itself to have received some very important information which it was bound to take

[1] I wonder how many people even now will recall the point of the cartoon in which a guest at a cocktail-party is remarking about a well-dressed young woman who is the centre of an animated group of males, 'I believe she once worked for a Mr Messina'.

[2] op. cit., pp. 78, 83. The kind of consideration here involved can, I think, be well illustrated with reference to the account of the feeding of the four thousand in Mark viii. 1–9. It is clear from the context that this account has been inserted into a narrative which originally passed straight from the end of chapter vii to verse 10 of chapter viii. Many modern scholars have therefore argued that the narrative is simply a second account of the feeding of the five thousand recorded in Mark vi. 31–44, which the evangelist later inserted into his Gospel under the mistaken impression that it described a different occurrence. It is pertinent to observe: (1) the possibility that the passage was a doublet will have presumably occurred to the mind of the evangelist himself; (2) he would hardly have sliced his gospel open and inserted the passage unless he had convinced himself that this possibility was in fact not borne out by such evidence as he had available; (3) what this evidence was we have no means of knowing, but we have no evidence bearing on the matter at all; (4) he may conceivably have been wrong, but as he was in a much better position than we are to get at the evidence we are in no position to say so. Nothing of very much importance turns on the question, but it provides a good example of the tendency which is all too common with modern scholars to assume implicitly that they have access to information that was not available to the evangelists. There seems also in some cases to be a confused impression that it is somehow easier to believe in one miracle than in two.

seriously whether the immediate relevance was obvious or not. The impression which the New Testament writings give is that the Church was scrupulously anxious to preserve and hand on the witness of those who had known Jesus in the days of his flesh and that there were people whose accepted function it was to remind it of this if it showed any tendency to forget it. It seems to me to be psychologically and theologically preposterous to suppose that, when the primitive Church found itself faced with some problem of belief or practice, it first of all made up its mind what it intended to do and then invented or garbled some utterance of Jesus in order to claim his support for its decision; what it would surely have done would have been to enquire into the tradition and testimony of the eyewitnesses in order to find out what there was in the teaching of Jesus that would throw light upon its problem and then, under the guidance of the Spirit, to see how this applied to the case at issue.[1] This will, of course, mean that what has been embodied in the Gospels is sometimes an inspired commentary or interpretation of our Lord's teaching, rather than a stenographic reproduction or a tape-recording of his actual words; but this does not mean that the substance of his teaching is distorted or that the Church's interpretation of it is partisan, perverted or superficial. Still less does it seem to be probable that the material which is brought together in the Gospels is simply the upthrow of an outburst of mythopoeic frenzy resulting from some mysterious and irrational 'Easter-experience' which attacked Jesus' disciples two days after his crucifixion and spread like a disease to those with whom they came into contact, so that the Church lost all sense of the distinction between fact and fiction as regards the facts of Jesus' life.

I am myself quite unconvinced that any purely natural explanation of the composition and nature of the Gospels does justice to their actual character and I shall say more about this later on. I do not, however, think that it is necessary to argue for verbal infallibility in the Gospels in order to rebut the position of the sceptics. In the Church God acts through human instru-

[1] Cf. R. M. Grant: 'Christians had disputes about keeping the Sabbath; they had them because Jesus himself had treated the Sabbath with considerable freedom. They were concerned about divorce because Jesus had been so concerned. The life of the Church was not completely disjoined from the life of Jesus.' (*Historical Introduction to the New Testament*, p. 302.)

ments and these are liable to err. The fact that the Spirit will lead the Church into all truth does not mean that the Church will never be affected by misunderstanding or will never diverge from the path along which God is directing it; it does mean that it will be protected from irreparable catastrophe. To vary the metaphor, the Church is like a stream which picks up from time to time a good deal of rubbish in its course, but sooner or later deposits it on some convenient sandbank. To change the metaphor again, the guidance of the Spirit acts like a negative feed-back, which corrects the loss of direction to which the Church is continually subject. Furthermore, even if we are prepared to admit for the sake of argument that in occasional cases, which we may or may not be able to identify, the Gospel writer has misunderstood or misreported some utterance of our Lord, this provides no justification whatever for the assumption that we cannot rely on the general account which the Gospels give of his teaching or that we shall be led into grave spiritual disaster if we assume as a general rule that he said what they say he said. To make an obvious comparison, in the ordinary business of life we constantly rely upon the statements that people make to us, although we know that they are sometimes deceitful or mistaken. The man who, on this account, refuses to believe anything that is told him will either die of starvation or end up in a mental hospital or both. In actual fact, we do accept what people tell us unless we have definite grounds for disbelieving them and only very rarely do we come to grief in consequence; if we refuse to do this we shall come to grief quite certainly and swiftly. Common prudence would suggest a similar attitude to the Gospels, on purely natural and untheological grounds. There are, however, one or two things to add. Even if we are misled by the Gospel writer (or by our misunderstanding of him) in a particular case, we are unlikely to suffer serious harm in virtue of what we believe about the Holy Spirit and grace. We are, on the other hand, very likely to suffer serious harm if we select and adjust the recorded acts and utterances of our Lord by some subjective criterion of our own. In saying this, I am not, of course, attacking responsible Biblical scholarship; I am only putting up a danger-signal where one seems to me to be badly needed. To summarise the main points, I would say (1) that the highly sceptical attitude of many Biblical scholars to the Gospels does not seem to be justified on objective grounds or to be confirmed by scholars who come to the New Testament from a professional training as ancient historians, (2) that this attitude is suspect as being highly congenial to certain philosophical or psychological presuppositions which have been adopted without adequate critical analysis, (3) that occasional inaccuracies or obscurities in the Gospel, whether they are identifiable or not, will not invalidate the Gospels as a whole, (4) that reliance on the Gospels, even if it may lead us into occasional error, will not result in irreparable catastrophe, whereas systematic scepticism about them will lead us into religious chaos or paralysis, (5) that there is all the difference in the world between raising a doubt for serious discussion and proclaiming it as the key for the understanding of Christianity by the modern man. But above all I would stress that, when one is dealing with a case in which a unique factor is alleged to be involved, namely the Incarnation of the Eternal Word, it is altogether illicit and hazardous to apply criteria of judgment derived from a general range of experience from which that factor is *ex hypothesi* absent. This is a matter not of theology but of methodology and of logic. I do not think it can be too strongly emphasised that any argument against the authenticity of some incident recorded in the Gospels is entirely valueless if it is based upon an explicit or implicit presupposition against the supernatural and the miraculous. Even if it can be shown—though the argument is very often circular—that in a later account of the event the element of the supernatural is, as they say, 'heightened', this will not settle the matter, for the later account may discern some characteristic of the event that the earlier account failed to discern or was unwilling to stress. The student of the New Testament will be well advised to ponder the following words of C. S. Lewis; they are taken from the Epilogue to his admirable book *Miracles*:

> When you turn from the New Testament to modern scholars, remember that you go among them as a sheep among wolves. Naturalistic assumptions . . . will meet you on every side—even from the pens of clergymen. This does not mean (as I was once tempted to suspect) that these clergymen are disguised apostates who deliberately exploit the position and the livelihood given them by the Christian Church to undermine

> Christianity. It comes partly from what we may call a 'hang-over'. We all have Naturalism in our bones and even conversion does not at once work the infection out of our system. Its assumptions rush back upon the mind the moment vigilance is relaxed. And in part the procedure of these scholars arises from the feeling which is greatly to their credit—which indeed is honourable to the point of being Quixotic. They are anxious to allow to the enemy every advantage he can with any show of fairness claim. They thus make it part of their method to eliminate the supernatural wherever it is even remotely possible to do so, to strain natural explanation even to the breaking point before they admit the least suggestion of miracle. . . .
>
> In using the books of such people you must therefore be continually on guard. You must develop a nose like a bloodhound for those steps in the argument which depend not on historical and linguistic knowledge but on the concealed assumption that miracles are impossible, improbable, or improper. And this means that you must really re-educate yourself: must work hard and consistently to eradicate from your mind the whole type of thought in which we have all been brought up.[1]

This does not mean that Lewis is advocating uncritical credulity. As he writes earlier in the same book:

> The philosophy which forbids you to make uniformity absolute is also the philosophy which offers you solid grounds for believing it to be general, to be *almost* absolute. The Being who threatens Nature's claim to omnipotence confirms her in her lawful occasions. Give us this ha'porth of tar and we will save the ship. The alternative is really much worse. Try to make Nature absolute and you find that her uniformity is not even probable. By claiming too much you get nothing. You get the deadlock, as in Hume. Theology offers you a working arrangement, which leaves the scientist free to continue his experiments and the Christian to continue his prayers.[2]

Lewis continues:

> We have also, I suggest, found what we were looking for—a

[1] op. cit., pp. 197f.

[2] ibid., p. 128. It is instructive to reflect on the enormous number of attempts that have been made by modern positivist philosophers (the heirs of Hume) to justify the principle of scientific induction, and on the gaps that their colleagues have invariably detected in their arguments.

> criterion whereby to judge the intrinsic probability of an alleged miracle. We must judge it by our 'innate sense of the fitness of things', that same sense of fitness which led us to anticipate that the universe would be orderly. I do not mean, of course, that we are to use this sense in deciding whether miracles in general are possible: we know that they are on philosophical grounds. Nor do I mean that a sense of fitness will do instead of close enquiry into the historical evidence. As I have repeatedly pointed out, the historical evidence cannot be estimated unless we have first estimated the intrinsic probability of the recorded event. It is in making that estimate as regards each story of the miraculous that our sense of fitness comes into play.[1]

I should indeed like to make Lewis's *Miracles* required reading for all New Testament scholars.

IV

When all this has been said, however—and it has been very important to say it—it is still true that the Gospels are works of a quite unique type, and differ, both in their construction and their purpose, from any normal biographical work. They are written not in order to give us a reasonably complete and balanced story of the life of Jesus from childhood onwards—as Professor Nineham remarks, with the exception of verse 13 of chapter i, everything related in St Mark's Gospel would fall within an aggregate period of three or four weeks[2]—but in order to demonstrate that Jesus was 'the Christ, the Son of God'. This does not mean that his life, as a process in human history, was irrelevant; quite the contrary. It does mean that a special and central relevance attaches to *some* of the events of his life, and that the rest of them are important not for the place that they hold in a continuous chronological account but for the light which they throw upon the significance of those. In discussing

[1] ibid., pp. 128f. Professor Nineham remarks, in his article on 'Eye-witness Testimony and Gospel Tradition', that 'Evidential force of direct attestation varies in inverse proportion to the intrinsic credibility of what is reported' (J.T.S., XI (1960), p. 259). But how do we estimate this intrinsic credibility in a situation alleged to be unique and in which direct intervention by God is alleged to be involved? This he nowhere considers.

[2] *Commentary on St Mark*, p. 35.

the differences between the synoptic Gospels and the Gospel of St John, scholars seem often to have overlooked what is much more striking, namely their essential similarity.[1] For, in spite of their differences, all four Gospels agree in consisting of a disproportionately full account of the events of the week in which Jesus was crucified, preceded by collections of biographical and didactic material which is chronologically ordered in only the loosest sense and which each writer has selected, arranged and presented in order to bring out the significance (or some primary aspect of the significance) of the Great Week as he sees it. It is the death and resurrection of Jesus that matters above all else; the rest of the Gospel is concerned in one way or another with who Jesus was and what his death and resurrection mean, though, the writers being human beings, we cannot rule out the possibility that they sometimes recorded an event simply because it had happened and they found it interesting.[2] Because the evangelists were not isolated believers in Jesus but members of his Body the Church, the form-critics are undoubtedly right in stressing that the Gospels are expressions of the Church's belief in Jesus and its experience of him. But we have only to look, for example, at the opening words of St Luke's Gospel or at St Paul's declaration in 1 Corinthians xv. 3–7 in order to see that the New Testament writers and the Church itself did not feel themselves entitled to indulge in speculation about the life of Jesus or in embroidering their Easter-experience with mythical fantasies, but conceived themselves as under a solemn duty to preserve the tradition as the eyewitnesses had delivered it. Far from the tradition being an outgrowth from the experience, the experience itself is under the control of the tradition.

Clearly, the peculiar shape which is common to all the four canonical Gospels (and which is in such marked contrast to such gnostic documents as the 'Gospel of Thomas'[3] and the 'Gospel of Truth') arises from the fact that the Church was convinced that the passion, death and resurrection of Christ together formed

[1] R. H. Lightfoot suggested that, so far from St John's Gospel needing a 'key', it may be designed as a key to the synoptics (*Commentary on St John*, p. 34).

[2] D. M. Baillie remarked that events may be recorded in the Gospels simply because they are true (*God was in Christ*, p. 57).

[3] i.e. the gnostic work of that name, recently discovered, not the earlier-known apocryphal gospel.

the mighty salvific act of God which had brought into existence the Church itself as the People of God, the New Israel and the Body of Christ. But equally important, I would suggest, though frequently understressed, is the fact that the Church's life was maintained in existence as a continuing reality by the weekly celebration of the Eucharistic mystery, the rite which the Lord Messiah, on the night before his passion, had commanded to be performed as his 'recalling', his *anamnesis*, and by which the salvific act was perpetuated in the Church's midst with all its efficacy unimpaired. The Gospels, with their unrelenting emphasis upon Holy Week and Easter, are in effect the Church's answer to the question 'What mean ye by this service?'[1]—a question to which every Christian had to know the answer if he was to make any sense of the extraordinary and otherwise altogether baffling religious meal on which he was assured his very existence as a Christian depended and participation in which was his inescapable duty. A number of liturgical scholars have pointed to the fact that the Liturgy itself formed an independent tradition parallel with the teaching tradition which ultimately crystallised in the Gospels.[2] Unlike the Reformers, the primitive Church in constructing its liturgical forms did not consult the Gospels (which did not at that date exist) in order to find out how to fulfil the Lord's commands; the liturgical tradition itself appears to have exerted a considerable control and counter-check upon the formation of the Gospels. But my present point is simply that the very shape of the Gospels reflects the Eucharistic outlook of the primitive Church. And the existence of the Eucharist as the central and focal feature of the Church's life must itself have exercised, no less than the presence of the apostolic eyewitnesses and their successors, a powerful restraint on any tendency to wander from the concrete facts of the life of Jesus into gnostic speculation or imaginative mythologising. Thirty years after the death of some remarkable figure in one of our ancient universities nobody would be prepared to stake anything of importance on the details of the anecdotes which were then being told about him, however much in

[1] Cf. Exod. xii. 26, where the question is asked in the context of the Jewish Passover, which foreshadowed the true Passover, Jesus Christ (cf. I Cor. v. 7f).

[2] Cf., e.g., G. Dix, *The Shape of the Liturgy*, p. 49; J. A. Jungmann, *The Early Liturgy*, p. 37.

character they might be; but it is relevant to remember that the atmosphere of the Eucharistic assembly of the primitive Church was not that of an Oxford common-room after dinner, and that the Church had controls over its tradition which the common-room has not.

I shall now draw attention to a feature of the Gospels which has indeed been noticed by a number of recent commentators, although I think it has been largely misunderstood and misinterpreted. This is the way in which they lend themselves perfectly naturally to being read on either of two levels, one being that of historical narrative and the other that of symbolic interpretation. This is characteristic of all the four Gospels, but it is marked most strongly in the case of St John, in whom both the elements—that of vivid factuality and that of symbolic depth[1]—are far more intense than in the synoptics, to the great bewilderment of many New Testament scholars. The point can be well illustrated with reference to the miracle of the man born blind, in John chapter ix. It is perfectly possible, and very edifying, to read the story as a highly symbolic expression of the themes of Jesus as the Light of the World, of conversion to Christianity as 'illumination' (cf. Luke i. 79; Heb. vi. 4), of the supersession of Judaism by Christianity and so on, and to conclude that the factual basis of the narrative is at most some one or more rumoured healings of blind men by Jesus, which the evangelist has worked up into a detailed and highly circumstantial account. However, when one reads the chapter in a perfectly straightforward way, one can hardly avoid being struck by the vivid impression of eyewitness reporting and by the extremely convincing characterisation of the persons involved. The blind beggar has all the features of the underprivileged and physically handicapped man, whose wits have been sharpened in the struggle for existence, who is easily frightened and yet quick to express his loyalty to the stranger who has done so much for him. His natural reaction to bullying is a combination of timidity and cheek, which can perhaps best be brought out if we parallel the stately periods of the Authorised Version not with the American R.S.V. or even the New English Bible, but with a simple rendering into cockney. Here are three examples:

[1] 'St John . . . uttered eternal mysteries with a louder trumpet.' (Ambrose, *De Sacr.* III.ii.11).

(1) 'Whether he be a sinner or no, I know not: one thing I know, that, whereas I was blind, now I see' (verse 25).

'*I* dunno whether 'e's a sinner, but I do know one thing. Yesterday I couldn't see a ruddy thing and now I can see orl right. Larf that one orf!'

(2) 'I have told you already, and ye did not hear: wherefore would ye hear it again? Will ye also be his disciples?' (verse 27).

'I've told yer once, ain't I? D'yer want me to tell yer again? I suppose *yore* thinkin' erbaht joining 'im now, ain't yer?'

(3) 'Why, herein is a marvellous thing, that ye know not from whence he is, and yet he hath opened mine eyes. Now we know that God heareth not sinners: but if any man be a worshipper of God, and doeth his will, him he heareth' (verses 30, 31).

'Well this is a rum go, ain't it? Says in the Bible, don't it, that God don't take no notice of sinners. But if a bloke says 'is prayers an' tries to keep straight, God'll listen to 'im, won't 'e?'

A further convincing note is added by the evasiveness of the beggar's parents, who cannot deny that he is, in fact, their son, but are quite determined not to get mixed up in the business. And is it shocking to suggest that the correct rendering of verse 34 is 'You dirty little bastard, who are you to lay down the law to us?'[1]

[1] Dorothy Sayers handled this incident with great skill in Scene II of the Seventh Play of *The Man Born to be King*; this is another of the books that I should like to see prescribed for reading by all students of the New Testament. I quote here the following passage from her Introduction:

> A loose and sentimental theology begets loose and sentimental art-forms; an illogical theology lands one in illogical situations; an ill-balanced theology issues in false emphasis and absurdity. Conversely; there is no more searching test of a theology than to submit it to dramatic handling; nothing so glaringly exposes inconsistencies in a character, a story, or a philosophy as to put it on the stage and allow it to speak for itself. Any theology that will stand the rigorous pulling and hauling of the dramatist is pretty tough in its texture. Having subjected Catholic theology to this treatment, I am bound to bear witness that it is very tough indeed. As I once made a character say in another con-

An equally good example of the point here involved is provided by the conversation of Jesus with the woman of Samaria, recorded in John chapter iv. But indeed this combination of vivid factuality and faultless characterisation on the one hand with a profound theological symbolical depth on the other pervades St John's Gospel from start to finish. And, with due allowance made for the differing emphases and literary idioms of the writers, this is no less true of the synoptics. Now, it has, of course, been recognised for some years that in all the Gospels narrative and theology are closely interwoven, and that this is as true of the matter-of-fact Mark as of the deeply contemplative John; indeed, the work of the form-critics largely took its rise

---

> text: 'Right in art is right in practice'; and I can only affirm that at no point have I yet found artistic truth and theological truth at variance.

Properly developed, this might provide a valuable technique for settling some outstanding biblical problems. Dorothy Sayers went on to say with some emphasis that the principle just stated does not in any way conflict with the equally important principle that 'the dramatist must begin by ridding himself of all edificatory and theological intentions. He must set out, not to instruct but to show forth; not to point a moral but to tell a story.' (*The Man Born to be King*, p. 19.)

I should like also to recall the following passages from Mr F. N. Davey's brilliant Introductory Essay to the original two-volume (1940) edition of E. C. Hoskyns's *Fourth Gospel*:

> The fourth Evangelist is safeguarded from the charge of inventing history, or of using it merely as symbolism, by three considerations. In the first place his whole conscious intention is to force his readers back upon the life of Jesus in the flesh and upon his death in flesh, as *the place of understanding*. . . . In the second place, what he is attempting to do, consciously, but as a theologian, is no more and no less than what is implied in the use made of the historical episodes and Sayings of Jesus by those who formulated the apostolic Gospel, so far as we can reconstruct their procedure from the synoptic gospels, and in the presentation of Jesus Christ as the sphere of God's revelation and salvation in the Epistles of Saint Paul and in the other New Testament scriptures. In the third place, his gospel, far from evacuating the observable world of anything but secondary importance, establishes it as the place where men, living in the flesh, are confronted by the last things of God: a strange procedure indeed if he regarded the history of Jesus in the real world as a pliable medium subject to his own theological insight. (P. xxxiv.)
>
> However positively we must maintain that there is no evidence that the fourth Evangelist invented episodes or Sayings of Jesus out of the air, it remains equally certain that his perception of the meaning of history forces him to set the history he narrates in the widest possible theological context, in the full light of his Christian perception of Jesus and with the fullest regard for the theological implications, not only of

from this. Nor do I deny that the evangelists have handled their material in such a way as to produce not a simple biography of Jesus of Nazareth—the prototype of the 'Life of Jesus' so hopefully sought by Liberal Protestants of the last century—but a profoundly theological presentation of his life and work. What I am concerned, however, to emphasise is that, when they have done this, the material has lost nothing of its vivid factual character, and that this is most striking in the case of the Fourth Gospel, in which the theological emphasis is strongest. It might, I think, even be argued that the two aspects, so far from con-

---

the isolated episodes and fragmentary Sayings, but of the whole apostolic Gospel. (P. xlvii.)

The distinguished archaeologist Dr W. F. Albright wrote in 1956:

There is . . . less evidence than ever to support the claims of Gnostic influence on Paul and John. There is no fundamental difference in teaching between John and the Synoptics; the contrast between them lies in the concentration of tradition along certain aspects of Christ's teachings, particularly those which seem to have resembled the teaching of the Essenes most closely. And yet, with all this superficial similarity, there is a wide gulf between the doctrines of the Essenes and the essentials of Johannine teaching, which the latter shares with the Synoptics and Paul. . . . There is absolutely nothing to show that any of Jesus' teachings have been distorted or falsified, or that any vital new element has been added to them. That the needs of the early Church influenced the selection of items for inclusion in the Gospel we may readily admit, but there is no reason to suppose that the needs of that Church were responsible for any inventions or innovations of theological significance. Whether the Gospel was edited by John the Presbyter of Papias and the First Epistle of John, or whether some other reconstruction is more probable, we may rest assured that it contains the memories of the Apostle John—regardless of whether he died in Jerusalem or in Ephesus, though the latter is so well attested by tradition that it remains most plausible.

And he adds somewhat piquantly in a footnote:

One of the strangest assumptions of critical New Testament scholars and theologians is that the mind of Jesus was so limited that any apparent contrast between John and the Synoptics must be due to differences between early Christian theologians. Every great thinker and personality is going to be interpreted differently by different friends and hearers, who will select what seems most congenial or useful out of what they have seen and heard. From Socrates to the most recent men of eminence there are innumerable examples. The Christian might *a fortiori* suppose the same to be true of his Master. ('Recent Discoveries in Palestine and the Gospel of St John', in *The Background of the New Testament and its Eschatology*, edited by W. D. Davies and D. Daube, pp. 170f.)

flicting with each other, reinforce each other in a most surprising way. It is, of course, logically possible to ascribe this to the genius of the writers, but, when full allowance has been made for the choice which God makes of human agents, to accept this as the full explanation seems to me quite impossible. The explanation surely lies not in the writers but in their subject. If the classical Christological definition is correct, that in Jesus of Nazareth there are two distinct and unconfused natures, a divine and a human, which concur and coinhere in one 'person and hypostasis', then an adequate account of his teaching and his acts will be expected to show this dual character. I am not, of course, putting forward the preposterous theory that the primitive Church obediently accepted the Definition of the Council of Chalcedon and wrote its Gospels in conformity to it. The truth is that the Definition of Chalcedon is based upon the picture of Jesus which is painted in the Gospels and which was repeatedly verified in the corporate experience of the Church and the individual lives of its members. What I am arguing is that a narrative which, without any suggestion of incoherence, can be read as either an extremely earthy human story or as a highly theological document, and this without in any way losing its unity, derives this extraordinary character not from the fact that its author was a literary genius of the highest order but from the fact that it is recording the impact made upon his beholders by someone who, while he was a completely unified Person, was nevertheless, in the unity of his person, fully human and truly divine. The Gospels therefore reflect in their very structure and their styles the divine-human character of him who is their theme. And if we do, in fact, accept the Chalcedonian definition it would presumably be very disconcerting and perplexing if the Gospels had not the kind of duality in unity on which I have remarked. Of course, if we approach them with Arian, Apollinarian, Nestorian, Eutychian or kenotic presuppositions, we shall find them baffling and shall be forced to improvise complicated theories to explain why they are the kind of things that they are; some interesting case-studies can be made along these lines, based upon the writings of modern New Testament scholars. There is nothing to worry us about the fact that the Gospels come to us out of the experience of the primitive Church, unless we believe that the primitive Church had no respect for the tradition of the apostles and the testimony of the eyewitnesses and was incurably prone to error.

V

In earlier chapters of this book I have discussed at what may have seemed to some readers to be almost excessive length two widely discussed attempts by contemporary writers to deal with the basic issues raised by the form-critical approach to the New Testament. I shall now, against the background of the position I have outlined above, turn to a third recent discussion, which has neither the sensationally gymnastic character of Dr Robinson's *Honest to God* nor the radically secularist bias of Dr van Buren's *Secular Meaning of the Gospel*. This is the extremely interesting and concise study by Dr John Knox entitled *The Church and the Reality of Christ*. Stating the basic problem of Christian theology as the question, 'how faith in Christ can be essentially related to historical fact and yet be as sure as faith must be', Knox remarks that, while his first impulse was to say, 'If we have only the Church we have nothing', twenty years later he has reached the point of seeing that in having the Church we have everything.[1] Clearly, a great deal will turn on how much 'everything' is found to include, but it must be said at the start that Knox is not implying that the historical existence of Jesus is unimportant and that all that matters is the experience of the Christian community. And his first chapter has the significant title 'The Church and the Fact of Jesus'.

Here he asserts that, even before the rise of form-criticism, it was widely recognised that 'the Gospels, in both intention and fact, are not the product of careful, critical research into the original facts, but are records of the Church's teaching: they bring us Jesus *as the early community thought of him*. The responsible Christian', he continues, 'could hardly see and acknowledge this fact without going on to ask, "But what about Jesus as he *really* was? Do I not need to know about *him*?"' And he further asserts that 'the problem has been deepened by the recognition, increasingly prevalent among historians generally, of the importance of subjective elements within history itself'.[2] Now, as it

[1] op. cit., p. 10.
[2] ibid., p. 15.

stands, this statement might mean no more than the rather obvious fact which I remarked upon earlier in this book, giving examples from Boswell and Macaulay, namely that *any* historical document is, in a sense, primary evidence for what the writer believed to have happened and is only secondary evidence for what actually took place. If this was all that was involved, such a book as that of Mr Sherwin-White, from which I have extensively quoted, would be of fundamental relevance to the issue. But this is what Knox would not be willing to admit. While refreshingly discarding the cliché, dear to the less rational type of modern theologian, that doubt is an essential element in faith, he maintains that 'even if we recognise an element of risk in faith, it cannot be the kind of risk involved in assuming the accuracy of a historical fact. If there is risk in faith, it must be the absolute, the eschatological risk. We are risking the possibility that the God of heaven and earth will in the ultimate and final reckoning fail to justify our trust in him, not that the chance discovery of an ancient document or a new conclusion of historians could conceivably rob us of it.'[1] It seems to me that Knox is positing a false alternative here. It is perfectly possible, and intellectually respectable, to hold, on grounds of faith, that, while conclusive evidence for some particular historical event would destroy one's faith, such evidence will never, in fact, be forthcoming and that, if at any time it appears to have been produced, there must be further evidence, not yet at hand, which will point to a different conclusion. (This is a point that was made very emphatically by Mr I. M. Crombie in *New Essays in Philosophical Theology*.)[2] Knox insists that, whatever risk the believer is or is not taking, he is not at any vital point dependent on the findings of historians. But then the question is raised, How can he be dependent on the fact of Jesus?

One answer to this question, Knox tells us, would be that no past fact can be essential to any present existence, so that, however important the career of Jesus may have been at its time, our own existence as Christians cannot now be dependent on it; this is the position which he ascribes to both Bultmann and Tillich. For Bultmann the 'Christ-event' began when something which is still being proclaimed was first heard (the '*kerygma*'), for

[1] ibid., p. 17.
[2] op. cit., p. 129.

Tillich it began when something which is still being seen was first seen. The simple factualness of Jesus cannot be denied, but what matters is not what Jesus did and said, but what he was 'seen' and 'heard' to do and say, the 'picture' or the 'kerygma'.

Now, Knox very reasonably refuses to accept this antithesis, nor is he willing to fasten it too firmly on Bultmann and Tillich. 'It belongs', he says, 'to our existence as Christians to affirm the actuality of Jesus' existence—and not merely the bare fact of it, but something of the full, distinctive quality of it.' But now, he asserts, we are driven into a dilemma. 'How can this be true in view of the existential certainty of faith, on the one hand, and the tentativeness of all historical findings, on the other?'[1]

I have already suggested a possible way out of this dilemma, but Knox's solution follows a different line. He states it thus:

> The solution of this problem—or, at any rate, an approach to a solution—lies, it seems to me, in our recognising, and accepting fully and without reservations of any kind, the radical significance of the early Church. . . . We need now to see that the Church's priority is not only epistemological, but actual;[2] that the basic, objective, historical reality underneath, and presupposed in, all primitive confession—picture, kerygma or whatever else—and the actual carrier of all the meanings being confessed was the early Church; and that, in consequence, the only adequate way to define the Event is to identify it with the Church's beginning. . . . The historical Event to which all distinctively Christian faith returns is not an event antedating the Church, or in any sense or degree prior to it, but is the coming into existence of the Church itself.

Now, even a theologian in the Catholic tradition may find this position somewhat startling, for it would seem to make it possible to eliminate Jesus altogether. Nor are the following words any more reassuring:

> To be sure, this 'coming into existence' must not be thought of as a momentary or 'simple' happening. It involved a complex interaction of persons, incidents and circumstances over a

[1] ibid., p. 21.

[2] i.e. the Church is not only that *through which* we perceive the fundamental datum of faith, but is the fundamental datum *which* we perceive (my comment).

period of time. But if we are asking what gives their characteristic significance to all of these factors, binds them together, provides the 'form' in which they have their being as historical event, then, I am suggesting, we can be content with no answer less inclusive than the coming into being of the Church.[1]

Now, there is, of course, a sense in which the Catholic Christian can readily identify the basic event of his religion with the foundation of the Christian Church; if, for example, he sees the Church as deriving its existence as the Body of Christ from the moment when, at his death on the Cross, Jesus breathed forth his Spirit on his Mother and the Beloved Disciple. But this assumes that Jesus is actually, even if not epistemologically, prior to the Church; whereas Knox's definition of the basic Event includes no reference to the historic person Jesus at all. It is true that he hastens to repair this omission. 'Elsewhere', he writes,

> I have described the Event of Christ as including the personality, life and teaching of Jesus, the response of loyalty he awakened, his death, his Resurrection, the receiving of the Spirit, the faith with which the Spirit was received, the coming into being of the Church. These are not items in a chronological series. It is clear, for example, that the personal character of Jesus, as well as his disciples' response to him, must be thought of as a constant, pervasive feature, and I am now pointing out that the 'coming into being of the Church' is a way of referring to the essential character of the whole Event. Still, these items do imply a certain temporal duration in the Event. This 'duration' might be indefinitely extended. One might think of the Event in such a way as that the Old Testament history would belong to it as well as the entire later history of the Church.[2]

It is, I think, entirely satisfactory to point to the fact that it is in the Church that we meet with Jesus and not only in the pages of the written or printed text of the Gospels. And it is true and important to stress with Christopher Wordsworth that 'there is one Church of Christ, from the beginning of the world to the end'.[3] The personal character of Jesus is indeed a pervasive

[1] op. cit., pp. 22f.
[2] ibid., p. 23.
[3] *Church History*, I, p. 1.

feature, communicated to the twentieth-century Christian no less than to the Apostles; it is the constitutive principle of the Church. But when Knox describes the *Event of Christ* as consisting of a series of items which he tells us 'are not items in a chronological series', the historic Jesus, the Lord who taught and healed and died in Palestine, seems to have vanished behind the experience of the Church. Are we, in fact, being offered this complex phenomenon which is called 'the Event of Christ' instead of Christ himself?

Knox faces this accusation quite frankly, but also quite impenitently. 'As Christians we affirm an Event in our human history in which God supremely revealed himself. . . . Since we actually know this action of God only in the Church, is it not simplest to identify the Event with the birth of the Church? Indeed, what ground have we for identifying it in any other way, and why, after all, should we seek to do so?'[1] To the accusation that his definition of the Event subordinates Jesus to the Church, he replies by making a relevant distinction between the definition of the essential character of an object and its content. The *content* of the Event, he insists, is dominated by Jesus, but the Event to which he and his career *actually belonged* was the emergence of the Church. Furthermore, he maintains that 'the Church' with which we are concerned is not just the early or primitive Church:

> The Church reflected in the New Testament documents is not the *primitive* Church only, but is the Church I know. As I read the passages in which its distinctive life is most clearly expressed, my primary experience is not that of *learning* something about the past, but of *recognising* something in the present. In a word, the Church is one, not only in space but in time—the one because the other. . . . To lose the sense of the reality—that is, of the actual existence—of the Church would be to lose the only conceivable ground for any distinctively Christian affirmation about anything. We may have some knowledge of God in our solitariness or through some other social or cultural medium, but our knowledge of God in Christ—of God as acting in and through the particular historical event—can reach us only through the historical community.[2]

[1] op. cit., p. 27.
[2] ibid., pp. 30f.

This is indeed finely said, and I for one would heartily endorse it. But it raises two questions of fundamental importance. The first is *how* the Church witnesses to the historic reality of Jesus. The second is *what* it tells us about him. And on neither of these, as I see it, does Knox give us a satisfactory answer.

To the former of these questions, which he identifies with the question raised earlier as to how a past fact can be in any true sense essential to a present existence, he replies by developing the notion of the Church's corporate memory. Indeed 'The Church and its Memory' is the subject of his next chapter, in which he adduces a number of parallels from the cases of families and nations to persuade the reader that the Church's *memory* of Jesus provides us with a presence of Jesus himself which gives us a present experience of him. I must confess that such a presence seems to me to be purely metaphorical and, if the notion is valid at all, to direct us only to a figure in the past, though I am very doubtful whether it does even that. My criticism of this central part of Knox's argument will run as follows: Knox is anxious to maintain (1) that the experience of the primitive Church has as its dominant content the career of the historic Jesus, (2) that our experience in the Church today is essentially homogeneous with that of the primitive Church. He offers, as a sufficient ground for both these theses the assertion that the Church has a continuing 'corporate memory' in which the career of Jesus is contained.

(1) Now, as regards the first thesis, Knox's theory would seem to be satisfactory if we could identify corporate memory with tradition and assume that the primitive Church received its information about Jesus from the apostles and eyewitnesses, has preserved it through the centuries and has handed it on from one generation to another. However, Knox explicitly refuses to make this identification, though he admits a relation between the two notions. 'The "memory" ', he writes, 'unlike "tradition", does not contain either factual data in the ordinary sense or doctrinal formulations. Its content is more concrete. So far as the original Event is concerned, it is only Jesus himself who is *remembered*.'[1] This would seem to imply that we know *less* about Jesus than the Gospels profess to tell us; nevertheless Knox maintains that 'whether the Church is deemed to have a right to

[1] ibid., p. 54, n. 1.

this knowledge or not, it has always known *more* of Jesus than the Gospels tell us—not, I repeat, more facts about him or his life, but more of the man himself. Its picture of Jesus has not been derived solely from the Gospels.'[1] 'There has come down within the body of the Church—in, around, and underneath the Gospel materials and reflected more directly in certain statements in the Epistles—an authentic remembrance of Jesus.'[2] Knox does, in fact, hold, as a matter of personal opinion, that 'however critical our methods may be, we are left with a very substantial residuum of historically trustworthy fact about Jesus, his teaching and his life', but he does not hold that the Church vitally requires this information, grateful as it must be for it.[3] The 'memory', which is what really matters, is concerned with the personal moral stature of Jesus and the relation of love in which he stood to his friends;[4] it is this that the Church 'remembers' and it goes far beyond anything that the Gospels say. To sum up, it seems to me clear that Knox quite fails to make the desired link between the experience of the primitive Church and the historic Jesus of the Gospels. As he himself says, in his view 'these [New-Testament] documents are more valuable for the testimony they bear to the existence and nature of the early Church's memory of Jesus than for any statement of more "objective" fact they may make about him and his career'.[5] He has clearly not succeeded, with his metaphor of 'memory', in turning the flank of the form-critics.

(2) It seems equally clear that Knox has failed to show the homogeneity of our present experience with that of the primitive Church. 'I suggest', he writes,

> that [corporate memory] provides the clue to the solution of our problem of how a past fact can in any true sense be essential to a present existence. Jesus is *remembered* in the Church, and has been from the beginning; and this memory is deeply constitutive of its being. Tillich and Bultmann are right in recognising that the actual human Jesus of Galilee and the first century can exist now only as an image in men's minds

[1] ibid., p. 53 (italics not in original).
[2] ibid., p. 54.
[3] ibid., pp. 52f.
[4] ibid., pp. 54ff.
[5] ibid., p. 49.

> and hearts. But they fail to recognise—or, at any rate, to attribute sufficient importance to the fact—that the image is of the characteristic kind that belongs to memory and therefore carries in itself, for those who hold it, the assurance of its own authenticity.[1]

This passage is extremely revealing, for it makes it plain that in Knox's view the presence of Jesus in the Church today is purely metaphorical. 'It carries the assurance of its own authenticity', but that is merely the assurance that something once took place in the past, not that in any concrete sense it exists in the present. It is like the memory which I myself have, fifty years later, of the outbreak of the First World War. We may find reasons later for believing that Knox does, in fact, look upon Jesus as someone who still exists, and if this is so it will sharply differentiate him from van Buren. But as far as his notion of 'corporate memory' is concerned it seems quite incapable of doing either of the tasks which he has set it, and to owe such plausibility as it has to the fact that, by a pure metaphor, we speak of something which we remember as existing in our minds. I cannot therefore conclude that Knox gives a satisfactory answer to his first question, namely *how* the Church witnesses to the historical reality of Jesus. His second question was *what* it tells us about him, and to this we must now turn. It is the concern of most of the remainder of the book, which begins with a chapter entitled 'The Church and the Resurrection'.

This chapter begins as follows:

> I have said that the Church would not, without ceasing to be the Church, conclude, or even consider the possibility, that Jesus never lived, that he whom it 'remembers' did not exist at all. The same impossibility of denying a past fact can be affirmed equally confidently at one other point, and, I believe, *at only one other point*; the Church without ceasing or having ceased to be the Church, could not deny, or even doubt, that God raised Jesus from the dead.[2]

[1] ibid., pp. 35f.

[2] ibid., p. 61. Somewhat similarly Dr John Macquarrie has written: 'What is the minimum [of historical factuality] which we would need to infer? Simply that there was someone who once exhibited in history the possibility of existence which the *kerygma* proclaims. We may of course believe more than that.' (*The Scope of Demythologising*, p. 93.) But Macquarrie seems to attribute more importance to historical research than Knox does.

This is indeed a sweeping statement, for, as the words which I have italicised show, it would, in fact, reduce the Creed to the single clause in which the Church proclaims her belief that Jesus rose from the dead. The reason for this is not altogether clear, even upon Knox's premisses, for, if (as I presume he would hold) the Creeds express the content of the Church's 'memory', they certainly go into more detail about the life of Jesus than this; and the Gospels go into very much more. Knox is, nevertheless, quite explicit on the point, and he adds:

> It is important to note that the grounds for the Church's assertions in both cases lie in its own life. The assertion of Jesus' existence rests, as we have seen, in its memory. It would be palpably false to say that the Church knows that Jesus existed because the historians have assured it that he did. The truth of the matter is, rather, that the principal argument the historians have for his existence is the Church's prior knowledge of it—that is, a memory of Jesus which can be traced back continuously through the centuries to the time when the Church first emerged into consciousness of itself. How, they ask, can this memory be explained if Jesus did not live? But the Church, which has the memory, does not need the argument. Its own existence being, so to speak, the major premise, it does not need to wait for the conclusion.[1]

Now, this statement of the historian's approach to the existence of Jesus does not seem to accord with the facts, at least in the case of such a scholar as Mr Sherwin-White. He certainly did not ask (though the question is a very sensible one) how the Church's memory was to be explained; he took the New Testament writings as documents of ancient history and treated them as such. We are not, however, concerned with this here, but with Knox's assumption (for I cannot find that he gives any reasons for it) that, apart from Jesus' existence, his resurrection is the sole fact that the Church needs to affirm about him.

The connection seems, however, to lie in the Church's experience of the Spirit. The Church, Knox tells us, shared from the beginning not only in a common memory of Jesus but also in a common experience of the Spirit, 'the Spirit being experienced as the Spirit of God, the Creator of the heavens and the earth, the Lord of all nature and history, and also as the personal

[1] ibid.

reality, the very being and presence, of the same Jesus who was remembered'.[1] How the Spirit was *experienced* in the cosmic functions is not made clear, but on the second point it is insisted that the Spirit is not a conception or the object of a conception but a felt reality and that 'just as the Church actually remembered Jesus, so it actually experienced the Spirit'.[2] It thus appears (1) that the Church has (or had) a more immediate acquaintance with the Spirit than with Jesus ('experience', as contrasted with 'memory') and (2) that the experience of the Spirit is taken as being identical with the knowledge of the resurrection of Jesus. Knox nevertheless goes on to say that the experience that the Church has of Jesus is also an experience of Jesus himself: 'The Spirit meant not only the actual presence in their midst of the transcendent God to whom they looked up in worship, but, equally inexplicably, the actual presence of the Jesus to whom they looked back in remembrance.'[3]

Now, all this is, of course, perfectly true from an orthodox standpoint, as far as it goes, but it seems to be very much less than the Church has, in fact, intended when it has asserted the Resurrection of Jesus. It is highly significant that Knox, while not denying the corporal restoration of Jesus to life and the emptiness of his tomb on the first Easter morning, does not think these to be of any real importance. He even goes so far as to disparage St Paul for trying to silence the doubts of the Corinthians by giving them an account of the visual experiences of Jesus had by his disciples, and alleges (most unconvincingly, in my judgment) that St Paul 'clearly implied' that, although he hoped these data would convince the Corinthians, they had not convinced him.[4] Knox well remarks that it is utterly beyond our power to visualise, or even to conceive, God's act in raising Jesus from the dead, but continues by saying:

> The simple notion that a corpse was revived is inadmissible, not because it is impossible, but because it is irrelevant. It would explain, to be sure, the existence of the living physical body of Jesus after his death (having 'flesh and bones', eating with his disciples, and the like). But that is not our problem.

[1] ibid., p. 62.
[2] ibid., p. 63.
[3] ibid., p. 65.
[4] ibid., pp. 67f.

> What we need is an explanation of how it can be that the one the Church remembers in the flesh it also knows as (or in) the Spirit. And a theory of resuscitation has nothing to do with the case.[1]

Here, I think, we come to the very heart of the issue, to the point at which traditional Christian orthodoxy comes into basic conflict not only with Knox, but with Robinson and van Buren as well. For all these writers, what an account of the Resurrection has to do is to explain the experience of the primitive Church (and, derivatively, the experience of the Church of succeeding generations). For traditional Christianity, it has to affirm that the Lord Jesus is restored to life and is glorified in the totality of his human nature (body and soul alike), as the firstfruits of the New Creation, in whom the whole human race and the whole material universe will ultimately be transformed as well. This does not involve *merely* the revivification of his corpse, but, to use an idiom of Professor I. T. Ramsey's, it involves that—*and more*. Knox indeed honestly admits that 'something like this' seems to be implied both in the Gospels and in St Paul; and, he says, 'if we find such a way of thinking congenial and convincing, well and good; certainly it cannot be refuted'.[2] This is going very much farther than van Buren and somewhat farther even than Robinson. But now comes the damning admission: 'Most modern persons, however, will have difficulty with it.'[3] So Knox, after all, is not, as we thought, expounding the belief of the primitive Church; he is offering us a reductionist theology. So it is not surprising that, after telling us that the Eucharist, 'if it was to be the central act of the Church's worship . . . *had* to embody a recognition of the two elements in the Church's essential nature—the devoted remembrance of Jesus and the joyous knowledge of the risen Christ', he goes on to say: 'The Resurrection is our way of referring to these two elements in the Church's existence in their relation to each other and to whatever must be pre-supposed when we think of them.'[4] Knox is far too careful a writer to be guilty of slovenly use of words, and I am sure we must interpret his sentences strictly. And here he has

[1] ibid., p. 69.
[2] ibid.
[3] ibid.
[4] ibid., pp. 66f.

told us, not that the Resurrection is an event that happened to Jesus, as the Church (including, as Knox has admitted, the Evangelists and St Paul) has consistently maintained, but that it is *our way of referring* to something, that is to say, a linguistic convention; not a fact about Jesus, but a mode of human speech. The only *fact* which is important for the Christian religion, as Knox told us at the beginning of his discussion, is the Church; now he adds that 'the Resurrection, in so far as it can be thought of as historical fact, belongs to the existence of the Church'[1] (note again, not in so far as it *is* an historical fact, but in so far as it *can be thought of* as one). Is it unfair to say that Knox reduces all theology to ecclesiastical psychology?

He develops this line of thought by arguing that 'to say that the Resurrection of Christ, in so far as it belongs to history, took place only within the larger event of the Church is not to deny its miraculous character . . . provided we recognise the miraculous character of the Church itself'.[2] Indeed, for Knox the Church, and the Church alone, is the primary miracle; in a secondary sense everything that happens within the Church shares in the Church's miraculous character, and it is therefore not surprising that 'in an earlier age, less scientific and less critical than our own', 'the realisation of the miraculous character of the whole Event . . . tended to turn every incident and circumstance within the Event into a separate wonder'.[3] However, we know better. And suddenly at this point Knox remembers that, right at the beginning of his discussion, he did, in fact, say that, apart from the Existence of Jesus, his resurrection was the one essential fact upon which the Church's existence depends. And now he tells us, emphatically and repeatedly, that the Resurrection is not, as he said it was, a mere linguistic convention:

> The Resurrection of Jesus, however, is more than a symbol of this miracle of the Church's life—more than the Virgin Birth and the empty tomb, which, whether they are thought of as 'happening' or not, must be recognised as having only symbolic significance. *The Resurrection of Jesus is a fact of the objective order, both indubitable and essential.* This cannot be said of any of

[1] ibid., p. 71.
[2] ibid., p. 72.
[3] ibid., p. 74.

the miracle stories—including the miracle stories which confirm or illustrate the Resurrection itself. [There follow assertions of the essential irrelevance of the Virgin Birth, the empty tomb and the story of the walk to Emmaus.] . . . But the Resurrection of Jesus is not of this kind. It is not a story which a Christian may find credible or incredible. It is not subject to confirmation or invalidation by historical research. . . . Actually we have to do here, not with a story at all, though stories, sagas and legends soon grew up about it, but with an essential implication of the existence of the Church itself. . . . The Church affirms the Resurrection because its own existence as the community of memory and the Spirit is the essential and continuing meaning of the Resurrection.[1]

The Resurrection, then, is not, after all, a linguistic convention; it is an objective fact. Nevertheless, unless I have altogether misunderstood them, the last two sentences, and indeed the whole of the passage, just quoted seem to make it plain that, for Knox, the Resurrection of Jesus is not an event that occurred in the concrete historical order of history, not something that happened 'under Pontius Pilate', as presumably his crucifixion did, but something that took place, and takes place, within the mind and 'memory' of the Church. I shall later on explain why such an interpretation of the Resurrection, and the even more 'reduced' interpretation that Knox gives to the other Gospel-miracles, seems to me to be totally inadequate to the requirements of the Christian Gospel.[2] Here I will simply remark that it can only be on account of his peculiar reduction of theology to ecclesiastical psychology (or should we rather say mnemology?) that he can write such a passage as the following:

The statement of the Creed . . . that Jesus was born of the Virgin Mary has *exactly the same value* for the Christian who doubts that it actually happened thus as for the Christian who

[1] ibid., pp. 77f (italics added).

[2] Cf. pp. 269f. *infra*. In contrast, the following remark by Dr Alan Richardson (*History, Sacred and Profane*, p. 212, n. 1) may be quoted with reference to an essay by Dr H. von Campenhausen: 'As an historian, he deprecates the setting aside of historical evidence to make way for psychologising and existentialist theories; he conducts a careful critical enquiry into the sources, and he concludes that Christ's resurrection and the empty tomb are to be regarded as real events in the light of a strictly historical assessment of the relevant evidence.'

accepts the literal truth of the statement with no question whatever, although the latter will probably have some difficulty in recognising this. . . . Actually, he finds *the literal truth* [*] of the miracle story even acceptable for the same reason his brother finds it dispensable: he has prior knowledge of a miracle which far transcends in scope and depth of significance the Virgin Birth or any similar wonder. For him as well as for his brother the real value of the story lies in its dramatisation of the supernatural character of the whole Event.[1]

I shall postpone discussion of this point to a later stage; but I have quoted the passage here for the further light which it throws upon Knox's attitude to historic factuality in relation to the Christian faith.

VI

In the following chapter, on 'The Church and the Incarnation', the matter becomes even more clear. Knox lays immense stress upon the notion of the Church as the Body of Christ, which has, of course, played a very prominent part in both Catholic and Protestant theology in recent years. But he interprets it in a very specialised sense. Former discussions—and one thinks in particular of Mersch's seminal work *Le Corps mystique du Christ*[2] and its sequel *La Théologie du Corps mystique*—have started from the union of human nature with the eternal divine Word in the womb of Mary the Virgin and have passed on, via the persistence of that union after the Ascension and the incorporation of men and women into the God-man, to the Church as the concrete historic reality in which the humanity of Jesus is now expressed and operates on earth. Knox's train of thought is the reverse of this. He insists that the Church is Christ's body, not metaphorically but in a most realistic sense. It is not, in his view, because Christ took human nature from Mary that the Church is Christ's body, but because the Church is Christ's body that the Church has produced myths about Jesus' origin. 'The Church is the historical locus, the "embodiment" of God's saving action within the temporal order. . . . To say that God's saving act was and is embodied in the Church's existence is to say (if we

[1] op. cit., p. 76 (italics, except those indicated by asterisk, added).
[2] Translated into English by John R. Kelly, as *The Whole Christ.*

wish to use the term in that connection) that it is "incarnate" there.'[1] This is not, however, as Knox goes on to admit, how the term 'incarnation' has commonly been used; it has referred to the human life of Jesus.[2] 'How, then,' he asks, 'do we see the relation of this "incarnation" to the "embodiment" which we affirm to have taken place in the Church?'[3] He rightly rejects the notion of 'two incarnations'. He also, revealingly, rejects the description of the Church as 'the extension of the Incarnation', on the ground that it says not too much, but too little, for the Church: *the* incarnation is, he insists, the Church itself. His own answer to the question is twofold. First, in the phrase 'the Incarnation of the Word', he wants to limit the meaning of the immensely polyvalent term 'Word' to 'the creative, revealing, redeeming *action* of God'.[4] Secondly, in line with his previous account, he wants to *include* whatever historical character the life of Jesus had *within* the 'Event' of the Church's coming into being. Now, in itself, such a mode of speech might be taken as a somewhat bizarre but, if properly controlled, a possibly fruitful linguistic innovation. But, as used by Knox, its purpose is to deprive the historic life of Jesus of any theological importance so far as anything beyond his bare existence is concerned. He describes the development of Christology as simply the progressive development and explication of the fact that the Church is Christ's body. 'This process of discovery and understanding involved what can only [*sic*] be called the gradual "mythologising" of the Event',[5] and the word 'myth' is used to describe such an apparently metaphysical statement as 'God was present' or 'God acted', as well as the stories recorded in the Gospels. Confirmation is thus given to the view previously asserted, that for theology, as distinct from historical science, the Church is really all that matters. Knox is a good enough logician to distinguish between a fact and somebody's awareness of that fact. Nevertheless, in answer to the objection that, whatever may be true

[1] op. cit., p. 86.

[2] Incidentally, Knox gives the sentence, 'Jesus . . . in the days of his flesh was "God incarnate" ', as a description of the traditional belief. That orthodoxy holds that Jesus is still God incarnate does not seem to have occurred to him.

[3] ibid., p. 86.

[4] ibid., p. 87.

[5] ibid., p. 90.

about the Church's *awareness*, Jesus and his Resurrection were *in actual fact* prior to the community, he writes:

> This can be granted about Jesus in some general objective sense, with which historical science may concern itself, and even about the Resurrection in some objective sense quite beyond our knowing (and it should be noted that, in what I am going to say, these 'objective' facts and their importance are being taken for granted), but it is decidedly *not* true of 'our Lord Jesus Christ'. The particular concrete reality denoted by that phrase exists only for the Church and within it.[1]

The words in parentheses may sound reassuring to the traditional Christian, but this impression soon vanishes when we see how they are understood. For Knox now to all intents and purposes abandons any profession of simply 'reinterpreting' the Church's traditional belief. He claims that his identification of the conception and birth of Jesus as Lord and Christ with the conception and birth of the Church will both 'relieve the Gospel tradition of an impossible pressure' and also 'free the humanity of Jesus from an intolerable strain'. This pressure on the Gospel tradition—'an arbitrary pressure which that tradition is simply not able to bear'—is, we are told, caused by 'the locating of the Incarnation, as a kind of static thing, in the individual personal existence of Jesus'.[2] And pressure is alleged to have been visibly at work in the period while the Gospels were being composed.

> As we move from Mark, through Matthew and Luke, to John, we can see the effort of the community, no less real for being unintentional and unconscious, to bring the account of Jesus' career into agreement with the developing belief that Jesus was God—to make the facts of history fit the view that in him, in his own discrete being, the Eternal Word become an actual human individual. But this effort did not succeed. Even in the Fourth Gospel, where it is carried furthest, some inconsistent 'facts' recalcitrantly remain; and Mark is full of them. . . .
>
> The Gospels, even as they stand, do not present us with such an individual as the identification of the Incarnation in this sense with Jesus simply and alone would require us to find. . . . Nor does the 'memory' of the Church help to make up this deficiency. The Church does not 'remember' the 'Word made

[1] ibid., pp. 93f.
[2] ibid., pp. 96f.

> flesh'; it 'remembers' the human Jesus, great and good and dying on a cross. If it knows the 'Word made flesh' (as of course it does!) it knows it in its own existence, where alone, so far as history is concerned, Christ in his fullness (which certainly includes the Resurrection) is embodied.[1]

I feel moved to the following comments:

(1) No reason is given why the Church, in its earliest days, should have felt itself under this extraordinary pressure to distort its 'memory' of the human Jesus in this way. Werner had at least some explanation why the Church invented a new doctrine of Jesus as divine. Knox has none, unless he intends to imply that the Church could not be content with its existential experience of Jesus, but felt itself bound to give this some historical basis. If such a process was psychologically inevitable and it was humanly impossible that the 'Event' could be left floating in an historical vacuum, is it not at least likely that the historical basis was there at the start? Must we suppose that the divine act of redemption was arranged by God in such an irrational way that the Church was morally certain to falsify it?

(2) Can we take the movement from Mark, through Matthew and Luke, to John as casually as Knox takes it? I suggest that much more serious attention needs to be given to Grant's point about the circular nature of this type of argument.[2]

(3) In what sense can the doctrine that Jesus was God incarnate be said to be 'static'? And why should 'static' in any case be simply a term of abuse?

(4) If Knox is right, the Evangelists were engaged upon a thoroughly disreputable task, in which fortunately they failed. Has Knox sufficiently reflected upon the inherent improbability of such an hypothesis? Or upon the implications which it will have for the character of the primitive Church upon whose 'experience' and 'memory' Knox places so much stress in building up his whole account?

(5) Can it be calmly maintained that the Gospels, *even as they stand*, do not present us with one who is, by the very nature of his acts and claims and by the impact which he made on his disciples, endowed with the authority of God himself and therefore, at least by implication, *homoousios to Patri*, 'of the same kind

[1] ibid., p. 97.

[2] Cf. p. 223 *supra*.

of being as the Father', to use the phrase of the Council of Nicaea?

(6) The contrast between the Church's 'memory' and 'knowledge' seems quite perverse and the statement made about these two faculties altogether unsubstantiated. It is not clear whether the Church referred to is the primitive Church or the Church throughout the ages, and the contrast between the Church's memory and its knowledge is, I think, introduced for the first time at this place, and without explanation. In any case, 'the human Jesus, great and good and dying on a cross' would seem to be the subject of the secular historian and not of the Church's memory, which previous statements would lead us to suppose was concerned with facts, like that of the 'Word made flesh', which (it was alleged) were outside the grasp of the historian. By substituting the psychological concept of the Church's 'memory' (a term which applied to a corporate body is in any case highly metaphorical) in place of the scriptural and patristic concepts of 'testimony' and 'tradition', Knox has given a description of the Church's attitude to her Lord which seems devoid of any basis. I can only ask the reader to consider carefully the last two sentences in the quotation above, to try to make sense of them and then to ask why we should suppose them to be true.

Very little more convincing is what Knox has to say about the strain placed by the 'static' conception on the humanity of Jesus. (By the static conception, we must remind ourselves, is meant one which sees the Incarnation as primarily referring to Jesus rather than to the Church.) By it, we are told, 'Jesus is required to be not only what the Gospels do not represent him to have been, but also what as a human being he could not have been.'[1] In view of what we have just been told about the Gospels, the former of these deficiencies might not seem, in Knox's view, to be very serious. The latter is redolent of the *decuit ergo fecit* type of argument that in other contexts scholars of Knox's outlook usually disown. How are we to say what are the capacities of human nature if it is assumed by God the Word? Somewhat surprisingly after this, we are told that the orthodox definition of the two natures in one Person is more satisfactory than those of the ancient heresies or of modern thinkers who have identified the deity of Jesus with an extraordinary degree of some human

[1] op. cit., pp. 97f.

quality. Nevertheless it is criticised as 'not fully satisfactory because of the manifest impossibility of a truly human existence actually having this character'.[1] Furthermore 'it requires him to be what we would not have wanted him to be—what indeed we cannot bear to think of him as being'.[2] I cannot help wondering at the reference of the word 'we' in this sentence. It certainly cannot mean 'the great body of Christian thinkers, saints and ordinary folk in the Church throughout the ages', for if it did the sentence would be manifestly untrue. Comparison with usage elsewhere in the book makes it unlikely that it is the auctorial 'we', meaning 'I, Knox'. It must, I think, mean Knox and those who share his general outlook. In any case what is asserted is that *no* doctrine of Incarnation can be applied to Jesus without denying his full, unqualified humanity, and that therefore it must be applied to the Church instead.[3] In maintaining this, Knox is, in fact, writing off as perverted and doomed to failure from the start the work of the great majority of the Church's thinkers throughout the centuries. Such a revolutionary thesis needs, I suggest, more support than Knox even attempts to give it. But in conclusion we must see what he proposes to substitute for the traditional view.

> The solution [he writes] lies, rather, in the recognition that the most appropriate form for holding and conveying the meaning of Christ is not a definition of him, but a story about him—the story of the Son of God who 'emptied himself' and took the nature of a 'servant', who was 'obedient unto death, even death on a cross', whom God has 'highly exalted' and made 'Lord' over Sin and Death. This story was the theology of the earliest Church, its Gospel or 'Good News', and no abstract statement could take its place or can ever do so. The concrete meaning of what God did in Christ cannot be expressed in the definition of a hypostasis; it must be 'told' as the story of an

[1] ibid., p. 99.
[2] ibid.
[3] Nevertheless, with a happy inconsistency, Knox can write, discussing the Atonement: 'The Church, therefore, is not only the "body" of the *Event*, or the "body" of *God's action*, but in a real and wholly unique sense it is Christ's own body and has its reconciling, uniting character because he himself lives in its life' (p. 107). The relevant question is whether this 'Christ' is merely someone experienced in the Church or whether he is also the Word by whom the universe was created and who (really and not mythically or symbolically) became man in Mary's womb.

> action. The definition in this case can be true, in the sense of shutting out other definitions less apt and adequate, and can be valuable, even indispensable, in guaranteeing the proper recognition of elements and proportions in the concrete meaning of Christ which might otherwise be obscured; but the fuller truth and the larger value must always remain with the story, where the inner reality of the Event—'things into which angels long to look'—was first expressed and where alone the ineffable fullness of its concrete meaning can be declared.[1]

There is much in this passage with which I can agree. That no statement about divine mysteries, however true, can be fully adequate is, of course, a commonplace of traditional theology; all our statements are analogical, and, even when the *perfectio significata* is familiar, its *modus significandi* eludes us. And orthodox formulas indeed rule out formulas less adequate than they. Again, important as it is to say, in so far as our feeble words can do it, what Jesus is, it is of not less importance to say what he has done. To use Knox's words, the 'story' and not just the 'definition' matters. What I must, however, dispute is his bland assumption that stories raise no problems; that 'the fuller truth and the larger value' remain with them, as they declare the ineffable value of the concrete meaning of the Event. They seem to me quite clearly to raise problems no less than the definitions do; and even the simple story which Knox quotes from Philippians chapter ii, when we delve into it, leads us on to the path which in the end will take us to Nicaea and Chalcedon. In any case we seem to have got away from the Church and its 'memory' and back to Jesus and the Gospels, in spite of what we were told about their persistent, though in the end unsuccessful, attempt to substitute another figure for him. The remaining two chapters of Knox's book, dealing with the Atonement and with the norms that are discernible in a divided Church respectively, are of great interest in themselves, but do not add anything of substance to the question which we have been considering. Before leaving my readers to form their own conclusions on Dr Knox's reconstruction of the Christian religion, I will briefly summarise my main points of criticism.

(1) If the notion of the Church's 'memory' is to be made a guiding principle, it needs much more careful definition and

[1] ibid., p. 100.

discussion than Knox gives it. The notion of the 'memory' of a corporate body, especially one whose membership completely changes as time goes on (for it is only the Church militant with which Knox is concerned), is not at all an obvious one.

(2) 'Testimony' (or 'eyewitness') and 'tradition' are factors of even greater importance. Knox's neglect of them is due to his determination to take as his starting-point for theological reconstruction the experience of the primitive Church rather than the person and teaching of Jesus. This leads him to an improbable view of the activity of the Evangelists and does not succeed, as it presumably is intended to, in turning the flank of the form-critics.

(3) Knox's attempt to by-pass historical research into the Gospel material by making the Christian religion independent of its results does justice neither to the nature of the Christian religion itself nor to the value for it of historical scholarship. It is contrary neither to faith nor to reason to hold that certain facts of history are essential to Christianity and that, although these are in principle subject to scientific disproof, such disproof will never take place.

(4) The reduction of the essential content of Christianity to belief in the existence of Jesus and his resurrection (the latter not necessarily including the empty tomb) is inadequate to the Christian Gospel, which is not just concerned with experience (even corporate experience) in the minds of Christians, but with the re-creation of the human race by the Incarnation, death and Resurrection of God the Son.

(5) The Church is the Body of Christ, not merely as the embodiment of God's Word, in the sense of God's activity, but as the organic whole composed of all those who have been incorporated into the human nature which God the Son took in the womb of his Mother. To treat the great mysteries of the faith 'symbolically' is thus quite inadequate, e.g. to identify the Incarnation with an Event in the life of the Church rather than with the beginning of the human life of Jesus of Nazareth.

(6) If the Church is the Body of Christ in the traditional sense rather than in Knox's sense, then the Church's 'memory' is primarily the content of the human mind of the ascended Christ. This memory, communicated to the finite minds of the Body's members according to their respective functions and their

spiritual perceptiveness (*quidquid recipitur recipitur ad modum recipientis*), is the basis of the Church's progress in the development of her understanding of the Christian religion. But the Church's 'memory' in Knox's sense receives nothing either from testimony and tradition on the one hand or from the mind of the ascended Christ on the other, since it is antecedent to both.

The attractiveness of Knox's position, as of other 'reductionist' versions of Christianity, lies in its alleged immunity to the depredations of New-Testament scholars upon the factuality of the events described in the Gospels. I am not convinced that this is an immunity that Christianity either ought or needs to claim, and I would add that it is only a highly selective attitude to New-Testament scholars that produces the impression of depredation at all. Nevertheless, New-Testament scholarship is, as I remarked earlier in this book, one of the three grounds on which reductionism relies. I shall therefore conclude with some further remarks about the crucial cases of the Resurrection and the Virginal Conception of onr Lord.

VII

The writers whose works I have been chiefly considering in this book—Dr Paul van Buren, Dr J. A. T. Robinson, and Dr John Knox—differ a good deal in their views about the factual character of such traditionally central objects of Christian belief as the virginal conception (commonly referred to as the 'Virgin Birth') and the physical resurrection of Jesus, though none of them holds them to be essential. For van Buren both of these, as facts of history, are simply incredible to modern secularised man and are therefore false. Robinson, as we have seen, is 'prepared to keep an open mind' about the 'biological details' of Jesus's birth: 'Nothing for me', he says, 'depends on them.' And the Resurrection was not something that happened to Jesus; it was an 'overwhelming experience' that happened to the disciples; whether the Resurrection involved a 'literal vanishing or transformation of the elements which composed the flesh of Jesus' or a 'vision of Jesus alive' or the appearance of an 'astral body', 'all this is quite secondary'.[1] Knox considers that the virginal conception has 'exactly the same value' for those who reject its

[1] Cf. p. 147f. *supra*.

historicity and for those who accept it; and, while insisting upon the importance and essentiality of something that he certainly calls 'the Resurrection of Jesus', is equally indifferent to the factuality of the empty tomb.[1]

Nevertheless, all these writers are anxious to accept both the virginal conception and the Resurrection as edifying myths, expressing aspects of Christian existence in a moving and evocative way. Thus van Buren writes about the Gospel stories of the Nativity:

> If it were insisted that they must be understood 'factually', of course, they would have to be rejected, for such an interpretation would indeed threaten the doctrine of the full manhood of Jesus specified in the Christology of Chalcedon. But the believers, sharing the wonder and thanksgiving of the shepherds (or of the astrologers in the other story), will not want these stories to be excised from the whole witness of the New Testament. As the angel said to the shepherds, 'This shall be a *sign* unto you'.[2] The story of the babe born in total poverty and weakness may be an occasion for the deepening or renewal of the Christian perspective, a sign pointing to the life of freedom in the midst of fearful men which ended on the cross.[3]

For Robinson, what the Virgin Birth means is that '[Jesus'] birth and life cannot *simply* be thought of as a biological event; his significance is much deeper than that'. For Knox,

> it is conceivable, easily conceivable, that the story [of Jesus' Virgin Birth] might never have been told at all. In that event, the Church would now lack one of its historic symbols, but would otherwise not be poorer. Perhaps some other story about Jesus' birth would have taken its place in the tradition and would have come to have precisely the same symbolic value.[4]

What precisely is the symbolism of the Virgin Birth, when it is not accepted as a literal fact, is not always easy to determine. Dr Thomas Boslooper, in a book which I have not mentioned hitherto, quite vehemently insists on the retention of the historic credal language which declared that Jesus Christ was 'born of

[1] *The Church and the Reality of Christ*, pp. 76ff.

[2] Although, on van Buren's view, the angel said nothing at all, for there was no angel to say it.

[3] *The Secular Meaning of the Gospel*, p. 165.

[4] op. cit., p. 77.

the Virgin Mary' and goes so far as to assert that its abandonment would result in a catastrophic impoverishment of the Christian religion. At the same time, he refuses to accept it as literally true and interprets it as meaning merely that God acted in history and that monogamous marriage is civilisation's most important social institution.[1] How, in fact, respect for monogamous marriage is to be promoted by using the term 'virgin' to describe someone who, in Boslooper's view, was not a virgin at all, is not altogether obvious; if respect for monogamous marriage was the main point at issue, it would seem to be better forwarded by a story about Jesus as the son of Joseph and Mary, and this would have had, on Boslooper's view, the advantage of being historically and not only symbolically true. The obvious symbolic interpretation that one might expect to be given to the Nativity stories by someone who did not accept them as factually accurate would be that they symbolised the incarnation of a pre-existent divine being. This, however, would be ruled out by the writers just mentioned as being impossibly supranaturalistic, but the interpretations that they offer are vague and unconvincing, neither does their witness agree together. What seems common to them all is a nostalgia for the childhood associations of the Christmas story. I can only say that, in the absence of the Catholic doctrine of the Word made flesh of a virgin, this seems to me to lead at best to an unhealthy sentimentality and at worst to downright superstition.[2]

When we turn to the Resurrection these writers have at least a more consistent case, for, in whatever precise sense they interpret the Resurrection stories (Robinson has offered us three or four in the passage above quoted), they agree in basing them on the experience of the first disciples. For van Buren, this 'peculiar experience which the disciples had on Easter' was 'an experience of seeing Jesus in a *new* way and sharing in the freedom which had been his. . . . On Easter they found that Jesus had a new power which he had not, or had not exercised, before: the power to awaken freedom also in them.'[3] We must

[1] *The Virgin Birth*, pp. 227ff., especially p. 235.

[2] The view that Jesus was the son of Joseph and Mary is a piece of pure mythologising. If the traditional view is rejected, the obvious unsupernatural alternative would be that Joseph's suspicions were justified and that Mary had been unchaste.

[3] op. cit., p. 132.

recall that, on van Buren's form of empiricism, Jesus ceased to exist after his death, so this new power began to be 'exercised' only when he existed no more; I do not find this convincing. For Robinson, on the other hand, 'the life they had known and shared was not buried with him, but alive in them. Jesus was not a dead memory but a living presence, making new men of them.' Jesus, then, was still alive, whether in a resurrected or an astral or a visionary body. Nevertheless, the Resurrection was not something that had happened to *him*: '*this overwhelming experience of the disciples* is the great historical event which we call the Resurrection'.[1] For Knox, also, the Resurrection means 'not the incident of the rising, but the Church's knowing the risen one'. This, it is fair to add, is asserted as not 'merely subjective'; 'it is not an idea or a way of thinking, whether about Jesus' death or about anything else', in spite of the previous statement 'The Resurrection is our way of referring . . .' Nevertheless, 'the Resurrection of Christ, insofar as it belongs to history, took place only within the larger Event of the Church's "becoming" '. The Resurrection, as distinct from the stories about it, is 'a fact of the objective order', but it is something altogether unknown outside the experience or the 'memory' of the Church.[2]

Now, before going on to enquire whether, on rational and critical grounds we are bound to reject or ignore the Nativity and Resurrection stories as mythical, it will be well to consider whether the account of the Christian religion which these writers offer us is substantially that of historic Christianity and whether it embodies the values which are those of the Gospel message. The common feature of all these presentations is that they start from a certain experience (an 'existential' experience, a 'confrontation', an 'encounter', to use some of the popular expressions) which the primitive Church had of the Risen Christ. The rest of the Gospel story is what earlier critics would have called a 'rationalisation', but what we are now told to call a 'mythologisation' of that experience. The basic event of Easter is thus not something that happened to Christ, but something which happened to the Church, and this experience is passed on to succeeding generations by some process that can be metaphorically described as 'contagion' or as the Church's 'memory'.

[1] loc. cit., p. 147 *supra* (italics added).
[2] op. cit., pp. 70, 67, 72, 77.

This is not, it must in fairness be stressed, an individualistic doctrine; in it (at least for van Buren and Knox; I am not so sure about Robinson) the Church is placed in the centre of the picture; indeed, for Knox the Christ-Event *is* the coming into being of the Church. But where, as it seems to me, this attitude is quite incompatible with that of historic Christianity is that it restricts the Gospel entirely to the sphere of redemption and has no doctrine of creation, and it fails to take seriously the material element in man and in creation as a whole.[1] It concentrates Christianity entirely in the Resurrection-Event; and everything else in the Gospels, including the details of the Event itself, is a mythological embroidering of it. The whole history of God's ancient people the Jews, the whole history of the human race from Adam, the whole history of the world from the creation is irrelevant to it. For St Athanasius, the Work of Christ was the re-creation of the human race by the Eternal Word and Son of God through whom it was made in the first place; for St Irenaeus, the Incarnation is the crown and fulfilment of creation, creation and redemption are parts of a single plan, and he who feeds our bodies with his flesh and blood in the Eucharist is also he who makes provision for the earthly needs of those same bodies in the order of creation.[2] This is not a doctrine for which it is irrelevant whether the Resurrection of Christ was the transformation of his physical organism or the adoption of an astral body or a mere spiritual vision. Nor is it a doctrine for which it is irrelevant whether the Eternal Word took flesh of a virgin to redeem the human race or whether monogamous marriage is civilisation's most important social institution. If the virginal conception is literally true, then it means that the Creator has assumed the nature of fallen man in its totality in order to renew and transform it: *tu ad liberandum suscepturus hominem non horruisti virginis uterum.*[3] If the empty tomb is a literal fact, then Jesus has

[1] In van Buren there is the additional point that in his system there is no such being as God and neither Jesus nor anyone else survives physical death; but I have perhaps said enough about this already.

[2] Cf. L. S. Thornton, *Revelation and the Modern World*, pp. 120 *et al.*

[3] I do not wish to imply that God the Son could not, absolutely speaking, have become incarnate by a non-virginal conception, any more than I should wish to deny that, God might, absolutely speaking, have redeemed mankind without becoming incarnate at all; it is always unwise to place limits to the power of God. What we can see is that both an incarnation and a virginal conception were thoroughly appropriate to the needs and

risen from death in the totality of his human nature, so that, by incorporation into it, we might be renewed in the totality of ours. But if the virginal conception is only a symbol and not a fact of history, it may symbolise almost anything; and some of the things that it might be taken to symbolise are definitely undesirable, the most obvious being that sex is nasty. And if the empty tomb is only a symbol, it is difficult to see what it can symbolise except that the flesh of Christ has been conquered by death, so that he survives, if at all, as a disembodied spirit. But, beyond all this, which would be true of *any* form of desupernaturalising of the Gospel, the particular form with which we are faced here, which concentrates Christianity entirely in the Resurrection-Event considered as an experience of the primitive Church, limits the concern of Christian theology to the Church itself and provides nothing that can justify, still less provide pointers for, Christian action in the social realm. Van Buren, indeed, as we have seen, declares that his presentation of the Gospel has not even any evangelistic or apologetic force; he is not concerned to make the Gospel either more intelligible or more attractive to the unbeliever, but only to provide comfort for the secularised man who finds himself inside the Church but does not find the Church secular enough. I cannot think that Robinson noted this aspect of van Buren's system when he gave it so appreciative a mention. Of course, if this dismal situation is the inevitable outcome of honestly facing the facts, we must make the best of it and face it with heroic pessimism. But if in this life only we have hoped in Christ, we are of all men most pitiable. In the reduced, secularised, demythologised Christianity which we are being offered in place of the historic faith of Christendom the most striking characteristic is its narrowness; there is in it nothing of the cosmic breadth of a religion which sees the whole universe as held in the loving hand of a God who created it and redeemed it. But now we must pass to the further

---

circumstances of the case and were more 'natural', in the sense of more appropriate, than the alternatives. I have discussed this at length in my *Christian Theology and Natural Science* (pp. 307ff.). In practice, denial of the virginal conception or inability to see its relevance almost always goes with an inadequate understanding of the Incarnation and of the Christian religion in general; and this seems to me to be particularly true of the writers whom I have discussed.

question, whether this wholesale abandonment of traditional Christianity is necessary.

Now clearly I cannot in the space at my disposal (nor, in fact, could I anywhere) give a full survey of the present state of New-Testament criticism. But it is very important to recognise that by no means all responsible contemporary New-Testament scholars accept the conclusions of the extreme form-critics and demythologisers. This is not always evident, on account of the regrettable habit, to which all scholars are subject but which seems for some reason to affect students of the Bible in particular, of expressing their own tentative, and often evanescent, conclusions as if they had been proved up to the hilt and were universally accepted by other experts in their subject. This, of course, does not take in their colleagues, but it often seriously misleads the general public and also puts the sceptic in an unfair position of advantage, since the conservative is always open to the suspicion of having vested interests to defend and in any case the denial of the traditional Christian beliefs is always more sensational than their affirmation. Man bites dog is news; dog bites man is not news.

Nobody but a fundamentalist would deny today that the Gospels as we have them, and the material which went into their composition, come to us out of the life and experience of the primitive Church, and that they embody in many places not just a bare 'photographic' and 'tape-recorded' account of the acts and words of our Lord but frequently a comment and an interpretation of those acts and words in the light of acts and words recorded elsewhere (or perhaps not recorded at all) and of the experience of the primitive Church. Much that today we should put in a commentary or in footnotes has no doubt been worked into the narrative itself. This should not trouble us unless we are, as certain theologians appear to be, dominated by the conviction that the Church is always, or generally, wrong.[1] If, for example, in the variant accounts given by different evangelists, we have interpretations of the same event from different points of view, this is only something for which we

[1] This position appears to be held on theological grounds, concerned with the radical depravity of man, by Dr Nygren and Dr Subilia, to mention only two (cf. p. 231 *supra*), but many others appear to hold it in virtue of a dogma of the general irresponsibility of early Christians.

should be grateful, for there is no reason to suppose that the acts and sayings of Jesus were so superficial as to have only one possible significance, and that a significance which lay plainly on the surface; indeed, the Gospels themselves tell us that the significance was often only understood at a later date and in view of subsequent happenings.[1] This does not mean, however, that the evangelists had no respect for fact; rather the impression that we receive is that they considered it very important to get the facts right before they interpreted them. I have already emphasised the place occupied by the element of testimony and tradition in the Gospels.[2] Knox has, I believe, gone thoroughly astray in his assumption that the Gospels are only concerned with Jesus as he was experienced in the Event of the Church's own coming into being. Mr G. H. Boobyer has well written, in a very valuable essay:[3]

> To accuse the gospel evangelists of indiscriminately submerging historical fact in a flood of miracle-mongering to serve the interests of theological propaganda would be outright injustice. They could, in fact, be remarkably objective in what they record. For example, the changes which are *not* made in order to bring the gospel traditions into conformity with the Christian beliefs and practices of the apostolic age are sometimes more surprising than those which are. In view of the background of apostolic thought about Jesus as the divine Son and heavenly Lord, how astonishing it is that St Mark's Gospel and St Luke's should keep the words, 'Why callest thou me good? none is good save one, even God.' Another illustration of the same point occurs in St Matthew's and St Mark's accounts of the Last Supper. Neither evangelist includes the words, 'This do in remembrance of me', notwithstanding the fact that they appear in St Paul's version of what Jesus said (I Cor. xi. 23–25)—a report written before the gospels and one which represented the widespread practice of the church. . . . The evangelists wrote to substantiate the Christian gospel as presented in their day; yet their interest in theology was infused with a concern for history.

The question of interpretation, while arising from all the four

[1] Cf. Luke ii. 50; xviii. 34; John xii. 16.
[2] Cf. pp. 232ff. *supra*.
[3] 'The Gospel Miracles: Views Past and Present,' in *The Miracles and the Resurrection*, p. 39.

Gospels, is, of course, particularly pressing in the case of St John, and all the commentators have given their views about it. I shall, however, quote a passage which comes not from a professional New Testament scholar but from a literary critic who was faced with the practical task of bringing the Gospels together in a broadcast play and who approached her task with the utmost conscientiousness towards the sacred writings themselves and at the same time with the peculiar intuitiveness derived from her own special expertise. The late Dorothy Sayers wrote as follows:

> It must be remembered that, of the four Evangels, St John's is the only one that claims to be the direct report of an eyewitness. And to anyone accustomed to the imaginative handling of documents, the internal evidence bears out this claim. The Synoptists, on the whole, report the 'set pieces'; it is St John who reports the words and actions of the individual unrepeated occasion, retrieving them from that storehouse of trained memory which, among people not made forgetful by too much pen and ink, replaces the filed records and the stenographer's note-book. [Many examples follow.] All through, in fact, the Gospel of St John reads like the narrative of an eyewitness filling up the gaps in matter already published, correcting occasional errors, and adding material which previous writers either had not remembered or did not know about.[1]

Now clearly if we are to accept the interpretation which the evangelists give to the events which they record, we must have confidence in their own reliability and in the reliability of the tradition and testimony which they received and of which they made use, though we ought not to forget that in some cases it was their own eyewitness that they were recording. This confidence clearly involves an act of faith, and, in the article from which I quoted above, Boobyer criticises both Dr A. M. Farrer and Dr Alan Richardson on this account. Richardson is quoted as saying: 'The answer to the question, Did the miracles happen? is always a personal answer. . . . It is the "Yes" of faith to the challenge which confronts us in the New Testament presentation of Christ—the only Christ we can know.'[2] Farrer is

[1] *The Man Born to be King*, pp. 33f. The whole passage is well worth detailed study.

[2] *The Miracle Stories of the Gospels*, p. 127, cit. Boobyer, p. 45.

quoted as speaking of 'the use of faith to confirm evidence' and as asserting: 'It is possible through faith and evidence together, and through neither alone, to believe that Christ really and corporeally rose from the dead.'[1] Again Farrer writes: 'What Christians find in Christ through faith inclines them at certain points to accept with regard to him testimony about matter of fact which would be inconclusive if offered with regard to any other man.'[2] Boobyer's criticism of this attitude is that, in fact, this 'is not faith confirming evidence, but faith bringing about a jump beyond evidence; and small though the jump may seem, conclusive proof is still lacking that we have come down on something true'.[3] We have, he points out, not even narratives written down by Jesus himself, but secondary sources compiled by others. (Strangely enough, Boobyer himself, at the end of his essay, seems to opt for the very view of faith which he has been criticising.) I would, however, myself maintain that the faith which co-operates with evidence in producing conviction of the reliability of the Gospel accounts is not simply an existential *acte gratuit* exercised by the individual in isolation, but is an element of his life as a member of Christ's body the Church. Admittedly this cannot be true of the primary act of faith which brings a man into the Church if he has not been in it from childhood; this is on any showing a highly complicated matter in which the calculation of probabilities by human reason, intuition acting beneath the purely rational level, and the hidden working of the grace of God are all involved in a way which varies from case to case and defies schematisation. When, however, the believer has found his way into the Church and has begun to participate in its sacramental and social life he will rapidly discover that the Christ whom he meets and in whom he lives, in the Church which is Christ's Body, is also the Christ of the Gospels whom the Church proposes to him for belief. Knox is, I think, quite right in holding that the Christ whom we know is the Christ of the Church, but he is, I think, quite wrong in assuming that he is not also the Christ of whom the Gospels tell and that there is an impenetrable barrier between the Church and the Gospel incidents. I would therefore hold that, when

[1] *Kerygma and Myth*, I, p. 220, cit. Boobyer, p. 45.
[2] ibid., p. 220, cit. Boobyer, p. 46.
[3] art. cit., p. 46.

faith is conceived in this way, faith and evidence cohere without difficulty. The interpretations of Jesus' acts and words which I find in the Gospels are the Church's interpretations, but then the Gospels are the Church's books produced in the setting of the Church's life. This does not exclude the examination of the Gospels by the methods of critical scholarship, but it does affect the presuppositions on which that scholarship should work. The critical scholar is not committed, within the area of his research, to accepting the Church's presuppositions about Jesus, but he should not be committed to accepting naturalistic presuppositions either. If he does accept the latter, then the results of his research will in all probability contradict the beliefs of the Church, but this is because he has begged the question from the start. In examining, for instance, the evidence for the virginal conception, if he begins with the presupposition that such an event is impossible he will end with the same conclusion; if he begins with the presupposition that it is possible he may end with the conclusion that the evidence for it is good or that it is bad or that it is inconclusive. This is as far as scholarship can take him. The Christian will accept the virginal conception as part of the Church's faith. And in the rare cases where faith appears to be contradicted by scholarship whose conclusions have not been prescribed from the start, he may be cast down but will not be destroyed. For he will know how temporary and mutable the conclusions of scholarship essentially are, and he will also be conscious that he himself may not have perfectly comprehended the Church's faith.

When all this has been said, however, it needs to be added that, on the purely rational level, the allegedly negative attitude of modern scholarship to the basic miracles of Christianity is largely a myth. To take the crucial example of the Resurrection narratives in the Gospels, it is frequently asserted that the accounts of the four evangelists differ so widely that they can only be understood as diverse mythological patterns embroidered upon the 'Easter-experience' of the Church. Minute attention to the stories, however, shows them to be markedly coherent. As long ago as 1920 the late N. P. Williams showed that, if allowance is made for two minor and easily explained displacements, the accounts are perfectly consistent.[1] Dr A. M. Ramsey,

[1] *The First Easter Morning.*

in 1945, came to a very similar conclusion, but laid more stress on the plan and purpose of each evangelist.[1] The evidence of Dorothy Sayers, who was faced with the practical problem of making the stories work together in a play, is of special interest. She wrote as follows:

> The playwright, in any case, is not concerned, like the textual critic, to establish one version of a story as the older, purer, or sole authoritative version. He does not want to select and reject, but to harmonise. . . . And in doing this, he is often surprised to find how many apparent contradictions turn out not to be contradictory at all, but merely supplementary. Take, for example, the various accounts of the Resurrection appearances at the Sepulchre. The divergences appear very great on first sight; and much ink and acrimony have been expended on proving that certain of the stories are not 'original' or 'authentic', but are accretions grafted upon the first-hand reports by the pious imagination of Christians. Well, it may be so. But the fact remains that *all* of them, without exception, can be made to fall into place in a single orderly and coherent narrative without the smallest contradiction or difficulty, and without any suppression, invention, or manipulation, beyond a trifling effort to *imagine* the natural behaviour of a bunch of startled people running about in the dawnlight between Jerusalem and the Garden.[2]

No fresh evidence has come to light in the meantime, only some fresh prejudices.[3] Or again, to consider the virginal conception. Here admittedly added knowledge of the associations of the literary forms made use of by Matthew and Luke throw fresh light upon the idioms in which the stories of Mary and Joseph are told. But the factual reliability of the accounts, as well as the centrality of the virginal conception to the Christian Gospel, has been convincingly argued in two thoroughly well-informed and well-reasoned articles by Dr Otto A. Piper[4] and Dr John

[1] *The Resurrection of Christ.*

[2] *The Man Born to be King*, p. 35.

[3] Besides the essay by Boobyer already mentioned I would draw attention to the admirable essay in the same symposium by Mr M. C. Perry entitled 'Believing the Miracles and Preaching the Resurrection'.

[4] 'The Virgin Birth: The Meaning of the Gospel Accounts,' *Interpretation*, April 1964, pp. 13ff.

Wilkinson,[1] which are all the more impressive for the fairness with which they state the arguments on the opposite side.[2]

[1] 'Apologetic Aspects of the Birth of Jesus Christ,' *S.J.T.* XVII (1964), pp. 159ff.

[2] While on the subject of the Nativity Stories it may be pertinent to remark that even the story of the Magi, which it has become customary to dismiss as an early Christian midrash, makes a far more coherent story if it is taken as a straightforward account of a journey across the desert. Unfortunately I have mislaid the reference to the article in which this has been shown, but the following is a brief summary of the argument. 'We have seen his star *en tē anatolē*' = 'at its flaring up'. The star was a super-nova, and the Magi divined that the great Event which it signified had occurred at a place where it was at that moment in the zenith. They therefore made their journey in a westward direction, steering their course so that the star passed through their zenith each night. This brought them to the neighbourhood of Jerusalem, but their observations were not accurate enough to fix the spot exactly. They therefore enquired about relevant prophecies, and were directed to Bethlehem. As they approached Bethlehem the star was coming up the sky ('went before them') and reached the zenith ('stood over where the young child was') as they arrived there. (When a star comes to the zenith it gives the impression of momentarily halting before continuing on the downward part of its path.) As far as I know, this is the only explanation that makes sense of the star's movement; most accounts seem to think of the star as luring the Magi like a carrot before a donkey's nose. The interesting consequence follows that the arrival at the earth of the light from the new super-nova and the Nativity of Jesus were timed to be simultaneous. This should inspire us rather than perplex us if we believe that the Nativity was an event of cosmic significance and that 'the Lamb [was] slain from the foundation of the world'. That the story is related in midrashic idiom is quite irrelevant; this may, for all we know, be the one midrashic story which is literally true, the midrash for the sake of which, in the providence of God, the whole midrashic style was devised.

It is interesting to notice that Dr R. M. Grant, in a discussion which shows an almost preternaturally detached attitude, says quite frankly: 'The ultimate difficulty with the whole narrative of the conception, birth and infancy of Jesus lies in the modern (and ancient, too) belief in the general regularity of natural processes. In early Jewish Christianity there were those who held that Jesus was the son of Joseph and Mary, though we do not know why they maintained this view. Theological ideas have varied in relation to this subject. . . . If one attempts to by-pass theological questions by an "appeal to history" it must be admitted that the historical method as such can provide little guidance on this problem.' (*Historical Introduction to the New Testament*, pp. 306, 308.) Not all New Testament scholars are as open as this. The ultimate question is whether one believes in the possibility of miracles and whether, if one does, one will consider that the Incarnation of the Second Person of the Trinity might provide an appropriate occasion for them. Cf. pp. 235ff. *supra*.

With equal detachment Grant writes about the Resurrection:

Obviously any historian who presupposes that death marks the final termination of human life will find this claim unacceptable. He will

I have remarked above that there is really no fresh evidence bearing on the historicity of the Gospels, but only new presuppositions and prejudices. This can be well illustrated from the discussion of the Ascension given by M. D. Goulder in his book *Type and History in Acts*. He states baldly that 'the detail . . . of the ascension story is almost wholly symbolical', and the context shows that this does not mean that the details are historical facts which are symbolic of religious truths (as the Church has always held), but that, although they are symbolic of religious truths, they are not historical facts at all: 'St Luke . . . had overwhelming reasons for inventing a story describing the ascension if one did not already exist, and his account supplies no reasons for thinking that he did not so invent one.' He continues, 'The rest of the New Testament provides overwhelming evidence that no incident occurred of the kind St Luke describes.'[1] When, however, we go on to examine what this evidence is, which leads him, as he says, 'to conclude therefore that the account of Acts i. 1–14 is quite unhistorical', we find that it is exactly the same as the evidence which led Dr A. M. Ramsey to no such conclusion.[2] Is a writer being quite fair to his readers when he uses the adjective 'overwhelming' in this way?

It should be noticed that Mr Goulder's approach, while equally sceptical on the question of historic factuality, is very different from that of most of the writers whom we have considered and is, in fact, difficult to reconcile with it. Whereas they see the supernatural element in the New Testament as due to the mythologising by the Church of its Easter-experience, he sees it as due to the passion of the writers for Old Testament typology. It is interesting, however, to see how he deals with St Luke's

---

have to explain why the disciples believed that Jesus was risen, but he can still proceed on the assumption that they misinterpreted the evidence they had. In our view, such a presupposition does not belong to historical analysis, which must take the evidence as it stands and try to understand the purposes for which it was transmitted, without making a preliminary judgment as to its modern significance or insignificance. Admittedly such a procedure is difficult, but unless it is viewed as a goal historical interpretation becomes nothing but modern propaganda. (ibid., pp. 367f.)

[1] op. cit., pp. 182ff.
[2] *The Resurrection of Christ*, pp. 41, 68ff., 121f.

well-established reputation for historical accuracy, on which, as we have seen, Mr Sherwin-White lays so much stress.[1] He lays down two criteria; the first is that *where there are no types, Acts is intended to be factual*; the second is that *the thicker the types, the less likely is the passage to be factual.* The mentality ascribed to St Luke, implying a normal conscientiousness in accurate writing, which progressively evaporates as the typological afflatus takes possession of him, seems, to say the least, psychologically improbable; it would seem to be more likely that St Luke was, as Sherwin-White's examination seems to show, consistently conscientious, though his interest in typology may well have led him to bring into the open typological implications where he could see them and to emphasise those features of an event in which they were most obvious. Strangely enough, Goulder is ready to admit that 'we can never be certain that type and fact do not coincide for any particular incident or detail', but, on the somewhat dubious ground that 'the early Christians were prepared to believe that Old Testament types had been fulfilled without adequate evidence', he sets up his second criterion according to which typological significance and historical factuality are roughly in inverse proportion, or even, it appears, mutually exclusive. Thus, he argues for the unhistoricity of the account of the Ascension simply on the ground that 'the symbolic content of the account . . . is almost 100%'; 'the detail, then, of the ascension story is almost wholly symbolical'.[2] The implication behind this is therefore that, if (as is certainly rationally possible) the factual features of some incident were heavily loaded with typological significance, it would have been impossible for St Luke to record them; he must either have omitted the typology and recorded the facts or else have expounded the typology and ignored or garbled the facts. To do justice either to typology in general or to Goulder's application of it in particular would require an extended discussion, and anyone who wishes to be fair to him should read his book *in toto*. But the example I have given provides an illuminating illustra-

[1] In the text I have quoted Sherwin-White's remarks on the Gospels; the greater part of his book is, however, concerned with establishing the reliability of Acts. Among earlier works manifesting the same general attitude may be mentioned W. L. Knox's *St Paul and the Church of Jerusalem* (1925) and *St Paul and the Church of the Gentiles* (1939).

[2] op. cit., pp. 181f.

tion of the way in which a prejudice against the supernatural can distort a writer's manner of reasoning.[1]

I have referred specifically to the Resurrection and the

[1] Typology is a very hazardous occupation. The leading living typologist, Dr A. M. Farrer, has felt impelled to write sequels to both his book on St Mark and his book on the Apocalypse in order to emend radically his original typological interpretations and replace them by new ones. On Acts the reader may be referred to the late C. S. C. Williams's Commentary for the note on typology in chapters x–xii (pp. 152f.), the quietly ironical flavour of which Goulder (op. cit., p. 177) seems not to have entirely appreciated. There is a very simple, but searching, criterion which it is useful to apply to any attempt to deny the historical authenticity of a narrative on mythological, typological or other stylistic grounds. It consists in asking the question: 'Supposing, as a pure hypothesis, that the events described had actually occurred, then, given the author's stylistic idiom, would he or would he not have been likely to describe them in the way he did?' If the answer to this question is 'Yes', then the fact that he described them in this way provides no argument against their historicity. To give an example, Goulder asserts that, in accordance with his ingrained addiction to typology and his detachment from historical factuality, Luke inserted the two figures in white garments into his account of the Ascension in order to replicate the figures of Moses and Elijah at the transfiguration and the two similar figures in the garden of the Resurrection. But, supposing there *were* two figures of this kind at the Ascension what, on Goulder's view, was poor Luke to do? If he left them out in order to avoid the accusation of falsifying the narrative, he would be omitting an important and significant detail. If he put them in, then on Goulder's view he would be assumed to have introduced two fictitious and purely symbolic figures. If he tried to avoid this by changing the number from two to three, he would no doubt then have been taken to be typologising on the theme of the three angelic visitors of Abraham. It may be added that Goulder shows a curious attitude to orthodox Christology. 'The spiritual reality that the ascension story represents,' he says, 'is, of course, not affected by this argument [i.e. the argument that the ascension did not occur]. Jesus had been a man, and after a while he was so no longer: he ceased even appearing to his disciples, and gave the Church abundant evidence of his reign in heaven.' (op. cit., p. 183.) The statement 'he was so no longer' is a direct contradiction of the teaching of the Epistle to the Hebrews (e.g. viii. 3) and of the Chalcedonian definition (*adiairetōs, achōristōs*); when, we are left wondering, did he cease to be man?

It is only right to add that Goulder recognises the need for the typological method to be kept under some form of control. Nevertheless many of his typological identifications seem to be extremely speculative; one is left with the feeling that, with sufficient ingenuity, the method could be used to reach any conclusions that one wished. And the general conclusion, that St Luke abandons factual narration altogether whenever he sees that he can make a telling typological point, even to the extent of fabricating completely the stories of Ascension Day and Pentecost, strains credulity to the utmost. As Goulder himself asserts, it means that 'St Luke was both a fundamentalist and a poet, and that he did not realise that there was any contradiction between the two' (p. 204). And, in view of the words with which he begins his Gospel, it would mean that he was also a liar of no mean order.

Nativity stories because of their outstanding importance; to develop the argument further would involve a detailed examination of the Gospels for which I have neither the space nor the technical equipment. Enough has, I think, nevertheless been said to show that the impoverished secularised versions of Christianity which are being urged upon us for our acceptance today rest not upon the rigid application of the methods of scientific scholarship nor upon a serious intuitive appreciation of the Gospels as a whole in their natural context, but upon a radical distaste for the supernatural. Even scholars whose own religious practice implies the acceptance of the supernatural are frequently so imbued with this prejudice that in their study of the New Testament they take it as a matter of course that the supernatural element is, if not to be totally denied, at least to be consistently minimised. I pointed out very early in this book that this attitude claimed support from three fields of study, namely science, philosophy and biblical study, and in the course of my discussion I have paid a good deal of attention to each of them. I have also analysed, in wearisome detail, the arguments of some of the most prominent exponents of reductionist theology, in its various forms. The conclusion to which I have found myself forced is twofold: first that what we are being offered is not a reinterpretation of the Christian religion but a substitute for it, and secondly that the arguments offered, from whichever field of study they have been drawn, are quite unconvincing. This does not mean that traditional Christianity has nothing to learn from the new techniques and discoveries; on the contrary, it can be revivified and enriched by them. This task should be enough to occupy fully at least one generation of theologians and one cannot prescribe in advance what its results would be. All I can hope to have done in the present book is to show that there is no valid ground for the failure of nerve which has stampeded many contemporary theologians into a total intellectual capitulation to their secular environment. Whether I have succeeded, my readers must judge.

INDEX OF PROPER NAMES*

*Biblical names and that of the present author are not included.